glitter stucco & dumpster diving

glitter stucco & dumpster diving

reflections on building production
in the vernacular city

JOHN CHASE

VERSO

New York · London

First Published by Verso in 2000

VERSO

UK: 6 Meard Street, London W1V 3HR
USA: 180 Varick Street, New York, NY 10014-4606

Verso is the imprint of New Left Books

DESIGN BY POLLEN
Printed by R.R. Donnelley and Sons
ISBN 1-85984-807-9

British Library Cataloguing in Publication Data
A catalog record for this book is available from the British Library

Library of Congress Cataloging-in-Publication Data
A catalog record for this book is available from the Library of Congress

contents

Dedicated to my sister, Laura Chase Robinson

This book stems from my fascination with the essential ambiguity and multiple identities of architecture as a discipline. Buildings are never just aesthetic objects. They have socially constructed meanings and utilitarian functions. Architecture cannot be reduced to only one eternal Vitruvian aspect, any more than a human being can be classified as only a spirit, only a mind or only a body. Since the analysis and appraisal of formalism in contemporary high art architecture is attended to by others, this book addresses the quite substantial remaining elements of building production.

In this book I try to prove that orthodox architectural culture doesn't fully explain the contemporary cityscape. High art architecture has divorced architectural form from function and social purpose. Abstraction is worshiped for its own sake, and the details that tie form to site, program and user are forsaken. But in fact there is an irreducible connection between life and architecture. In architecture the concrete and the abstract are manifestations of each other.

Similarly the conventional wisdom of urban designers, planners and architects doesn't necessarily account for what people really want out of their house or out of their city. Since reform is about telling other people how to lead their lives, there is a streak of the oppressor in every good reformer. City planners, urban designers and architects often try to get the American public to live their lives less for personal benefit, and more for the group. The customary recipe is more public transit, higher density and less autos. Wonderful, fabulous, but often at odds with most people's healthy sense of self-interest.

When I am out and about, or for that matter even looking out the window, I want to know why the cityscape I see, the city around me, is laid out the way it is, why the buildings are built the way they are. Since buildings perform a function and have an economic role I want to know what that function and that role are. Since taking a detailed look at the sum total of building production is rather impractical, I have chosen to analyze two smaller case studies groups of buildings such as the stucco box apartment houses of the 1950s, and small houses remodeled by interior decorators in the 1950s and the 1960s.

These investigations have motivated me to argue for the importance of the specific forces that cause buildings to come into being and to organize and classify buildings according to those forces. Hence the idea that buildings are produced in the context of consumerism. The nature of their relationship to consumerism has a lot to do with what they are, how they operate and how they look. Similarly the idea of looking at building production and building type allows further ordering of buildings brought into being by forces other than consumerism.

While much architectural criticism has become eviscerated in its pursuit of untrammeled abstract form, I want to pursue my investigations equipped with the full range of human emotions. That is why I have included such wantonly subjective pieces as *A Curmudgeon's Guide to Urban Living*, and *Trashy Space, Trashy Behavior and Trashy People*. Whenever someone claims they have pinned down the exact nature of a place, I get nervous. Places and spaces can never be entirely defined because they are lived and perceived so differently by different observers and participants. Space only exists as a kind of geographical physics.

In this book I have tried to demonstrate that in a building, as in a person, there are always another 10,000 aspects of identity to be considered. Human identity, human space and building production are not single undifferentiated entities, but simultaneous and multiple in their essential being. Urban history becomes personal history; the petty and the profound are mirror images in the world that surrounds us. The urban landscape is a multifarious field of activity that often has contradictory identities. The disposition of trash, the everyday lives of the homeless, and changes in building codes and building technology all are determinants of built form and inhabited space. Urban space is at once subcultural space, real estate transaction and consumerist by-product.

In these essays I try to answer not what is a good building or what is good architecture, but rather what category does a building belong to, and how does it fulfill its mission within that niche. All aspects of the cityscape have meaning and purpose that can be explained with sufficient analysis and research. I have attempted to write about these subjects as parts of the skein of cultural activities and artifacts with which we cover the earth.

Therefore I have deliberately employed the tools of conventional architectural history on buildings that exist outside conventional architectural culture. The infamous Woolf doorway deserves the same scholarship as the work of celebrated modernist R.M. Schindler.

Architecture and man-made space are forms of material culture and lived history. Since the built environment is sometimes supposed to serve the role of historian and educator by revealing past practices, cultures and values, I wanted to know just what ought to survive and what ought to be sheltered in the immediate past.

In using examples of building types, urban development and life from Southern California, I have followed Reyner Banham's understanding of Los Angeles as a series of ecologies, in which microclimate, local geography, history, ethnic composition, economics and social caste melded to create communities with radically different personalities. Settled as a set of separated individual communities, Southern California has long been an amalgam of experiential and psychological possibilities: eccentric outposts such as Venice, ethnic regions such as East Los Angeles and enclaves of wealth such as the hillside communities of the Hollywood Hills and Santa Monica Mountains.

By considering the everyday, the multiplicity of human need and identity that buildings answer, I hope to demonstrate to the readers of this book that there may be redemption, and a place, not necessarily for everything, but for more of the built environment around them than they might at first expect.

acknowledgments

It was Mike Davis' idea to publish my collected writings as a book.

It honestly would not have occurred to me without his suggestion. Mike's enthusiasm and the mere fact that a writer who packed a real punch was willing to sponsor the project as an editor had a galvanizing effect on me. Thanks to Mike Sprinker who battled back from repeated dire illnesses to save me from, among other things, mistitling the book, and to Colin Robinson of Verso for supporting and realizing this project.

Much of the intellectual life I have enjoyed for the past 15 years has been due to the always probing and prescient Margaret Crawford, who has a mind at once widely and deeply informed, combined with enormous creative powers to synthesize ideas and concepts. Also contributing to my continuing education has been the frighteningly articulate John Kaliski. Special thanks to Allan Hess, Jeremy Kotas, Skip Shaffer, Elizabeth McMillian, Lorraine Wilde and Tim Street-Porter for their support of my writing and to book designer Denise Gonzalez Crisp. Las Vegas would have lost its sparkle without co-author Frances Anderton, who brings a fresh and sunny openness, curiosity and relish to any project she touches and whose charm was a major asset in production of our books on Las Vegas.

I truly miss my late cohorts in California architectural history who were very much alive when I first started writing: the incomparable gimlet-eyed aesthete and raconteur Esther McCoy, the ever industrious and kind beyond words David Gebhard, the gentle and cultivated Alson Clark and, finally, that gonzo guru of love and architectural mayhem, the matchless Pied Piper, John Beach.

I owe thanks to John Pastier and Barbara Goldstein for assistance in writing and publishing my work, Mildred Freidman of the Walker Art Institute for the chance to do an issue of the *Design Quarterly*, Michael Delgado of the now vanished *Los Angeles Institute of Contemporary Art Journal*, Gary Kornblau of *Art Issues*, Julie Silliman and Deborah Murphy of the Los Angeles Forum for Architecture and Urban Design for encouragement and their support for the Monacelli *Architecture and Urbanism of Everyday Life* book, the patient and forbearing Natalie Shivers in her role as my editor in the *Forum Newsletter*, *Offramp* editors Mark Skiles, John Colter and SCI-Arc publishing wizard Margie Reeves for their help in realizing the "Pirate" article, and Nan Ellin for including a revamped version of that essay in the *Anthology of Fear*.

Earlier versions of the following chapters in this book were originally published in the following books and magazines.

"Las Vegas: Pirates! Volcanoes! Neon! Welcome to the Capitol of Non-Glamour!" was compiled with Frances Anderton from *Las Vegas: a Guide to Architecture* (1997) and *Las Vegas: The Success of Excess* (1998) both written in 1995 and both published by Ellipsis Press, London, a division of the German publishing house Koneman.

"Finding Los Angeles in the Movies" and "Knocking Off the Knock-Offs" originally appeared, footnoted, as Chapter 3 of *Exterior Decoration: Hollywood's Inside-Out Houses*, published by Hennessey & Ingalls in 1982 as part of a series of monographs on California architecture edited by David Gebhard.

"How Can I Miss You When You Won't Go Away?: Convention Versus Invention and the Survival of Period Revival in Southern California" originally appeared under the titles "How Can I Miss You When You Won't Go Away" in Oct.–Nov. 1990 in the *Newsletter of the Los Angeles Forum for Architecture and Urban Design*, under the editorship of Natalie Shivers.

"A Curmudgeon's Guide to Urban Living: Paranoia, Pagoda, and Pirate Cave" originally appeared in the 1996 issue of the SCI-Arc journal *Offramp*, edited by Mark Skiles and John Colter, under the title "The Pet, the Pagoda and the Pirate Cave" and a different version of it later appeared in *The Architecture of Fear* under the title "Paranoia Informs Place-Making," an anthology edited by Nan Ellin and published by Princeton University Press, 1997.

"Trashy Space, Trashy Behavior and Trashy People" was originally written in another form in 1997 for the anthology *The Architecture and Urbanism of Everyday Life* for Monacelli Press compiled by myself, Margaret Crawford, and John Kaliski, published in 1999. The version in this volume also includes material transferred from the several earlier versions of the "Curmudgeon" piece.

"The Stucco Box," with John Beach, originally appeared in *Home Sweet Home: American Domestic Vernacular Architecture*, Craft and Folk Art Museum, Los Angeles; Rizzoli, New York, 1983, edited by Charles W. Moore, Kathryn Smith and Peter Becker. It also appeared in a condensed version with photos by Judy Fishkin in Barbara Goldstein's Arts and Architecture magazine, 1984, vol. 3, no. 3, pp. 42–47.

"The Making of Mountaingate" originally appeared as a two part series in the November, 1978 and January, 1979 issues of *LA Architect* during the editorship of Margaret Bach.

"You are What You Buy: The Consumerist Imperative in American Building Production" is a conflation of the following articles: *The Garret, the Boardroom and the Amusement Park* and *Five Basic Classifications of Building Production*, published in the Spring 1983 *LAICA Journal* of the now defunct Los Angeles Institute of Contemporary Art, Los Angeles; "The Garret the Boardroom and Amusement Park" reprinted in the November 1992 issue of *Journal of the Society of Architectural Education* and "The Role of Consumerism in American Architecture" in the same journal in August of 1991, both articles under the editorship of Diane Ghirardo; "Unvernacular Vernacular" in *Design Quarterly* 131, 186; "All Consuming Architecture" in *Art Issues*, December 1989/January 1990; "Buy or Die: Some Categories of Consumer Oriented Architecture" in *Art Issues,* Summer 1991, edited by Gary Kornblau; and "Shopping for Architecture: The Sequel" in *Proposals: 33-D6-E6, Rethinking the Beverly Center*, 1990, a pamphlet of the Los Angeles Forum for Architecture and Urban Design originally published in the *Newsletter of the Los Angeles Forum for Architecture and Urban Design* Dec. 1989 under the editorship of Natalie Shivers.

PART ONE
THE SOUTHERN CALIFORNIA HOME AS COMMODITY

6110 Saturn Drive, Los Angeles. Built for Mark and
Jeanette Lefko, 1960. The fins are a method of disguising a
rectangular box.

the stucco box

with John Beach

I: the stucco box

Although commercial vernacular architecture often borrows from high architecture, it nonetheless has a life of its own complete with its own vocabulary of forms, design methodology and set of individual designers.

The stucco-surfaced speculative apartment house is a symbol, for good or ill, of that golden age of Los Angeles, the 1950s. It was a time when Southern California seemed to come into its own, as a place where social and economic mobility combined with a benign climate to create a mythic good life, accessible, it seemed, to almost everyone. The stucco box apartment house reflected at once the pragmatic and hedonistic character of Southern California.

It was ruthlessly expedient, made out of the cheapest materials, by the simplest construction methods, allowing a maximum number of units to be shoehorned onto a single lot. At the same time, these buildings were glamorously packaged consumer objects that often permitted more contact with the outdoors, easier access to the auto and greater recreational opportunities than had Los Angeles' earlier tenement-style apartment houses. Some stucco boxes were more daringly abstract and more completely modernistic than others; these are the buildings that are the focus of this essay.

The stucco box apartment houses were generally two- or sometimes three-story wood-frame, stucco-finished, four- to 16-unit buildings on single or paired 50-foot-wide lots (though some had as many as 70 units), stretching far back from the street. They were built by small investors, contractor/owners or investment syndicates. Their interiors were functional and, if one discounts the occasional decorative detail such as the swag lamp or the exotic glitter-surfaced ceilings, rather minimal.

The stucco box was constructed as in-fill housing in already established neighborhoods, in the metropolitan core from Echo Park through Santa Monica and out to the San Fernando Valley, as well as in the still developing suburban areas of Los Angeles like Orange County and the South Bay. It reached its fullest development as a type during the years from 1954—when it was spurred by the popularity of modernism, the Post World War II housing boom and the mass-production of aluminum-frame sliding windows— to 1960, when more rigorous parking requirements and changing tastes signaled its eventual demise.

The ornamental components of the stucco box were normally confined to the publicly visible surfaces: the street elevation, and, when there was one, the courtyard. The sides and rear were treated in the most pragmatic and economical manner possible, resulting in large areas of smooth stucco wall, rhythmically repetitive window patterns and cubic forms that hover over the voids of the carport.

Windows were mass-produced, metal-frame units placed at the surface of the wall with no reveal. These windows created the image of a depthless plane, a light, technologically advanced membrane. The front of the stucco box was seldom austere (although there were exceptions), but from the side or rear most examples would have seemed quite in keeping if transported to one of the purist German "Siedlungen" housing exhibitions of the 1920s and '30s. The concept of building a simple, boxlike structure with the most easily available construction materials and methods and then fronting it with an elaborate facade was nothing new, especially in Los Angeles. The boxy utilitarian building had been used in residential and other construction ever since the Spanish first settled the region. Turn-of-the-century brick or wood tenement buildings were often completely unadorned at their side and rear elevations.

Prior to the stucco box, stucco had been more frequently applied to thick masonry walls, as in the Spanish Colonial Revival, than used to express its actual paper-thin thickness. Local precedents for this new use include such examples as Lloyd Wright's 1926 Sowden house, in which fragments of elaborate ornamentation are added to the exterior of an otherwise ruthlessly plain stucco surface.

The chief difference between earlier tenements and the stucco box was that the materials used in the latter lacked the scale and three-dimensional depth of the brick or tongue-in-groove siding used previously. Both brick and wood siding are composed of small elements and possess reveals or overlaps between the individual units of material that demonstrate their depth. Not only did the materials of the stucco box lack any sense of weight, plasticity or physical presence, the manner in which they were treated made no attempt to hide this fact. The honesty of the stucco box was inadvertent,

658 N. Hayworth Avenue. Designed by Sam Reisbord and built for Jerome M. White and Assoc. Like the automobiles of the same generation this 1958 West Hollywood apartment house comes equipped with fins.

Goldwater Vista Villas. 2060 Vista del Mar, Hollywood Hills, c. 1960. When the stucco box encounters an obstacle in the form of an oddly shaped lot or a change in grade it usually meets the problem head on and conquers it through the most direct possible means. The ad hoc solutions of the stucco box builders and designers to such problem sites often create the most visually complex boxes because of the dialogue between the specific demands of the site and the builders' determination to have these special features distort their standard formula as little as possible.

2488 Beachwood Lane, Los Angeles. Built by Marcus Shipman, Jack Chernoff, architect, 1957. A basically rectilinear stucco box is made to appear expressively configured by a butterfly room profile and a sloped carport ceiling.

born of the ease with which a speculative developer could disguise economic necessity as modernistic chic.

There was nothing precedent-setting about the use of overtly modern imagery for speculative apartment houses in Los Angeles. The Streamline Moderne of the 1930s used rounded corners, pipe railings and flat roofs to suggest the excitement of the machine age. And the use of modern imagery, albeit of a different order, became even more common in the postwar 1940s. But the stucco box designers developed a whole battery of highly original abstract effects that arose directly out of the nature of stucco as a medium. They scored it, in stripes and in grids, and painted it in contrasting colors. They scattered dark-colored sand or grit over light-colored walls to create a smoky overlay, and they imbedded small chips of pumice in the surface to give it textural interest analogous to chocolate-chip ice cream. Color was an integral part of the appeal of the stucco box, for much of its decoration was painted on rather than built.

The colors themselves were often intense pastels, some of them never before used with such abandon in domestic architecture, especially not in these drop-dead combinations: for example, black and pink or turquoise and gold. In fact, the colors of the stucco box had more in common with colors popular in automobile, fashion, advertising, industrial design and Modern art in the 1950s than they had with previous residential building color palettes (with the possible exception of Victorian polychrome). Some of the lower-budget stucco boxes were so stripped, their chief boast was that they did come in assorted colors, like Easter eggs or Christmas tree balls.

As Thomas Hine wrote in his book on post-World War II consumerist design, *Populuxe,* "To the simple mass-produced artifact that was known to be at the heart of every consumable, from salt-shaker to house, was added an overlay of fantasy of personalization, of style. Americans reveled in a kind of innocent hedonism, buying objects in vibrant two-tone combinations of turquoise and taupe, charcoal and coral, canary and lime." A choice of colors created product differentation in refrigerators, autos and apartment buildings alike. The colors were part of an explosion of consumerism that had kicked into high gear by 1954.

The roof of the stucco box was usually flat, though hipped or low-pitched roofs with the gable end facing the street were used where it was necessary to project a more conventional ideal of domesticity. When pitched roofs were employed, they were often exaggerated and stretched to great lengths, with the gable and the body of the building expressed as a single volumetric whole. Butterfly roofs that pitched up, rather than down at the ends, were sometimes incorporated to signify modernity. When the butterfly roof was used, it was often terminated by a flat, horizontal sunshade/entablature, as though the thin roof plane had simply folded down at a right angle. Frequently found in modernistic coffee shop buildings contemporaneous with the stucco box, it was a roof form borrowed form the expressionistic Modernism of Frank Lloyd Wright. The same roof also appears in the work of Southern California Modernists. A short list of buildings that incorporate this roof includes: 1938–59 Taliesin West, John Lautner's, Googie's Coffee Shop of 1947 and R.M. Schindler's Van Dekker house of 1940, Rodriguez house of 1941, and Richard Neutra's 1942 Nesbitt house.

Access to the apartments was most frequently provided in smaller buildings by a two-level exterior corridor along one side, and in larger buildings by a central courtyard, wholly or partially surrounded by the open corridor. Ideally, the courtyard would contain a swimming pool, though more often it did not. In either case the courtyard or linear passageway garden was landscaped and paved to appear as a communal patio.

The stucco box could either be classified as a 1940s garden apartment denuded of much of its garden or as a miniature tenement that has gained a garnish of landscaping. The vocabulary of the 1950s stucco box and especially of its site planning was more like that of the suburban garden apartment commonly found in sections of the San Gabriel or San Fernando valleys. The imagery is that of the resort, redolent with an air of escapism, which might refer to the tropics or, just as readily, to an outer-space journey. This notion of being on vacation all year round was symbolized by the landscaping, the lighting, the graphics and the outdoor access to all the units. The lack of overhanging eaves made the brilliant expanses of wall seem to reflect the smoggy glare of the California sunshine with redoubled intensity. For this reasons of association, the stucco box is a descendant of courtyard housing—even though many of the boxes had nary a courtyard, nor even a real side yard, to call their own, and often equaled or surpassed the high ratio of lot coverage achieved by the tenements of the 1890 to 1930 era in Los Angeles.

The lighting and landscaping of the stucco box were as exhibitionistic as the ornament. Plants were selected for their dramatic silhouettes, such as dracaena, sago palms and agave, or for their luxuriant tropical foliage, such as philodendron and rubber plants. They were frequently isolated as sculptural elements or graphic accents. Exotic specimens, such as a split-leaf philodendron or a giant bird-of-paradise clump, might be displayed not only as part of the landscape ensemble, but as an isolated abstract pattern, elaborately outlined and pierced against the even color field of the stucco surface. At night the wall was further enlivened by the intense shadows cast by colored "Malibu" spotlights concealed in the front lawn or planter bed. The notion of completing a building with its landscape is reminiscent of the 18th century aesthetic of the Picturesque, but the way it was accomplished was pure Hollywood.

The name of the stucco box, written in large plywood script, was frequently one of the key design elements in a largely blank front. A name might be balanced compositionally by a star-burst lamp or a horizontal series of bathroom windows. The buildings were packaged objects, just as much as album covers or cologne bottles, and the name was the label that signaled how to read the rest of the accouterments.

14025 Moorpark Street, Van Nuys, built by Dr. Albert Zdenek, A.J. Arnay architect, 1956. The modernism of the stucco box was sometimes tamed through the use of rustic materials and a garden setting. Photo by Regula F. Campbell.

The name of the stucco box was an integral part of its image, and the naming was an important event for its owner. In the 1950s and '60s, Los Angeles rental property was an attractive investment for the reasonably well-off small investor. In many cases, the stucco box represented the life savings of its builder and was a solid, publicly displayed symbol of personal success. Pride in this accomplishment accounts for the frequency with which stucco boxes were given human names, just as a boat might: the Melody Ann, for instance, in Inglewood, or the Muscat Apartments in Echo Park.

Sometimes the name evoked other places, other times, both future and past: Telstar in the San Fernando Valley, or the Algiers in Rosemead. Or the name might refer to the location of the building, such as the Cinema in Hollywood, or the Starlet across from Warner Studios in Burbank. It could be a pun on the street name, as in the Rocks of Gibraltar on Gibraltar Street in Baldwin Hills or the Fountain Bleu on Fountain Avenue in West Hollywood. The Beverly Wilton, standing at the intersection of Beverly and Wilton, seems wistfully to aspire to Beverly Hilton-hood. Many of the names offered escapist references to resorts or Las Vegas casinos—the Sands,

The Danielle Apartments. 209 S. Rampart, Los Angeles, c. 1959. The Danielle illustrates both the popularity of Mondrianesque motifs and the ephemeral materials employed in the adornment of the stucco box.

Palms, Dunes and Capri. Not surprisingly, in a place and time when pride in the suburban yard was so important, quite a few stucco box names included the talismanic word "garden."

The stucco boxes were not anonymous developer buildings. Many of them had architects, and their type and style were clearly defined as a genre of commercial vernacular architecture. Jack Chernoff, an architect who has designed some 2,000 apartment buildings, many of them stucco boxes, is probably as good a person as any to illustrate the usual experience of a stucco box designer. Chernoff's typical client for a stucco box apartment was "a guy in the nee-

8600 W. Rugby Drive, West Hollywood. Built by the Monica Estates Corp., Herman Fidler, architect, 1957. This building constitutes a virtual cram course in the decorative vocabulary of the stucco box. It combines fins, rocky-road ice cream-like panels of lava rock and the dented fender-like panels used as balcony railings.

dle trade, maybe a small manufacturer, who pulled together 10, 15, 20 thousand dollars to buy a lot." Many of these buildings had an approximately equal number of 650- to 700-square-foot one-bedroom units and 900-square-foot two-bedroom units. "Hopefully it [the apartment building] would make the investor a living, but it would not make him rich," Chernoff noted. At some points in the post-World War II period, there was an oversupply of units on the housing market, and apartment owners were forced to offer two or three months free rent to their prospective tenants. Many of Chernoff's clients lived in the rear units of their four- to six-unit buildings, some of them for 20 years or more.

Using a set cost of eight to ten dollars a square foot, Chernoff would attempt to "pack" the building as full of units as the parking requirements would allow by eliminating hallway space and by opening up the kitchen to a living-dining room. This idea, of the combined living and dining room open to the kitchen, was not adopted until the 1940s in Southern California (aside from one-room efficiency apartments) and did not become widespread until the 1950s. An early example is Sumner Spaulding and John Rex's "Apartments for Nurses" published in the November 1948 *Arts and Architecture* magazine.

Speaking of some apartments he had then recently designed, Chernoff was quoted in a 1972 *Los Angeles Times West* magazine article saying "We're looking for some dramatic punch that'll bring tenants in. Most important is an attractive exterior. We give them enough to get them in, not more. We don't waste any money on exteriors. Once they're in, they have to love these apartments. We give them the illusion of space. We'll cram in as many units as we can. I ask myself what can I cram in here and still get a nice feeling?" Chernoff went on to state that the buildings had flat facades and flat roofs because the two went together nicely and because they were the most economical choices possible.

The stucco box was well-suited to the newcomer in Los Angeles, and during the stucco box era there was no shortage of newcomers: Los Angeles' population increased by two million during each decade of the 1940s and the '50s. The boom tapered off to a increase in population of a mere million in the 1960s. Apartment construction reflected this trend: greater than ever numbers of them were built in the period from 1952 to 1966, peaking in 1962–63 at 2,300 permits per year. Apartment building then dwindled to only 300 permits per year and the pace of construction continued to be slow until 1975.

The stucco box inhabitant was often single or newly married, and upwardly mobile. He or she might not have considered the apartment as a permanent way of life, as may have been the case in denser American cities. So the stucco box maintained some of the social amenities of the bungalow court, a type initially developed, in part, as carefree vacation accommodation. These apartments were viewed not simply as a place of temporary shelter, but as an introduction to the near mythic, and much written about, social, sexual and climactic conditions of California living.

The automobile was an important influence on the stucco box. It became, in effect, part of the building, on display in the carport. The need to accommodate it helped to determine the form of the building and how much area would be left available, or rendered unavailable, for landscaping.

Parking was most frequently provided at grade level, on the periphery of the building, as an open carport that was recessed along one or more of its sides. If parking was required along the street facade, the second floor would often float on thin pipes above the void of the carport to become a light technological object, separate from the landscape in characteristic high-art Modernist fashion. In some cases this arrangement took on the uncanny aspect of a pop homage to Le Corbusier's villas of the 1920s and '30s, particularly when a series of small individual windows were united as a horizontal band by a picture-frame molding surround. The window frame facing, exaggerated to appear as a frame, was a legacy of the 1940s. In the 1950s the frame was often extended to include more than one window, creating an ambiguity of scale. These surrounds sometimes incorporated a grille, which partially concealed the architectonic order of the windows and the wall behind it, creating a new, superimposed cosmetic order.

Placing the garage at the front of a residential building was nothing new in Los Angeles—it had become commonplace in projects by Modernist architects such as the Laurelwood apartments of 1948 by R.M. Schindler or the Strathmore apartments of 1937 by Richard Neutra. Still, however much the garage or carports were on display, the automobile itself was invariably hidden behind screens or garage walls and doors. It was not until after World War II that architects and speculative builders began taking the doors, and sometimes the side walls, off garages so that the automobile and the negative form of the garage space became part of the design.

The advantages of this approach were several: it was economical, it eliminated the maintenance of garage doors and it made it easier to get the auto in and out of its parking space. Stylistically, the airiness and insubstantiality of the open garage fit easily into both the aesthetic of the postwar, post-and-beam school of high-art Southern California modernism and the aesthetic of the developer's stucco box apartment. Speculative builders may, in fact, have been a step or two ahead of the high-art architects in their use of open carports, though projects incorporating carports, numbering among their designers Greta Magnusson Grossman, Carl Louis Maston, Raymond Kappe and Craig Ellwood, were published in *Arts and Architecture* magazine during the first half of the 1950s.

Parking was the chief limit on the size of stucco box developments. According to the ratio of floor area to building-lot area permitted by the zoning code, most stucco boxes could have held more units than they actually

4450 Murrietta Avenue, Van Nuys. Built for Kibrick and Wilson, 1956. The most popular alternative to the flat roof for stucco boxes was an elongated pitched roof with the gable end facing the street.

did, but it was often impossible to provide the parking spaces necessary to build up to this limit. Doing so would have meant the inclusion of a concrete subterranean parking garage and a third or fourth story at greater expense. This type of larger apartment house with three or more stories over sunken parking became more common in the 1960s, because of intensified development pressures and changes in parking requirements.

After World War II, parking requirements held even at one space per each unit of more than three habitable rooms until 1958, when additional spaces were required per unit. In 1968 the requirement was upped again, so that a unit of more than three habitable rooms required two spaces, and each three-room unit required 1.5 spaces. Another change in parking laws during the 1960s outlawed a favorite stucco box device, back-out parking. Back-out parking often had taken up all the street frontage,

1035 Sierra Bonita Avenue, West Hollywood. Built by Glassman, Singer and Ecker, John Day architect, 1956–57. Individual windows, groups of windows and sometimes entire stucco box facades were often enclosed with picture frame or shadow box surrounds.

as well as the entire front yard setback and the sidewalk, for use as the back-out access area for parking tucked under the second story. This kind of parking effectively eliminated both curbside parking spaces for the public and the parkway strip with its attendant landscaping. When these buildings with tuck-under back-out parking were built next to each other they created an instant asphalt and concrete wasteland.

As important as parking in determining the look of the stucco box were its surface materials: the stucco finish of its walls, the ornament and trim added to these walls and the aluminum-frame sliding windows. In the United States the introduction of metal-frame sliding windows was closely linked to the introduction of custom sliding-glass doors, which began to appear just before World War II. The early sliding doors were hung from the bottom of their frame and often jammed. Sliding windows had been made of steel in the late '40s and early '50s, but they, too, frequently jammed. Architect Carl Dumbolton designed an improved bottom rolling door for the Arcadia Metal Products Company. Advertisements for steel-frame, metal sliding doors by the Glide and Steelbilt Companies first appeared in *Arts and Architecture* magazine in 1948. The early doors were first made of steel, later of wood and steel, then wood and aluminum, and finally all aluminum. The

1720 N. Bronson Avenue, Hollywood. Built for Mike Baum in 1955. It perches on the brink of the Hollywood freeway. The wing above the carport shows the stucco box at its boxiest.

steel sliders were replaced by aluminum sliders, in part because the use of aluminum in the war effort had helped lower its cost. The first advertisement in *Arts and Architecture* magazine for aluminum-frame sliding windows appeared in *Arts and Architecture* in January 1954 for Ador, followed shortly by the Miller, Panavision, Glide and Slideview product lines.

Alcoa manufactured aluminum double-hung windows as early as 1950. By 1954 the use of mass-produced aluminum-frame sliding windows and standard sizes (6 feet by 6 feet, 8 inches) for sliding doors became widespread. In effect, the nail-on aluminum window was pushed almost flush with the wall plane, emphasizing the overall flat appearance. Another common aluminum-frame window treatment of approximately the same era was a large pane of fixed glass flanked by panels of louvered jalousies.

Stucco as a material, regardless of its particular application, has gotten very bad press. The stucco box is no exception. The "Whited sepulchre," the Biblical metaphor for a suave surface concealing unspecified corruption, is perhaps the earliest slur. And today there is the illogical but apparently ineradicable attitude that since stucco is purely a surface material, what it covers must be unhealthy or immoral. Perhaps the ease with which stucco can be used to fake other materials, such as marble, brick, and even wood bark, is responsible for the general suspicion with which it's treated by critics and historians. However, the versatility and economy of stucco have made it a valuable material for vernacular builders and for many high-art designers in Southern California, including Wright, Schindler, Ain and Neutra.

In California stucco was first employed as one of the many finishes found in Queen Anne buildings of the 1880s, principally in small panels in the gables of houses. Buildings partially or entirely sheathed in stucco did not begin to appear regularly until the 1890s, as part of the Mission Revival, when stucco was used on wood-frame buildings to suggest adobe construction. The plainness of its surfaces also lent it Craftsman associations, as in, for example, some of Irving Gill's earlier buildings. By the 1920s, California was a stucco Eden. Its stucco surfaces had evolved into a well-defined vernacular, wood-framed construction type with a standard set of techniques, details and costs for its finishes.

This pragmatically determined building type was arrayed in the style of Modernism, popularly adapted from the world of high-art architecture. A high-art style that ventures into the vernacular world must have a series of trademarks that can be immediately grasped by those with no architectural training or knowledge. These trademarks are not mere stylistic gestures; they are metaphors for a wide range of aesthetic, psychological and historical associations, in short, a complete set of attitudes about life and art. In the case of Modernism, these peripheral but indispensable associations include abstract art, the stream of consciousness novel, Freud, plastic, speed, cinema and technological progress. This same set of associations has been evoked at successive stages of the stucco box's development by periodically updated sets of images and details.

The trademarks of vernacular modernism in the 1950s and '60s were taken from four primary sources: high-art architecture, abstract art, automobile design and interior decoration. It is no coincidence that the most ebulliently Modernistic apartment houses were built during the 1950s, while Detroit was turning out the most flamboyantly Modernistic automobiles in history. The moxie of 1950s auto design, seen in such details as two-tone paint jobs or harlequin patterns on the dashboards, set a benchmark of sophistication and daring that other artifacts of that decade had to meet, even as the auto stylists themselves were influenced by the prevailing fashions of

175 S. Oxford Avenue, Koreatown. Built by J. Howard and J. Greenberg, Max Starkman, architect, 1958. The front facades of the stucco box were often blank, given over to abstract/graphic designs in which the address was often an important element.

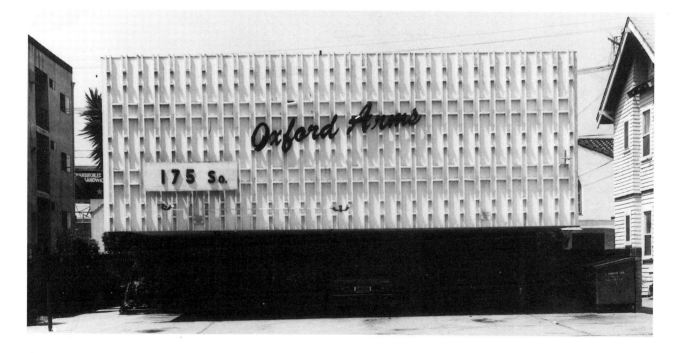

the times. Both the tail-fin on the automobile and the star-burst light on the stucco box were indications that the consumer products they were attached to were new, exciting and up-to-date.

George Nelson's splashy, star-burst clocks may have served as a precedent for the innumerable star-burst lights on the front facades of the stucco boxes. Typically these shallow, bowl-shaped clocks, first advertised in *Arts and Architecture* magazine in 1951, were mounted nearly flush to the wall surface and lit from behind. The surface was pierced with tiny holes, so the light exploded outward in a halo of long spikes.

Borrowing from the local tradition of high-art architectural Modernism, apartment builders converted the exhibitionistic expression of John Lautner and Lloyd Wright into a graphic language of pattern and decoration. One commonly used motif was a bas-relief or semidetached rectangular plane, surfaced with fieldstone or a scored grid pattern. It had formal precedents in the constructivist tendencies of local work by Schindler and Neutra, as seen in Neutra's Kaufmann house of 1946, which displayed a constructivist, latter-day de Stijl attitude to the International style by contrasting stone with stucco walls. The visual and spatial explosion of the box was further popu-

920 El Centro Avenue, Hollywood. Built by Guy and Josephine Welch, 1958. When the stucco box engaged itself to the public streetscape, it often did so out of necessity, because of a narrow lot. This communication with the street frequently took the form of outdoor stairways, or as here, rows of balconies.

larized in the early 1950s work of Carl Maston, Ray Kappe, Thornton Ladd and Greta Magnusson Grossman.

A major influence on all popular design of the 1950s and one much loved by the builders of the stucco box was the abstraction of comtemporary high-art painting and sculpture. Starkly counterposed rectangles, á la Mondrian, were likely to appear in the design of clocks, jewelry, ceramics, magazine layouts and stucco box facades.

Less popular, although still common, were the biomorphic boomerang and kidney shapes of coffee tables and ashtrays a lá Miro, which also turned up on fabrics and Formica. Counterposed rectangles and boomerangs appear in the stucco box primarily as two-dimensional cutouts mounted on the wall plane, but they also occur as entrance canopies, planters and swimming pools. These carefully irregular forms were freely employed to enrich the appearance of the building, but they were almost never used to shape the structure itself; unless distorted by environmental circumstance, the stucco box remained rigidly orthogonal because of traditional economies of construction.

The cardinal rule of cosmetic architecture is that the fabric and the architectonic order of the building do not determine the visual impression made by the building on its viewers. Look, the building says, I am just a piece of paper, acting as a canvas for graphic or abstract patterns. This decorative approach is easier and less expensive than trying to unite the plan and elevation of the building as a single architectonic whole.

It was precisely because of this customary orthogonal conformity that the infrequent stucco box exceptions to this rule are so appealing, having as they do both plastic and graphic interest. Occasionally a change in grade might cause the ceiling of a car-port to be sloped rather than flat or, rarely, the edge of the building above the car-port might be chamfered. In some cases the stucco boxes were given fins or appendages that made them appear to be sculpturally configured. Apartments built on steeply sloping lots, or triangular lots left over from freeway construction, were often given added character by their straightforward accommodations to these circumstances.

Although the entire stucco box facade was frequently treated as an environmentally scaled abstract relief, it was also common practice to treat the elevation in the manner of an interior decorator, with objects placed in the same manner as they might be upon a shelf or mantel as might be found in a living room. The swag lamp, the wall sconce, the picture frame, the ornamental plaque and the shadow box were all staple devices of interior decoration that were placed on the street facade as if to symbolize the quasi-public nature of the interior life that was led there. The shared courtyard and the walkways that functioned as balconies, with or without a swimming pool, served in the literature of the period, and not infrequently in actuality, as outdoor rooms for parties, barbecues and general socializing.

One variant of the stucco box building type, used either to indicate an especially high level of poshness or to accommodate an elevator, featured a vestibule in which the street wall was almost completely glazed. This glazing created a space not unlike the one-wall-removed convention of traditional set design. Inside were the real icons of interior decoration, carefully chosen and arranged for public view: elaborate flocked wallpaper, an ornamental plaque large enough to be seen from the street, a chandelier or swagged hanging lamp—overscaled and of complex design—and at least one indoor plant capable of casting dramatic shadows. This entry-cum-showcase distributed its éclat equally among the inhabitants of the apartment house. Usually the tone was Modernist, though some of its parts clearly aspired to the Baroque, particularly the light fixtures and wall coverings.

In the parallel universe of high art architecture, blank facades were also being created, just as in the stucco box. Craig Ellwood's iconic Hunt house of 1955–57 at 24514 Malibu Beau Road, Malibu. The facade is composed of a pair of garages flanking a glass courtyard.

The abstraction and minimalism inherent in the stucco box, combined with its utilitarian bent, produced some facades that were simply blank walls, interrupted only by the entrance, the address, two or three lights and perhaps a few bits of scattered ornament. By the 1950s in Los Angeles the need for privacy was more important than any desire to maintain contact with the street. The cheapness and the Modernistic cachet of these dazzlingly blank facades allowed the stucco box designers to ignore orthodox notions of welcoming domesticity that the inclusion of windows on a facade might have conveyed.

In Southern California the stucco box was part of a regional vernacular of Modernism. Despite the fact that we are frequently informed nowadays that Modernism was never popular, the phenomenal sales figures for free-form ashtrays, Finnish dinnerware and wire-basket chairs during the 1950s and early '60s prove otherwise. Expressionistic Modernism had the power to engage the popular imagination because it could serve as a vehicle for personal

764 Doheny Road, West Hollywood, 1959. Designed by Kenneth S. Iwota for Paul Wexler and Harvey Gerry. It would have been unthinkable for decorators to horse around dressing up a blank facade with chess pieces and super-scale quoining even ten years earlier.

fantasy. It dominated commercial vernacular architecture in Southern California for more than a decade.

From the late 1950s until the mid-1960s Modernist high-art buildings were publicized in Southern California newspapers as well as in the professional magazines. Almost every issue of the Home section of the Sunday *Los Angeles Times* would feature at least one Modernist residence, which may also have appeared in the banner carrier for Southern California Modernism, the magazine *Arts and Architecture*, available at many local newsstands alongside *Time* and *The New Yorker*. One publication that may have influenced stucco box designers was *House and Home*, which published the infamous article on '50s expressionist architecture, "Googie architecture," in February 1952. Other relevant projects published in the

111 Oxford, Koreatown, c. 1960. A wooden grille covers the windows, imposing a cosmetic architectural order on this apartment house. Cosmetic architectural order has been characteristic of a significant amount of commercial vernacular building in southern California.

magazine were Raphael Soriano's Colby apartments, Kenneth H. Lind's Sunset Apartments in Pacific Palisades and Elliot Noyes house at New Canaan, Conneticut.

These published buildings were studied, interpreted and reinterpreted by clients, developers and builders who probably owned a component hi-fi system, a slat-bench coffee table and a reasonably late model automobile. Some of these partisans of the Modern felt that historical reference in their personal environment was at best dishonest and at worst unsophisticated. They formed a public that was highly self-conscious of living in the 20th century and they demanded an up-to-date backdrop for their everyday life. It was not a rigorous, theoretical or high-art Modernism that they wanted, rather, it was accommodating, inexpensive and vernacular.

However, while the decoration of the stucco box celebrated Modernism, there was less enthusiasm for the vitality of its architectural vocabulary than there was for its cheapness. The grilles, frames and panels that were applied to the stucco box could even be made out of scrap wood. It was possible to use such ephemeral effects on the stucco box because its decoration was flat and graphic. The inexpensive materials worked well because the aesthetic of the stucco box did not demand that they appear to be anything other than additive, abstract decorations, for which the pattern was much more important than the material from which it was made.

Sometimes, the basically Modernist stucco box was overlaid with period revival elements, usually exotic ones, ranging from Aztec to Assyrian. But the designers did not attempt to create a complete period-revival environment of another time or place, as was the fashion in the 1920s or '30s. Rather, they would place a few signifying fragments of the style in question at some crucial focus, normally the entrance, in an otherwise modernist facade, just as an archaeological artifact might be displayed on a pedestal in a white-painted room in a museum.

The neutral box could also accommodate decoration that symbolized other themes. In the 1950s the imagery of the "Modern Colonial" and the suburban Ranch-style house, with its mock-hand-hewn siding and diamond-paned windows, was a distant runner-up in popularity to Modernistic themes for smaller apartment houses in Southern California. The 1960s ushered in a period of renewed stylistic eclecticism, rivaling that of the 1920s and '30s in California in the breadth, although not the depth, of its references.

Polynesian and Oriental motifs were popular during the early 1960s. Motifs adapted from the Hollywood Regency style, such as false-fronted mansards and the vertically exaggerated, arched doors originated by John Woolf, were widespread. The mansard theme, which has proved extremely durable in Los Angeles, has passed into the general vocabulary of the area's popular architecture, combining with and symbolizing a variety of styles. Stucco box architect Jack Chernoff readily incorporated the motif in his work.

When first widely employed in Southern California, in the second half of the 1950s, the mansard signified two specific, but diametrically opposed,

Hong Hong Apartments, 17433 Vanowen Street, residential, built by B.B. Morris, 1961. Period references, particularly Polynesian, Oriental and French references became common in the early 1960s. Photo by Regula F. Campbell.

tendencies. Traditionalists saw it as the signifier of French elegance. Modernists, leaning designers and developers could relate its heavily simplified form to the sloped shapes found in Frank Lloyd Wright's work of the 1940s and late 1930s, such as Taliesin West, the Pauson house and the Audbrass Plantation.

As a product of rapid changes in fashion, the stucco box is representative of the commercial vernacular category of building production. While high-art architecture influenced the remodels and, to a certain extent, legitimized the ruthless utilitarianism of stripped side and rear walls, the stucco boxes were chiefly influenced by each other. Some vernacular modes of building have evolved over a long period of time, but the vernacular of the stucco box was couched in the quickly changing, media-popularized styles of a consumer society.

As the post-World War II era perplexingly and obstinately refused to resolve into a technological utopia, and as concern about the toxic side effects of technological processes spread, Modernism began to slip down the architectural Top 40. Changed attitudes toward technology have had an effect upon the form as well as the imagery of the speculative apartment block.

Earlier buildings, and even entire neighborhoods, have been bulldozed for new, multiple-unit speculative buildings that are bigger, denser and blander than the stucco box, just as the stucco box itself had often replaced earlier single-family houses. The generally larger buildings of the 1960s intensified the problems of scale and density inherent in multiple-unit housing without offering a commensurate level of amenities. There was still a significant degree of playful Modernistic invention, but it became less frequent and less imaginative by the end of the 1960s.

Los Angeles' popular Modernist stucco box has become an artifact, representative of relatively stable social values, faith in technological process and an endless upward mobility. Everyone knows what American automobile design of the 1950s represented—fins, chrome and swelling curves combined with sharp angles for sex appeal. It is equally clear that the average Toyota from the 1970s just wasn't trying as hard to seduce, or even to appeal to a broad audience.

The same decline occurred with popular Modernism, especially in Los Angeles during the same eras. The exuberant, Modernistic design of the 1950s described so well in Allan Hess' book *Googie*, is already receding into the past. Many of its major monuments, including the downtown Googies and the Sunset Strip Googies themselves, have disappeared. But just as turquoise trapezoids disappear around the bend, the need for Modernistic ornamentalism rears its triangular neon-lit head once again.

Current [1982] Postmodernist sensibility, while sympathetic to most vernacular phenomena, rejects associations with Modernism because it considers Modernism passé. Buildings with cosmetic Modern facades have in part resulted from the renewed kick that Postmodernism has given to Modernism, permitting a greater degree of disparity between different design elements and a renewed appetite for the flamboyant. In certain respects the stucco box designers were only a link in a series of Modernist cosmeticists, from the Art Deco apartments of the 1930s through to the pop neorationalism of the 1980s. These architects for Southern California residential speculative builders have taken roughly the same tack when confronted with the same problems. They have addressed the same need to compose and style a building that consists of ruthlessly packed units, whose

Robertson Apartments, Robertson Boulevard, Los Angeles, c. 1956–64. Rendering of a lavish courtyard plan, apartment complex designed by Jack Chernoff.

arrangements are dictated by the pragmatic concerns of the speculative market. In each case they superimpose an arbitrary decorative geometric pattern or motif over the basic building envelope and its fenestration.

Modernism has been defined by many critics in such a way as to avoid seriously evaluating such nonpurist variants of orthodox high Modernism as the stucco box, despite its Modern image and its matter-of-fact acceptance of the most readily available technology. In the vernacular fashion, the stucco box grafted the new upon the old to create a product that was simultaneously forward-looking and comfortably familiar.

Its ability to symbolize Los Angeles and to symbolize Modernism in the minds of the critic, the vernacular builder and his or her client alike underlines the significance of the stucco box as a case study in vernacular architecture from the recent past. The stucco box provided a living environment that was a clean, well-lighted space at a human scale, for a reasonable price and with the popular approval to which high-art Modernism aspired, but too seldom achieved.

II: beach and the box

Sixteen years ago I wrote the above essay with John Beach for a catalog about the vernacular house edited by Charles Moore, Kathryn Smith and Peter Becker, *Home Sweet Home*. John Beach the teacher, the lecturer, the writer, the architect, the historic preservationist and Art Deco collector is a now a ghost. He is a ghost because he leaves behind such an extraordinary and palpable after-image, credible as a mythic figure. To take on the role of chronicler always has the potential to cripple one's capacity for action. In John Beach's case his talent for epic interaction with and recording of the environment overpowered all else. He had the ability to edit the raw material of the urban landscape into persuasive and original narratives, containing new subsets and commonalities that one never knew existed until he pointed them out.

Most of John's oeuvre is recorded only by the massive jumble of slides he left behind; most of the categories he created for them, the anecdotal material that fleshed them out and the creative, analytical and syntactical context they fit into died with him.

The live John Beach would rise from a bed littered with slides, a fourth glass of Jack Daniels in hand, and gather up a seemingly random collection of slides from window sill, chair seat and bedspread, simultaneously berating himself and moaning aloud, and then proceed, almost on time, to his speaking engagement. Once he made it to the podium, John would hold an audience of three hundred spellbound, plunging them into the previously unheralded world of, say, vaginal topiary or sleights of hand such as the infamous fake skyscraper on Wilshire Boulevard, six stories high at the front and one story high at the back. John himself probably could not have told you half an hour before a lecture which of a thousand story lines and sequences he might pursue that night.

The creation of complex or difficult visual relationships can be accomplished by a highly creative observer looking for things other people would not think to find. This process is just as meaningful as that of intentional design by an architect. The random single event becomes part of a meaningful collective, and the seeming orphan is matched to previously unknown brothers and sisters. The joke was that Beach's jokes were real: all of these extraordinary things—an entire slide show of buildings whose architectural features formed a face—existed both in their environment as a part of an everyday world and ennobled by their altered context and understanding in Beach-land. Instantly a seemingly random combination of windows and doors became, undeniably, a wall-eyed monster, and not only that, a building that was part of a collection of wall-eyed monsters.

In his slide lectures the audience became Columbus encountering a new world, but magically, and unlike Columbus', a world that existed right under their noses. These other worlds were always challenges to the sense of order and hierarchy presumed by traditional, high art architectural culture. By the end of a good John Beach lecture you hardly dared to go outside the lecture room, because you wondered if you would be up to the welter of new cultural and visual implications that would surely await you on the drive home, as the previously unexceptional took on a entirely new cosmic identity.

There have been other observers of the vernacular environment, such as John Margolies, who have helped create appreciation for genres of buildings, but no one ever logged as many miles of residential and commercial byways in California as John Beach, no one ever pawed through as much of the raw material as he did. And, most importantly, no one else was looking with his eye, no one else was looking for the types of relationships within the pieces of an individual building or between one building and a similar building elsewhere. The study of Modern, vernacular, commercial and consumerist architecture requires this kind of treasure hunt. One looks for published buildings because one has been told what they are and where they are. Vernacular buildings wait silently for you, with no clues as to their location. You don't know what you want to find or what there is to find until you find it. Least of all do you know where it might be.

To his audience, the transformation of glitter stucco to golden narrative was enchanting. No one with a capacity for the appreciation of metaphor or visual character was untouched by this miracle. If high-art architecture supplies heroes, then John Beach, with his finding of equally cogent and complex products in the world of vernacular architecture (such as the drive-through Donut Hole in La Puente), supplied the other personae that any decent novel or movie requires: the fascinating villains and the memorable character actors. These Beachean universes made a compelling argument for considering high-art architecture as merely one part among others of a system of production and consumption of the built environment, rather than the top of a pyramidal value structure.

Bearded and robustly fat, a tangle of greasy, long locks brushing the shoulders of his wildly patterned polyester dashikis (sewed for him by his mother

Mariposa Avenue, Los Angeles, c. 1958–62. Designed by Jack Chernoff. Rendering of Mariposa Lanai.

in Norman, Oklahoma), his smashed and taped-together glasses slipping off his nose, John Beach projected a monumental indifference to worldly conventions. His dedication to his favorite pastimes and his altruism and lively interest in others' lives made him lovably, and tragically, vulnerable.

Of his habit of going barefoot Esther McCoy remarked, "Those bare feet of John's, they look so tender, like little pink pads." And, indeed, since looking at the environment for its own sake an act, untranslated into other products, had no financial reward, those bare feet were an example of just how innocently and unguardedly John traversed the world. Tasks could be set aside at a moment's notice. He was always ready for one more ride through the San Fernando Valley, or one more desk-side chat with a student about Bruce Goff's incorporation of ashtrays, lumps of coal or indoor-outdoor carpeting into his work.

A true saint always makes others pay for that sainthood. His smell, for example. Whatever the frequency and methodology of John Beach's bathing procedures, they never seemed to work. Being near John was like having your face thrust into the crotch of a homeless street person who had been on a ninth-month bender. The odor was a crucial test, such a violation of a widely held social contract that it could only be endured by a true devotee. You could say it was a passive-aggressive control mechanism or you could say it was dégagé, a matter of concentration on ideas and visual stimuli rather than on more routine concerns.

John's inability to deal with some of life's requirements and his impulse to take care of you before he took care of himself meant, finally, that others had to be there to help him. John disliked that his endless browsing through and curating of the built environment, his sharing of his findings in conversation, would invariably have to be interrupted by the eternal nuisances of routine personal maintenance. A tendency to procrastinate, to delay the consummation of a the finished product, meant that it was no easy trick to get writing out of John. He was known to hide out at friends' house so that the people he owed articles to could not find him. He wasn't entirely pleased with me for summarily turning in a version of the above article we wrote together that he still did not considered finished; nor was he happy with all of my editing decisions.

His view of the stucco box? Love at first sight, of course. It was one of the countless worlds in the galaxy of terra incognita that John colonized. After he got out of the army he came to California, finding work at the Equitable insurance company. The Southern California of the 1960s was a splendid blast furnace of material and recreational consumer enjoyment, its new freeways stretching out into still developing territories. Vast and glittering Modernistic supermarkets confronted virgin, acres-wide parking lots. Walls of glass displayed rows of fluorescent lights above and the serried ranks of merchandise below. In 24-hour coffee shops, for the price of a Denver omelet, one could dine in a total design atmosphere of exhibitionistic Wrightian exuberance.

The commercial vernacular architecture of the period was a celebration of appetite: appetite for color, for abstract form, for the momentary triumph of unbridled Modernism in the domestic realm, for mobility and a life of poolside and beachfront recreation. The escapism of the stucco box packaging and presentation was a sign that Southern California was the place where you decided who you wanted to be, rather than who you had been told to be. Boredom was forbidden. There were no forbidden colors, textures or forms. The splashy naming and adornment of the pragmatic stucco-box shell was liberating and exhilarating to John. In the stucco box, the elitist connotations of foreign travel, of far-away places, of abundant leisure time and of control over one's identity were made egalitarian, available to the renter as well as to the tycoon.

Rendering of stucco box apartment by Jack Chernoff, c. 1957. The design mixes a nearly international style basic structure with decorative pattern making, in the degage manner typical of the genre.

III: when all that's glitter has been beiged over

If ever there was coziness this is it—I am for the moment ensconced in a canal boat on the upper Thames. The view of cows hunkered down for a nap is framed by William Morris—print curtains while low-hanging willow limbs sweep the water on the other side of the boat. On the stove is a teakettle, next to it on the counter a jelly jar of wild flowers plucked from the shores of the river by my niece. Planted every 20 yards along the banks is a fisherman with net and line. Passing canal boats come equipped with English sheepdogs, children scampering along their sides and flowerpots on the roof.

The canals and rivers of England, once part of the landscape of production, are now part of the modern landscape of leisure, consumable as a recreational experience precisely because they are disconnected from the everyday world of automobiles, industry and commerce. The chief signs of agricultural production are the spherical bales of hay, like pieces of taffy-colored Tootsie Roll, that lie in the fields as we pass by.

Each of the canal boats is an independent, cast-your-Winnebago-upon-the-water settlement, surrounded by glorious open space, placed in the most intimate contact with the English brand of highly domesticated nature. The painting and decoration of the long and narrow (six and a half feet wide) houseboats is folk-artish with lots of curlicues, outlining of panels and floral adornment.

While the current tourist-life of the canal boats is possible only because of their technological obsolescence as a transport mechanism, the stucco box apartment houses were only made by possible by advances in technology. The use of exposed steel poles, the development of the nail-on aluminum frame window and the acceptability of putting the automobile on display made the stucco box possible. But, like the canal boat, the naming and painting of these buildings made them qualify as a recreational experience, albeit an everyday one and one that required the use of a good deal of imagination.

Neither canal boat nor stucco box is more or less "vernacular" than the other. Both a canal boat builder and a stucco box builder knew perfectly well what to do. They did not have to read instructions or depend on a body of theory to do what they did, since there was a widely accepted way of doing things, with a set mode of construction, colors, shapes, materials and forms in each case. But, nonetheless, even in the supposedly enlightened year of 1983 when the Craft and Folk Art Museum in Los Angeles put on its series of "Home Sweet Home" shows, it was still a battle to persuade the organizers of the show that the stucco box actually was vernacular. It would have been much easier to lobby for canal boats.

I understand why I had a difficult time with the museum. In a sense, the inclusion of a genre of work for study by an architectural historian is a form of legitimization that implies approval and canonization. But the modern urban environment is the product not of the culture of high-art architecture, but rather of the forces of mass production and consumption. Any serious attempt to understand that environment must inevitably account for building types, styles and genres because of their ubiquity and the information they tell us about the culture that made them—not because they should necessarily be imitated. A study of 20th century architecture laundered of building types such as the tilt slab warehouse and the stucco box would be very much like a history of the twentieth century bereft of the influence of television shows, tabloids and shelter magazines. Behavior and beliefs simply could not be explained. Or, indeed, if one takes into account how construction of bottom-rung stucco boxes devastated the fabric of existing single-family neighborhoods in Los Angeles, leaving the stucco box out of architectural history is akin to leaving out war, famine and plague from a social history.

After all, the stucco box is no different than any other residential building type. The delightfulness, or not, of living there depends in part on good, old-fashioned real estate values such as location and size, determined by the income strata for which the apartments were built. Like being better dressed, making a better stucco box just required spending more money. Bigger budgets were required to get pitched roofs with open, high ceilings and clerestory windows, as well as a bigger lot that would accommodate those angled stairways, rubber trees and the turquoise-blue swimming pool.

The urbanism created by the basic stucco box, crammed in on its lot, set-back line to set-back line, could be downright nasty. After all, part of the point of the true small and cheap stucco boxes was the divorce of building form and ornament. The configuration of the box and the placement of its windows were purely expedient. The cosmetics were the pieces that made visual sense out of the basic nonorder of the building. The names, the lights, the plants, the whiz-bang stucco textures and mouth-watering colors were there to distract the observer from just what a brutally cheapskate product the stucco box usually was. If ever there was a pill that needed its sugar-coating, the stucco box is it.

Curb cuts to accommodate back-in parking wiped out the possibility of sidewalk-adjacent landscaping and street trees. Windows in the stucco facades of opposing buildings, unrelieved by any articulation or detail, stared each other down across narrow side yards. Huge windows facing east, west and south placed without regard to long, hot summer days, required being covered with aluminum foil to lower heat gain. If you could have replaced this housing with something better—you would have! To suggest that new housing couldn't offer a higher level of amenities would be absurd. Is it worth making people live in these things so that connoisseurs of popular Modernism and anyone else who wants to learn from the built environment can be entranced by scored stucco in racy colors, star-burst lamps and aging dracaena? Certainly not, if that means preserving living environments that don't make people happy.

In aging sections of Los Angeles, like the eastern portion of West Hollywood, densely packed stucco-box neighborhoods have quite a different meaning to their current occupants, often recent immigrants, than they did to their original occupants. The connotations of star-burst light fixtures, swag lamps and cursive script that boldly spells out "Capri" or "Sands" does not necessarily work its full magic on an elderly émigré from St. Petersburg. So stucco finish with integral, aggregate color is painted over. The plywood cursive script delaminates and is removed. Roses grow between the agaves. In front of the fleur-de-lis concrete block wall is a gaggle of kerchiefed shoppers laden with parcels from the Russian delicatessens on Santa Monica Boulevard. The linkage between image and self-identity that the stucco box once offered is broken. The boxes are now valued simply as commodities, for the amount of space and light they contain and the walking distance to the deli and the synagogue.

We may be coming to the era when key genres of buildings from the recent past, from post—World War II consumer culture, are no longer attractive enough to enough people to make the preservation of these buildings, and districts of these buildings, morally or politically possible. As first Modernistic coffee shops, and then modernistic supermarkets, disappear as a genre from the Southern California landscape, the possibility of understanding what life was like in the 1950s and '60s from the surrounding environment will also disappear.

One wonders just what constituency the stucco box will have, given America's distaste for apartments.

In the long run even the inspiringly shameless and brazen cosmetic conceits of the stucco box will probably not be enough to let the myth survive—to the public at large it will simply be one genre of older apartment types among others. But as an observer, rather than a potential tenant, I still can't help seeing them through John Beach's eyes.

A NOTE ON THE BIBLIOGRAPHY OF THE STUCCO BOX

The first publication of stucco box houses was in Ed Ruscha's *Some Los Angeles Apartments* in 1965, followed by a *Los Angeles Times West* magazine article, "The Blooming of the Plastic Apartment House" in 1972.

Reyner Banham offered up the stucco box under the cheerful pejorative term "dingbat architecture" in his 1973 *Los Angeles: The Architecture of Four Ecologies.* Stucco boxes are also depicted in Charles Jencks' *Daydream House of Los Angeles.* David Gebhard discussed the role of the neutral stucco box in his *Art in America* article "L.A.: The Stucco Box," in 1970, and the term stucco box was employed in my 1982 book, *Exterior Decoration.*

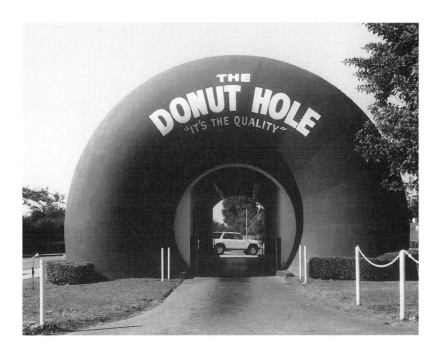

The drive-thru Donut Hole, 1968, John Tindall, Ed McCreany, and Jesse Hood, 15300 East Amar Road, La Puente. A John Beach favorite.

From wilderness to trash dump to subdivision, Mountaingate in 1978.

build your castle upon the trash

the making of mountaingate

Mountain gate as a real estate development is a prime illustration of the kind of misplaced and misconceived urbanization that has so aggravated the social and ecological problems of the region. There are three themes in this essay; the despoilation of wilderness, the paranoid social isolation of the wealthy and the nature of building production as consumerist consumption.

At night it is the line of powerful street lights marching up the hill that catches the eye, breaking the long dark stretch of the Santa Monica Mountains at the Sepulveda Pass. The road looks like it might have something to do with some massive government enterprise, such as the Los Angeles city Department of Water and Power. During the day it is the buildings on the ridge which become prominent, perched like an Italian hilltown far above the road.

The road and the buildings are part of a development constructed for the Barclay Hollander Corporation, a subsidiary of Castle & Cooke, Inc., by Southwest Environments, Inc. Castle & Cooke is an international corporation with land holdings throughout California. Barclay Hollander is a land development subsidiary of Castle Cooke. Southwest Environments administers the Barclay Hollander Corporation. Carl McLarand of Santa Ana is the architect.

The development occupies a ridge overlooking a golf course constructed on a completed landfill *and* the site of a future golf course to be constructed on another landfill. Beyond are spectacular views— smog and weather permitting—of the San Fernando Valley and the Los Angeles Basin. The first phase of this development is a pop-traditional seventy-two unit row-house condominium project called "The Ridge," well under way to completion. With town-houses selling for $325,000 to upwards of $400,000, The Ridge has a conventional, suburban subdivision, plot plan.

In its attempt to create an ersatz version of a place that seems to have been there much longer than it actually has. The Ridge at MountainGate is patterned after traditional, affluent westside Los Angeles neighborhoods according to its promotional literature. It boasts that "Plans call for millions of dollars to be spent on landscaping throughout the development period, so that residents of MountainGate will not have to wait years for their community to achieve the look of permanence and charm." And in the same fashion, pains were taken to make MountainGate's architecture appear to be as established and traditional as possible.

As in other environments of this ilk, such as Forest Lawn or Fisherman's Village, the project is intended to communicate with its audience by simplifying the semiotic qualities of the project as a network of signs and symbols. This network is calculated to tell the viewer what to see and how to experience the environment through design, programming, and, perhaps above all, marketing.

"The concept of creating a product for a market goes back to the beginning." explained MountainGate Marketing Director Michael Harper. Even the names for this development and the four model types in The Ridge are nearly as important as the architecture itself. English names—"The Bristol," "The Coventry," "The Ashford," and "The Dorchester"—are employed for a decidedly non-English architecture. These names reflect the fact that the design and marketing of luxury developments like MountainGate is in many ways similar to the design and marketing of that archetypal consumer item—the luxury automobile.

The promotional literature for MountainGate claims that "MountainGate Drive is lined with a stately wreath of olive trees symbolizing the fortunate lifestyle which awaits at the top." Elsewhere it compares the drive "to a famous drive in Italy just outside Florence that leads to a town where Michelangelo once lived." And perhaps predictably, the brochures perpetuate the mystique of Los Angeles' Westside—a place of "wealth, success and establishment" thus confirming Denise Scott Brown's observation in "Suburban Space, Scale and Symbols" in *Via III* that "The overall image of the community is as important to the people who live there as their own house or street."

At MountainGate, the code word for this mystique is "the Brentwood look," As conceived by the developer and architect, this aesthetic—when translated into architectural terms—is difficult to understand because the terms of translation are vague and confused. The architecture of MountainGate appears to be a montage of the more elegant and classic features of the architecture of Brentwood and Bel Air displaying a few of the more basic period devices, casually appropriated, and largely misunderstood.

Architect McLarand says that he used the work of Wallace Neff as a departure point for his design. (See essay on Wallace Neff on page 93.) Without knowing this, it would be impossible to tell that the memory of Neff's work had anything to do with MountainGate. By itself, the placement of the garage in front of the house is enough to make the Ridge unrecognizable as a stepchild of period revival houses in the pricier neighborhoods of the Westside.

Perhaps the most interesting aspect of the MountainGate exteriors is the device of using a combination of pitched and flat roofs in an attempt to create attached housing that doesn't look attached. The pitched roof elements appear more autonomous when separated by flat roofs. This individual articulation of the units in an eclectic pop style has become a major mode of developer rowhouses in such places as Houston and California.

The interiors of the units at MountainGate do not so much belong under the heading of architecture proper, but rather under the heading of "luxury features and appointments," once again much in the same sense as the provision of optional features in the interior of a Cadillac convertible. While the interiors have good row-house plans which take intelligent advantage of double-height spaces for living, dining and entry areas, and have some fairly theatrical spindled staircases a la Hollywood of the '30s, they can most conveniently be summed up as a standing inventory of the features currently in vogue with the home-buying public.

As important a part of the MountainGate package as the location, the image, and the recreational facilities, are the elaborate security provisions undertaken. "If MountainGate is besieged the Security Center is ready," reads the brochure. Just what could produce such a siege mentality, short of Charles Manson coming up for parole, is left to the private fears of the potential MountainGate customer. "The project is designed for security maximization," which, one supposes, differs from the 'maximum security' prison because it keeps threats to society out and not in.

The security system at MountainGate is monitored from a Security Center at the entrance to the residential section. It includes such features as "Raytek Bi-Spy Intrusion Sensors," "Panic Buttons," and "Product of Combustion" (i.e., fire) detectors. The piece de resistance of the security system must surely be the "unique security-oriented trash disposal—a standard feature wherein a resident does not have to leave the locked confines of his own area to dispose of his daily rubbish,"—an activity which now apparently merits the same degree of privacy and security previously reserved for bathing and sex.

It may seem unfair to belabor in this manner developer housing, a genre which has to date largely escaped the attention of critics, probably because the goals of a development like Mountaingate are so different from the normal goals of criticism within architectural culture. The Ridge calls down this kind of attention on itself by virtue of its location, its price range, the environmental issues it raises, and the fact that—on first impression when seen from the freeway—its hill town aspect seems to promise some special qualities of place which are found to be lacking upon closer inspection.

MountainGate in many ways epitomizes contemporary housing tract development in Southern California. The concept of the locked-gate community, the neo-traditional vocabulary of forms, the aura of prestige, and, now, the offering of attached housing in a price range formerly reserved for detached housing and the complete separation of residential use from any proximity to other users—none of this is unique to MountainGate. In recent years authors such as Mike Davis and Steven Flusty have written about this architecture and urbanism in Southern California as a major force that shapes the form of cities and buildings. Locked gate developments are features of other American cities as well, as discussed on page 136 of the Las Vegas chapter of this book.

This attention to display and to amenities is not wasted on the potential MountainGate buyer. "This is what makes a house, said a woman to her daughter as she surveyed a MountainGate model, "a good entry." In the world of the developer, the machine for living has become a stage set for consumption.

The first time I went to MountainGate I couldn't get in. But no one else could have gotten in either, without prior permission. The Ridge is a locked-gate development. During my next visit, MountainGate did let in some unannounced guests—but they were potential buyers in a Rolls. That second time I went to Mountain Gate—with an appointment this time—the hill across the San Diego Freeway from the subdivision was burning. Little rivulets of orange flames were charring the grassy slopes. The spectacle was showy enough to slow traffic on the San Diego but it was certainly nothing to compare with the big Mandeville Canyon fire a month later.

All the same, the fire I saw was a sign to me of the other side of MountainGate, a side that was not apparent in the developer's presentation of the project. The issue of fire hazard is only part of the network of environmental and social issues which call into question the wisdom of permitting this kind of urbanization of the wild and flammable Santa Monica Mountains. It is not that MountainGate is especially easy to burn The shingles are treated with fireproofing and the buildings are surrounded by lavish irrigated planting. Yet MountainGate could have burned —the Mandeville Canyon fire started near the golf course. At the time, the Ridge phase of the project was still being framed and looked out over cliffs that were mostly covered with highly combustible native chaparral.

Rather, the issue is whether or not it made sense to take relatively undisturbed terrain in the Santa Monica Mountains, dump trash in it, and fill it in, and then go on to build golf courses on the fill and an upper-class enclave of luxury condos on the cut-over ridges, in an area with difficult access and high fire-protection needs. The project, with its golf courses, consumes large quantities of water. Some of this water percolates down the layers of garbage and dirt—known as a sanitary land-fill—to augment moisture from rainfall, creating a contaminated liquid effluent known as leachate. At the same time, the fill is generating large quantities of colorless, odorless—and, under certain conditions, explosive—methane gas. Below the fill—as much as 240 feet below in some spots—lie the graded remains of the original canyons numbered five through eight, their natural contours obliterated underneath a mountain of refuse. And beneath that northern layer of trash and dirt fill topping run three, major, though not active, fault zones.

If MountainGate has a birthday, that day might properly be September 8, 1943—"Black Wednesday", one of Los Angeles' first smog attacks. Because of the city's air pollution, backyard incinerators, which had burned much of Los Angeles' trash, were banned in 1957. That year, filling began in the Mission Canyon landfill which abuts MountainGate on the north. MountainGate did not become a sanitary landfill site until 1964-65, shortly after Barclay Hollander purchased the site. The reason that has been given for the switch from the Mission Canyon landfill, only half-filled to capacity and already publicly owned, to the MountainGate site was that the County Sanitation District wanted to make use of the private site while it was available, holding the Mission Canyon site in reserve.

Ironically, the District has not been permitted to go back in and fill Mission Canyon to capacity. A 1974 request for renewed landfill operations was denied. Construction of residential developments immediately adjacent to the Canyon landfill site in the interim have made such a development politically infeasible.

As a result, Barclay Hollander's agreement with the County for dumping rights have continued, with the latest agreement for Canyon Eight having been made in 1978 for the sum of three million dollars. Barclay Hollander's original 1964–65 agreement netted them $2,800,000 for dumping rights, tax payments, and fees. In 1966, the District agreed to pay Barclay Hollander some $900,000 to purchase 125 acres to be used as a source of clean cover material for the landfill.

The amount of the payments has been one of the major points of contention between Barclay Hollander and its chief critic, the Brentwood Community Federation, a coalition of seven Brentwood-area homeowners' associations. Members of the Federation have charged that the initial payments for the dumping rights and tax payments alone were more than Barclay Hollander paid for the land in the first place. Barclay Hollander claims that the purchase price for the MountainGate property was approximately five million dollars, or approximately five thousand dollars an acre for what was originally a thousand acre parcel.

In addition to the amount of the payment, the Federation has maintained that the value of the County's grading—a figure they place at ten million dollars—is also in excess of the purchase price. They argue that the County Sanitation District vastly increased the value of the property by increasing the useable area;. This regrading accommodated recreational uses on the fill and housing on the truncated ridges— transforming land that would have previously sloped far too steeply to be useful into revenue generating property.

Barclay Hollander has replied that the costs associated with the land-fill have far out-weighed the benefits that have accrued to the company. The MountainGate landfill is designated as a Class II Sanitary landfill which accepts household waste and building demolition material. A landfill site should have an impervious base which separates it from underlying groundwater. It should also be free of active faults. Mountain sites such as MountainGate are often preferred because the canyons can be used as dumping grounds and the hillsides can be cut-over for clean fill.

As the fill is placed in the landfill, it is layered in cells, which separates the refuse into small units. At the end of each day, these are covered over, and the process is repeated the following day. Together with watering, compressing, and tidying up loose rubbish, this procedure is intended to eliminate the problems of flies, rodents, odor, mosquitoes, and subsidence that an unsupervised garbage dump can create.

While the basic principles of sanitary landfill are well understood, it is difficult to view even the most advanced sanitary landfill operation as a known quantity. Both the landfill site and the composition of the garbage dumped in the landfill can vary so much that the environmental impact of a landfill can be unpredictable to a significant degree.

"You see, we really didn't know much about landfills on this scale. They never existed before fifteen years ago." Lester Haug, deputy assistant chief engineer for the Los Angeles County Sanitation District was quoted in a 1972 *Los Angeles Times West* magazine article called "The Trash Cometh." Establishment of a landfill has several major environmental impacts. It effectively destroys the existing ecology of the site on which it is placed. If there are people living nearby during the construction of the site, they may be subjected to increased noise levels, windblown debris, and odors.

But the most serious problems connected with a landfill result from the rotting and settling of the garbage and fill. According to an Environmental Protection Agency study, as water percolates through the fill, it passes through refuse and "becomes grossly polluted both chemically and biochemically with the various constituents present in the solid waste." The resulting liquid is known as leachate.

The production of leachate generally occurs a few years after completion of a landfill when the fill material has become so saturated with water that it sheds the excess. One of the indicators of contamination in water is the Biological Oxygen Demand (BOD) and Chemical Oxygen Demand (COD). which shows the approximate oxygen depletion of water by contaminants. Raw sewage in the Los Angeles region generally has a BOD between three hundred and three hundred fifty parts per million (ppm). Leachate at its most toxic may reach BOD levels many times that of raw sewage. Leachate from Canyon Four in the Mission Canyon landfill ranged from a BOD of 179,000 ppm in 1967 down to 60 ppm in 1973.

Because of the variations in rainfall the leachate flow is also variable. While areas west of the Mississippi are generally considered suitable for landfills due to their low rainfall the precipitation in Southern California is concentrated in winter months, thereby increasing the effectiveness of what rainfall there is to create leachate. While rainfall at the Mission Canyon landfill in 1964 was only six inches, the next year rainfall measured forty inches.

Man-made moisture can also produce leachate. The Mission Canyon and MountainGate landfill sites were both designed to be completed with plantings requiring irrigation, although the heavy mantle of earth at MountainGate is supposed to prevent this moisture from entering the landfill itself.

While a California Department of Water Resources document included in the Mission Canyon Environmental Impact Statement (EIS) states the Mission Canyon landfill is "no threat to the quality of downstream waters," it also makes the observation that surface runoff could affect wells in the Santa Monica ground-water basin, although it could take years to happen. "Shallow alluvium extends from the canyons on the site down Sepulveda Canyon where water wells tap the ground water for domestic, industrial use, etc."

The generation of methane gas from sanitary landfills is a second major hazard found in sanitary landfills. Methane gas is a colorless. odorless, lighter-than-air gas which is explosive when it constitutes between 5% and 15% of the air. It is formed by anaerobic bacteria (bacteria which live in an airless environment) in the refuse. This means that the fill itself will not explode from the considerable quantities of methane gas generated because the gas will not be forming while air is present. Nor is there much chance of a golfer on the MountainGate course lighting a cigarette and getting blown across a sand trap as a result (although there are reports of small flare-ups from time to time).

The methane gas dissipates readily in the large volume of air above the golf course, making it unlikely that large amounts of it will occur in the concentrations necessary for an explosion. The catch is that any methane gas which is not burned off joins the atmosphere to become yet another constituent of the grey-brown fumes that daily fill the Los Angeles air basin. It is when methane gas finds its way into enclosed spaces such as meter boxes—or houses—via lateral migration that it becomes a hazard.

The consultant firm of GeoScience advised the developer in the MountainGate EIS that "under certain conditions however it [methane gas] could migrate laterally into soils at the boundary of the landfill, or because of fractures in the native bedrock, into the cut-over ridge proposed for development. Underground piping and bedding may also provide transport paths for gases unless preventive methods are taken." For this reason, preventive measures were taken by the developer to preclude the possibility of gas infiltrating the residential area.

In 1963, approval had been granted for 482 single-family units on a 2.665-acre site that includes the present MountainGate property. In 1970, Barclay Hollander requested a zone change for its property from single-family to townhouse and condominium zoning, with a maximum 1,338 units. The zone change was granted for a maximum of 1,170 units. The year before, Barclay Hollander had been purchased by the large multinational firm of Castle & Cooke.

Because of the complexity of the project, there were several special conditions attached to the zoning which went into effect under the provisions of the "Q" or Qualified Zoning district. In Q zoning, any uses permitted in the previous zoning are permitted as well as any uses specified in the Q zoning, as long as the conditions are met within a two-year period. If these conditions are not met within that period, the zoning lapses back into the original category. MountainGate has had its Q zoning extended in 1972, '73, and '74.

Q zoning has been criticized on the grounds that it often gives the developer a chance to gain approval for a cosmeticized version of a controversial development. and then to proceed to build the project as originally conceived by waiving or changing the terms of the Q conditions. This is what has happened at MountainGate in the view of Santa Monica Mountains Commission member Nita Rosenfeld. "The Q conditions that have been approved for the MountainGate subdivision have been eroded by variances, conditional use permits, and zoning boundary adjustments," she said. Some of the changes Barclay Hollander has requested, or has been granted, include substitution of access roads, elimination of a neighborhood commercial center, and conversion of the recreational clubs—originally intended for the exclusive use of MountainGate residents—to public use, with its potential for increased traffic.

Two years after receiving the Q zoning, Barclay Hollander submitted a tract map for 870 units. The EIS was prepared in 1973, and the project came before the Los Angeles Planning Commission in 1974. Barclay Hollander came under fire from the Brentwood Community Federation, which claimed that Richard Barclay of Barclay Hollander was also a partner in E.L. Pearson, the firm which executed the EIS.

The most alarming aspect of the EIS process was the way in which the leachate problem was ignored by the City Planning Department and denied by the County Sanitation Department. Despite the fact that leachate flow at MountainGate was verified by the Water Quality Control Board that year, the City Planning Department declared in the draft EIS that there wouldn't be a leachate flow from the property. In public testimony MountainGate lobbyist Myron Nosanov claimed that any leachate at the project would be so harmless that he offered to drink it.

The project was approved by a two to two tie vote of the Planning Commission. That decision was appealed to the City Council by the Brentwood Community Federation. The council denied the appeal, and the Federation took its case to Superior Court where it won a decision that the city had not made the proper findings during their deliberations on the project.

The Council reconsidered the project and approved it once again. Lack of funds prevented the Federation from appealing the decision. The history of the MountainGate development, in its broad outlines, is not unique. It demonstrates that large projects of its type are no longer in the realm of simple private enterprise. The large-scale development has entered a grey area of involvement with and dependence on governmental agencies, procedures, and politics, and has little to do with any larger notions of what constitutes intelligent land use in the long run. And finally, once the project is built, the enviromental and social consquences are hidden from the consumer by marketing, styling and the overall process of presentation.

PART TWO

ILLUSION AND DELUSION IN LOS ANGELES

The Paramount Globe, corner of Melrose and Gower in Hollywood. Movie studio sound stages appear on city streets as massive blank walled boxes.

finding los angeles in the movies,
finding the movies in los angeles

los angeles, in the movies

Some critics say that the audiences complain about the movies because the movies do not reflect reality; it is this writer's suspicion that more people lament the fact that reality does not reflect the movies.

—Kevin Brownloe

The most tiresome misconception about Los Angeles is that Los Angeles is a one industry town, where everything revolves around the entertainment industry. Most Southern Californians are no more connected to the movies than are the citizens of Davenport, Iowa. Yes, the entertainment industry is an important employer, yes, many people do have a connection to it either directly or indirectly, and, yes, it amounts to a lot of money and power concentrated in one place. But Los Angeles is a vast metropolitan area with many industries and many other important roles to play—such as landing spot of choice for immigrants from around the world. That one category of commingled cultures and new residents striving to make a living has much more to do with what the city is like in the 1990s than does the movie business.

Robert Stern's 1995 Animation Building at the Burbank Disney
Studios. The sorcerer's apprentice hat is a landmark visible from
the Ventura Freeway.

Even the fact that countless spots in Los Angeles have appeared in countless movies and TV shows still does not give them an irreducible double
identity or a guaranteed fictive resonance to the average Angeleno passing
by on their way to work or the corner convenience store.

However, having made my disclaimer, it is definitely possible to see Los
Angeles in a movie-mad way that surpasses what is possible in any other
city on the planet, *if* you want to. Everyone sees the world he or she needs
to see. In Southern California it is possible to construct a world synthesized
from shadows of the big and small screens and fragments of the local environment. By the side of the road are buildings that have multiple identities
as both real place and movie backdrop. The double life of everyday identity and mythologized identity is more ubiquitous in Southern California
than anywhere else in the world.

Southern California as a whole is not necessarily one big outdoor movie
location. However, at least in the swath of territory from Malibu to Culver
City to the San Fernando Valley and Pasadena, no resident would be shocked
to spot the light reflectors, grips and trailers that signify a movie, TV commercial or video shoot. As I write, it is possible for me to head down the
Venice walking street where I live and see harsh movie lights shining on a
temporary roadhouse constructed on the sands of Venice Beach. Built as a
movie set, it won't be there next week. On the way to work I drive past a storefront, Joe's Barbershop on Abbott Kinney Boulevard, that has been used in
movies (*Get Shorty*, for example) dozens of times. On the walk to lunch from
work in West Hollywood a string of storefronts has been commandeered for
a Sharon Stone movie. Part of this reengineered movie location is actual
stores, part imaginary businesses, a melding of the real and the theatrical.
When I watch a movie that has been made here, I see the place refracted back
to me through its new character in the movie. Driving the freeway during the
Rodney King riots and watching the towering columns of smoke on either
side was eerily reminiscent of the shots of Los Angeles in Ridley Scott's
Blade Runner, where smoke rose from mega-story skyscrapers above a poly-
glot city with a crumbling infrastructure.

Historian and critic Mike Davis has focused attention on the concept of
Los Angeles as a disaster-destined locale for cinematic and literary holo-
caust in his book *The Ecology of Fear*. He argues that in disaster flicks like
Volcano and *Earthquake*, part of the point of the movie was the excitement of

seeing the metropolis destroyed. After all there is a certain joy in seeing the Beverly Center mall engulfed by molten lava.

Norman Klein writes with energetic disgust of the movies' treatment of inner city Los Angeles as an apocalyptic/noir universe in his *The History of Forgetting: Los Angeles and the Erasure of Memory*. Discussing the role that fiction and the movies have had in shaping Southern California's attitudes toward the inner city, he argues that the movies have often been used to portray Downtown as shady, crooked, a lost netherworld. Klein believes that this portrayal contributes to the general public's idea that the center of Los Angeles is uninhabitable.

After the collapse of the market for Downtown real estate in the '90s Klein writes Downtown areas became "recoded" as "sites for 'die-hard' disasters, and the birth of civil wars (*Strange Days*). The Bonaventure (hotel by John Portman) has been anointed twice as suitable for assassinating a pres-

This 1930s building at Twentieth Century Fox Studios at Century Ciy was built as movie star quarters. The primary volumes and attenuated columns of the Hollywood Regency style as deployed by Douglas Honnold is evidence that studio buildings reflected period Los Angeles style.

ident or vice-president (*Line of Fire* and *Nick of Time*). And with *Escape from L.A.* Downtown finally becomes an island prison." noted Klein.

At the same time the movies have left their mark in real time and space. The relative simplicity of residential building construction in Southern California has allowed designers outside the field of architecture, including stage set designers, to produce some structures that reflect the theatricality of the movie industry. Equally important in the ready production of fantasy has been Southern California's long history of freedom to choose from a multiplicity of local stylistic predilections. Los Angeles' relatively loose social structure has allowed for the ready gratification of individual will in building.

In Los Angeles/Hollywood movie sets can become buildings, and buildings turn up in movies as stage sets. When a modest West Hollywood bungalow remodeled with bits of pasted on classical ornament turns up on the Dean Tavaroulas' sets for Francis Ford Coppolas' 1982 film *One from the Heart*, it takes on another life, as part of a universe of borrowed finery. In the 1933 movie *Female*, the use of shots of Frank Lloyd Wright's Ennis Brown house in the Hollywood hills as the first scene of the heroine's home and the Frank Lloyd Wright knit-block-like stage set creates a city in which this architecture plays a much larger role than it actually did in real life.

Small houses in West Hollywood remodeled by interior decorators are an attempt to reconcile grand ambitions with limited means through the use of stage-set artifice. (See following chapter.)

This house, at 8960 Vista Grande Street, was remodeled in 1965 by George Barnes. In 1982 it was reproduced as part of a real stage set of a Las Vegas street in Francis Ford Coppola's movie *One from the Heart*. This house has since been remodeled again.

In a February 3, 1998, *New York Times* article, Joseph Giovannini noted "When its Time to Start Filming, a House Can Become a Star": "The grandfather of all modernist houses used as sets is Frank Lloyd Wright's Ennis Brown house, a majestically terraced, Mayan style structure. By the count of its eighth owner, Gus Brown, it has been the stage for about 60 movies, commercials and fashion shoots since he bought it in 1968"—including the movies *Day of the Locust*, *Grand Canyon*, and *Black Rain*. An extreme example of movie reality overtaking everyday reality is the case of Carlotta and Buck Stahl, who are the present and original owners of a Case Study house by Pierre Koenig, built in 1960. Their house, famous for its tautly minimalist

The Ennish-Brown house 2665 Glendower, Hollywood Hills, 1924.
Frank Lloyd Wright's theatrical knit block houses have often shown up as a real life set in the movies.

lines that thrust out off the hillside in the Hollywood Hills over a magnificent view of Los Angeles, is so popular with filmmakers that it has become the sole source of their income, according to Giovannini.

Because of the ubiquity of location filming, and the actual looming presence of the blank-fronted studio buildings where movies and videos are shot, there is a special kind of cross media synergy that happens only in Southern California. When *Clueless's* Alicia Silverstone, in her role of a Beverly Hills teenager Cher, strolls by the Spadena house, the inclusion of that house is a reference to the coexistence of movie sets and real life architecture. The Spadena house was originally constructed as Hansel-and-Gretel-like dressing rooms and offices for Irvin Willat Productions in Culver City by art director Henry Oliver. In 1931 it was moved to its present site at the corner of Carmelita and Walden Drives in Beverly Hills.

9336 W. Washington Boulevard, Culver City, 1915. This office building at the Culver Studios, originally built in 1915 as the Thomas Ince Studio Building, was often used as a movie backdrop as well.

"The walls and sharply pitched roof were purposely built to look old and sagging as was the exterior woodwork, which was burned, charred, scraped—and left unpainted; roof shingles were all different shapes, sizes and colors. No two leaded glass-windows were alike, and the shutters were hung askew," wrote Charles Lockwood in his book, *Dream Palaces: Hollywood at Home*.

Similarly, *Pulp Fiction*'s rock and roll milieu of 24-hour coffee shops, cheap motels and late-night clubbing was composed out of equal parts real location and invented stage set. Once viewed on the big screen, the streets, storefronts, tenements and suburban backyards mythologized in *Pulp Fiction* never look quite the same again in real life—they have been layered with narrative possibility.

Hollywood has customarily been the villain faulted for the visual excesses of the Southern California cityscape and for the vulgarity of its status symbols. But it hasn't been a one-way street. Southern California and Hollywood have influenced each other. Hollywood's penchant for cliché, pretension and skin-deep glamour have made easy targets for critics of the local pop environment.

"Neutra and other apologists for elitist 'high art' architecture have used 'low art' film as a convenient scapegoat" for the period architecture deplored by purists, historian David Gebhard has pointed out. The shallowness of this historical perspective is revealed by even the most cursory glance at California's history. The state has been viewed as a special place ever since the gold rush era. And California became established as a tourist stop by the completion of the cross-continental railways after the Civil War.

Nineteenth-century California nurtured much that was mad and wonderful in architecture. The sudden influx of population in combination with the relative lack of previous development gave architects unparalleled opportunities. This is the situation in which the wild inventions of the Newsom family and the eerie, cute and threatening scale manipulation of Ernest Coxhead flourished. The amusement park environment of seaside resorts such as Venice and the antic eclecticism of Greene & Greene's pre-Craftsman work all preceded the establishment of the movie colony in Hollywood.

The state's receptivity to the new and unconventional led to the proliferation of unusual religious movements in California, beginning at the turn of the century with establishments such as Katherine Tinguely's Theosophical colony at Point Loma, near San Diego. Hollywood has its own Theosophical settlement, Krotona Court, on 15 hillside acres. According to Charles Lockwood in *Dream Palaces*, the complex sported " . . . a Moorish-Egyptian occult temple, a psychic lotus pond, a vegetarian cafeteria, several small tabernacles, a metaphysical library, and a Greek Theater. At Krotona the faithful lived in apartment buildings with Islamic domes and horseshoe arches . . . " By the late teens, Krotona was so popular that its founder, Charles Powell Warrington, " . . . rented a hall on Hollywood Boulevard to teach courses in Esperanto, the Esoteric Interpretation of Music and Drama and the human aura."

According to a 1905 promotional book, the houses of Hollywood came chiefly in three styles: Mission Revival, Swiss Chalet and Bungalow. The book featured two examples of the dreamlike architecture that later came to be associated with Hollywood in the movie era. Artist celebrity Paul de Longpre's house was a twin-towered Mission Revival confection. The house, its gardens and the artist himself were important attractions, required destinations for tourists of the period, in much the same way that movie stars' homes became important sights for tourists of a later period. Similarly, Dr. A.G. Schloesser's Sans Souci castle in the Hollywood Hills could be considered a predecessor of the Hearst Castle at Cambria. The Sans Souci piéce de résistance as described in *Dream Palaces* " . . . was a Gothic hall, fifty by twenty feet, with a twenty-five-foot high beamed ceiling, stained glass windows depicting scenes of chivalry, suits of armor and an organ loft."

Another local landmark was the Japanese-style house built in 1913 by Oriental art importers, brothers Eugene and Adolph Bernheimer, in the Hollywood Hills. The grounds were terraced and landscaped as a Japanese garden replete with an antique Japanese pagoda.

Given the existence of extravagant showplaces like Sans Souci and the Bernheimers' house it is clear that the myth of California as lotus-land preceded the establishment of the movie industry. Admittedly, there were many factors involved in the relocation of the movie business from the East Coast to the West Coast. An East Coast energy shortage, the stranglehold monopoly of the Eastern Motion Picture Company and abundant sunshine were all key factors in resettlement of the movies to Hollywood. But the diversity of California locations for shoots also played a role. The founder of one of the earliest movie studios to locate in Hollywood proper, David Horsley, even went so far as to claim that "The one greatest factor in bringing him to the west was the history of California by Mr. John Stephen McGroarty depicting the great variety of scenery . . . as well as the vast variety of architecture in which every state and nation had here expressed itself."

New Calvary Cemetery and Mausoleum, Downey Road and Whittier Boulevard, East Los Angeles, Ross Montgomery, 1927.
A stage set worthy of D. W. Griffith. Photo by Regula F. Campbell.

building the myth: the movies' influence on los angeles

While it was California that allowed the moviemaker's imagination free rein, this imagination in turn had a profound effect upon Los Angeles. The relationship of Hollywood, the concept, and Los Angeles, the place, can best be described as symbiotic. The influences of Hollywood on Los Angeles have been many. The visual presence of the studio back-lots around the city, though now negligible, was once considerable. In *Hollywood Babylon* Kenneth Anger describes the drama of the set for D.W. Griffith's film *Intolerance* as "A mare's nest mountain of scaffolding, hanging gardens, chariot race ramparts, and sky-high elephants, a make-believe mirage of Mesopotamia dropped down on the sleepy huddle of mission style bungalows that made up 1915 Hollywood."

Although joyful plagiarism from the past is something that has been a characteristic of American architecture in general, the spirit of Southern California architecture after the arrival of the movies seems to have only increased the role of fantasy. Architect Ross Montgomery's extraordinary stucco mausoleum for New Calvary Cemetery in East Los Angeles, or Morgan, Walls & Clements' Uniroyal Tire factory in the city of Commerce, dressed as an Assyrian palace, could have worked very nicely as sets for D. W. Griffith's *Intolerance*. One wonders whether these Los Angeles' landmarks would be possible without the example of the movies.

Set design and the architecture of Hollywood each sometimes functioned as models for the other. Director Howard Hawks was so entranced by the set for the Cary Grant comedy *Bringing Up Baby* that he used the design as part of the house that Myron Hunt designed for him. Alternatively, Marilyn Monroe's uncompleted last picture, *Something's Got To Give*, was shot in a set that was a replica of Jim Dolena and William Haines' house for the movie's director, George Cukor.

The importance of the movies has been not so much in the origination of styles, but in their popularization. The vogue for storybook fantasies in a charmingly underscaled medieval setting became established just prior to 1920 in northern California, growing out of the romanticism inherent in the Bay Area tradition of architecture. Southern California Hansel and Gretel architecture may have a papier-maché, movie-set quality and a theatrical exaggeration that exceeds the Northern California brand. However the underlying sensibility is much the same. One is the storybook cottage from a children's story, the other is the storybook cottage as exaggerated for the movie screen.

Art director William Cameron Menzies captured the unique character of movie reality when he wrote, "If for instance you photograph a romantic location, such as a picturesque European street, you will have an accurate reproduction minus the texture and color. Hence it is always better to substitute a set that is the impression of the street as the mind sees it slightly romanticized, simplified, and over-textured." The vision of reality presented in the movies had to be edited and stylized in a kind of heightened image of the original, in order to make it appear lifelike or larger than life. The enormous fireplace in Xanadu, Orson Welles' mansion in *Citizen Kane*, is monstrously overscaled. In Fred Astaire & Ginger Rogers' movie *Top Hat*, the palazzo and canals of Venice have been simplified and given a Hollywood Regency treatment compatible with the urbane Deco imagery associated with the couple in the 1930s.

The special needs of set design have resulted in a style of architecture unique to the movies. The lack of constraints of structural stability, functional requirements and marketability gave movie architecture the ability to represent features simply not found in the real world. The lessons Southern California learned from movie design is that a building doesn't necessarily have to function, or be constructed in a particular way, or built out of a special material—as long as it looks as if it were.

The entertainment industry has been important as a tastemaker in another sense in Southern California: as consumers, rather than producers, of design. Celebrities' tastes have had a significant influence on interior design and architecture in Southern California. The celebrity client is often able to pay for an expensive commission and frequently has a strong thematic requirement that has been selected to enhance their media image. As an example of this purchasing power 65 percent of the 241 homes on Los Angeles' west side that sold for over 2.5 million were bought by entertainment industry buyers, according to Ruth Ryon in the Jan. 10 1999 *L. A. Times* "Hot Properties" column.

"I like to work for show biz people because you can do more dramatic interiors for them," observed interior designer Anton Vogt. The late architect Frank Israel explained in a 1979 interview that working for a celebrity client makes special demands on an architect: "Even the ones with good taste have poor manners. Everyone in Hollywood wants to be someone else—the scriptwriter wants to act, and the actor wants to direct, because they all think they can do everything. Because of this they're dictatorial. They're the designer, and you (the architect) are just performing a service for them, by helping to get their design built."

Furthermore, Israel pointed out, "In Hollywood they design more for effect than for purpose." And because "everybody wants to be someplace else, Paris, Tahiti or New York, but never Los Angeles," there are often demands for more eclectic styles and features than the average client would request.

Hollywood observer Leo Rosten wrote, "It is often suggested that the movies are an escape for the masses. It is rarely suggested that they are also an escape for the movie-makers." Given the preoccupation with self, and the concept of self, as a salable product, fostered by the entertainment industry, it is not surprising to find this psychology reflected in interior design and architecture. The self-made quality of many successful Hollywood careers, the tradition of itinerancy and the theatric creativity of the entertainment industry are all factors that contribute to the freedom to create idiosyncratic environments.

Filmmaker Kenneth Anger's tabulation of movie star personal paradises in *Hollywood Babylon* includes Valentino's hilltop Falcon's Lair with its black-marble-bridge-spanned swimming pool and Barbara La Mar's enormous sunken bath, with its gold fixtures in her all onyx bathroom. The hedonistic celebration of self and the daily playing of a big-screen-scaled role at home is a central subject of Arthur Knight's book, *The Hollywood Style*. Knight's illustrations of Natalie Wood curled up in a director's chair in her study surrounded by pictures of herself, or of Gypsy Rose Lee's boudoir, which resembles a stage backdrop for a stripper, make a strong case for the existence of the Hollywood home as personal movie set. For Joan Bennett, architect Wallace Neff produced drop-dead glamor, Hollywood Regency Style—curvaceous window lintels conjure up the tapered limbs of a boudoir armchair. The central hall is oval and double weight, its recessed balcony is perfectly positioned above the fireplace as a fram for the star to make a momentary appearance before gliding out of view down the enclosed stairs, allowing her to make a grand appearance at their base.

Charles Lockwood's *Dream Palaces* cites Jayne Mansfield as a star who was trying for the old-school style of Hollywood excess. In her 1950s redo of Rudy Vallee's old Spanish Colonial Revival mansion in Holmby Hills, "the wall around the estate, the stucco facade, the heart shaped bathtub and even the heart shaped toilet seats were all pink." The only nonpink notes were "the plush purple-upholstered sofa, white and gold piano, crystal chandeliers, religious statuary, and pictures of Jayne."

Edward Grenzbach's Egyptian Revival house for Cher in Benedict Canyon is an example of a building that is part and parcel of a star's mystique. Regardless of the amount of publicity the house will receive, it contributed to Cher's consistently exotic public image in much the same way that her flamboyant Bob Mackie costumes did. There is no question as to the influence of the entertainment industry on this particular building. "The architect and I got a lot of ideas from the souvenir book that came with the TV movie Jesus of *Nazareth*," Cher told *People* magazine. While stars' homes like Cher's Egyptian house, Dolores Del Rio's Art Deco house and Barbara Streisand's Art Deco Revival Malibu house have been influential in the popular architecture of Southern California, such houses have nevertheless been the exception.

The most celebrated movie encounter with architectural high-art Modernism is undoubtedly Richard Neutra's 1935 house in the San Fernando Valley community of Northridge for director Josef Von Sternberg. The streamlined shapes of the International Style house were extended into the landscape by a curving aluminum patio wall. In *Richard Neutra and the Search for Modern Architecture*, Tom Hines writes "An advanced sprinkler system around the curving wall produced varied effects from a gentle mist to a battering rainstorm. Surrounding the wall and, in broken stretches, the entire house, was a shallow moat . . . .An actual ship's searchlight over the porte cochere together with the moat and front wall imparted a wittily 'nautical' air."

Historically, the majority of homes inhabited by movie stars have been indistinguishable from those inhabited by other Southern Californians of comparable income brackets. In this sense, the genre of the "movie star home" simply does not exist. For the most part there are no identifiable differences between the supposed "homes of the stars" listed on the notoriously unreliable maps of the stars, and their starless counterparts next door. Furthermore, the concept of the "movie star home" does not distinguish between the home built or altered for a movie star and an existing house that a movie star merely lives in for a time. A home specifically designed for a star, such as Will Roger's home in Pacific Palisades, is obviously going to reflect the star's image more strongly than a house that is merely purchased.

Just because movies were a hometown industry didn't make Los Angeles exempt from being influenced by the movies. Here, as elsewhere in the America, the effect of movie theaters as palaces-for-the-masses was a powerful influence in combination with the milieus presented in the movies. As

Edwin Turnblhad observed in *California Arts and Architecture* magazine "Films have created vogues of interior decoration far from Hollywood. Picture goers request plans and details of a home or an interior they have enjoyed on the screen. It is likely that the Elizabethan decoration in the forthcoming Fred Astaire picture 'A Damsel in Distress' may cause much inquiry about the period of design."

There is no more literal medium than the movies for the introduction of a new style or the revival of an old style. In the movies, the styles they present

Drop-dead glamour for a movie star by Wallace Neff. The hall fireplace of his 1938 house for actress Joan Bennett in the Holmby Hills section of Los Angeles. (Photo: Henry E. Huntington Library and Art Gallery)

are intimately bound up with the excitement of plot, dialogue and celebrity. It takes very little imagination for the moviegoer to evaluate the style of the clothes or the furniture in a movie for his or her own use.

The popularization of Moderne architecture by the movies is a case in point. The luster of Deco fit Garbo's roles. It was also important for Ginger Rogers and Fred Astaire's pictures of the 1930s. Their smooth and sleek style of acting and dancing needed the chic, streamlined Moderne style to complement it. In Cedric Gibbon's set designs for pictures such as *Grand Hotel* and *Our Modern Maidens,* the Moderne was defined as the natural setting for young jazz-age sophisticates. As Donald Albrecht has noted, these movies geared their depiction of "American technological modernism for young professionals" to an "upwardly mobile audience" who aspired after the glamour they saw on the screen.

Another example of the movies' power to set styles was noted by *The Wall Street Journal* in 1980 "because of a movie called "10," a braiding fad has stretched its way across the country. . . . Suddenly perfectly sensible women are spending scandalous sums and enduring finger-wearying hours to turn themselves into walking head curtains." In another case of life imitating art,

Entertainers homes are often indistinguisable from others of the same period. Johny Mathis's c.1965 house at 1469 Hollywood Hills has much in common with other houses inspired by John Woolf's Reynolds House. (See page 88.)

William Dalyrymple, in his 1999 book, *The Age of Kali*, writes that one of the Tamil Tiger guerilla fighters in Sri Lanka informed him that "our camps are equipped with television and video war films. War films are shown three times a week and are compulsorily viewing. We often consult videos like *Predator* and *Rambo* before planning our ambushes."

Los Angeles has been influenced not only by the movies themselves, but by their makers, with filmmakers such as Cecil B. De Mille bringing their armies of "celebrated designers, interior decorators, hair-dressers and set decorators to Los Angeles," noted his brother William C. De Mille. Los Angeles was bound to be affected by these members of the movie support trades. It is not surprising that art directors, who might easily "be asked to design castles of palaces at work decided to build a few real structures as well. And, as might be expected, their choice of style was correspondingly eclectic.

Art director William Cameron Menzies designed his Beverly Hills home in a Tudor Revival style filled with winsome features, such as stenciling in the upstairs hall. ABC set designer Samuel Jay remodeled his house into a small apartment building that could be considered a Southern California version of Corbusier's Villa Savoie, by way of New Orleans. The symmetrical formal facade, hiding a confused jumble of roof-lines behind it, is typical of the cosmetic, but often bluntly effective approach, of set designers to architectural problems.

Many buildings, such as the Jay apartments, use the vocabulary of the decorators to create their intended effect. The influence of the movies may have been all-pervasive in creating a demand for certain styles, but it was the profession of interior design that supplied the totems and the code that really determined the look of so much popular architecture in Southern California after World War II.

Not only did the movies and the design professions influence each other in Southern California, but many designers and architects practiced both in and out of the movies. Some movie art directors, such as Austin Cedric Gibbons and Van Nest Polglase, had previously studied or practiced architecture. Gibbons was the son of an architect and worked in his father's office before working for artist/muralist Hugo Ballin. After World War II he moved to Southern California and drew set designs for Samuel Goldwyn. From 1924 to 1956 he was the first head of MGM's art department. Gibbons cut a stylish figure in Los Angeles, driving a white Duesenberg and marrying movie star Dolores Del Rio. Gibbons himself designed the interiors of their home in Santa Monica. The architects for the

Gibbons home, Douglas Honnold and George Vernon Russell, had met while both were working at MGM. They launched their partnership with a house for studio executive Samuel Goldwyn.

As Donald Albrecht describes the Gibbons/Del Rio house, it had the theatrical aspect of a sound stage. Movie setlike aspects of the house included " . . . water sprinklers on the copper roof above to create the sound of rain, and a recessed light projector to cast the illusion of moonlight on a wall opposite." Other architects who crossed over into film were Lyle Wheeler and Carl Julius Weyl. Wheeler made his movie debut in 1937 with the sets for *A Star Is Born*. Weyl was an architect who designed quite a few buildings in Hollywood. In 1935 he became an art director for Warner Brothers.

Henry Oliver, the art director who created the Spadena house " . . . left art directing entirely and designed fanciful apartment buildings throughout Southern California, plus the original Van de Kamp's bakery windmill logo," noted Charles Lockwood in *Dream Palaces*.

Frank Lloyd Wright's son, architect Lloyd Wright, Jr., was in charge of the Design and Drafting Department of Paramount Studios in 1916 and 1917. While movie set design is only one of many influences on his career, it seems quite possible that it is one of the sources for the theatricality of his 1920s residential work. To create his wide range of effects, "he utilized many tricks of the theater; stucco-covered wood, stud walls which appear to be solid concrete, or even, as in the Harry Carr house (Los Angeles, 1925), where he stenciled on geometric patterns reminiscent of precast block because the client could not afford the real thing," wrote David Gebhard in his exhibition catalog, *Lloyd Wright*.

The same generation of German and Austrian emigration that brought modernist architects Richard Neutra and R.M. Schindler to Southern California also brought German-speaking set designers and set architects to Hollywood. Hans Dreier, a German emigre who had studied and practiced architecture, made Paramount "a Bauhaus-like workshop of local architectural school graduates and fellow émigrés, most notably two of Southern California's leading modernists, Jock Peters and Kem Weber," wrote Donald Albrecht.

Before coming to Hollywood, Peters had worked in the architectural office of Peter Behrens, where Mies van der Rohe and Walter Gropius had apprenticed as well. Peters' Southern California architectural production outside the movies was small, with the landmark Bullock's Wilshire Department store, a triumph of Zigzag Moderne styling, being his masterpiece. According to

Albrecht, both Peters and Weber found employment in the movies because architectural work was slow for them at the start of the Depression.

Nevertheless, a stint in the studios did not have a predictable effect on an architect's career. Architect William Pereira came to Los Angeles because of the movies. His wife, Margaret, had signed for a minor part in the John Barrymore movie *Reunion in Venice*, and he found a job with Paramount as a production designer in 1938. During his career there he was able to stage the burning of Atlanta for *Gone with the Wind*, win the first special effects Oscar for an underwater squid fight in *Reap the Wild Wind* and produced two more movies himself. After he left Paramount he went on to found one of Los Angeles' big corporate architectural firms, whose work was not discernably influenced by the movies.

Frank Israel is representative of the architect who has worked inside and outside of the movies simultaneously. Israel, the foster son of Kitty Carlisle and Moss Hart, came to California in 1977 after having worked for architectural firms on the East Coast and in London. Among his other projects in Los Angeles, Israel designed a remodel for actor Joel Grey and an addition for entertainer Rita Moreno. Israel was the art director for Roger Vadim's movie *Night Games*. The movie's lurid atmosphere called for props such as red lights and dry ice in the steamy bathtub scenes. He also made unsuccessful attempts at writing a movie script and worked on the sets for several television commercials such as the Dr. Pepper/Picasso ads.

Of Hollywood's effect on him Israel said, "Hanging around Hollywood has influenced me to the point of where I think talking about architecture is abhorrent. It has enabled me to transcend the intellectual." His experiences in the movie industry have strengthened his already strong sense of irony and taste for fiction, ambiguously, almost interchangeably, mixed with reality. In a show at the Yale School of Architecture, Israel combined photographs of existing buildings by other architects with his own drawings of projects such as a proposed remodeling of a West Hollywood apartment house for artist David Hockney.

Perhaps because the practices of interior design and fashion design in the movies had more in common with their practices in the outside world than did architecture, the influence of the movies in these fields has been stronger. Many of the best known California fashion designers made their reputations at the studios, such as Adrian at MGM, or Jean Louis at Columbia.

Careers that involved interior design both inside and outside the world of movies and the theater were common. Lady Mendl, Elsie de Wolf, was one of the earliest decorators to make the switch from acting to interior design. She was a stage actress in the late 19th century, who also knew her way around the backstage, designing sets and scenery for the productions she acted in. Her first major interior design commission came her way in 1905, five years after she quit the stage. Architect Stanford White gave her the commission to decorate the interior of the exclusive Colony Club in New York. After her success with trelliage and chintz there Lady Mendl recalled, "I received commissions to decorate women's clubs all over America and they were done carte blanche, and I became famous and made a fortune."

Driven from Europe by World War II, and finding New York too difficult to live in lavishly on less than lavish means, Lady Mendl arrived in Beverly Hills in 1941. "The company too, was extraordinary. During the Depression Hollywood had drawn writers, artist and performers from around the world, lured west by the enormous salaries that studios paid. The war had increased the migration, bringing newcomers who were attracted by the climate and the company as much as by the chance to work in films, and the colony on hand to greet the Mendls in Beverly Hills included Aldous Huxley, Erich Maria Remarque, and Arthur Rubinstein, as well as longer established residents such as Mary Pickford, Anne Warner, and Hedda Hopper. George Cukor became one of Elsie's favorite gin rummy partners," wrote Jane S. Smith in *Elsie de Wolfe: A Life in the High Style*.

Lady Mendl was a huge social success due to her elegance, originality and assurance. Her approach to her own house in Beverly Hills, remodeled in 1941, was nothing if not theatrical. In *Elsie de Wolfe*, her biographer Jane S. Smith described, in a white stucco garden house that Elsie constructed conceal the view of an alley and a neighbor's trash can: "The whole structure was an illusion: the fancy scroll of the front roof had nothing behind it, the windows were blind, and the interior was really only a shallow recess in the arch of the door, shaded by a huge green and white-striped awning but barely large enough to hold a wrought iron table and two small chairs. The entire inside wall was lined with a large plate glass mirror, however, so if you sat there you felt you were enclosed within a garden."

Lady Mendl was a key figure in an influential group of decorators and movie people who set the tone for the decorator high style of the the '30s and

'40s in Los Angeles. She was friends with actor-turned-decorator Bill Haines and with the young artist-turned-decorator Tony Duquette.

Haines had been a popular star of the silent movies when he traded professions to become a highly successful interior decorator. Haines launched his interior decoration career in 1933 with his redecoration of Joan Crawford's Brentwood house, just prior to Crawford's divorce from Douglas Fairbanks, Jr. According to Anita Loos, as quoted by Anger, studio mogul Louis B. Mayer told Haines, "I'm going to give you a choice. You're either to give up that boyfriend of yours, or I'll cancel your contract." Haines choose love over the movies.

Haines befriended director George Cukor shortly after Cukor's arrival in Hollywood and the two became the center of a gay salon that included actors, decorators, architects, writers, real estate agents and architects

In the 1930s, working out of an office on the Sunset Strip (currently occupied by Le Dome restaurant), "He introduced French and English antiques, a welcome antidote to often gloomy Spanish Colonial interiors of the previous decade. He then began to add touches of chinoiserie—which he particularly loved—and Regency, as well as an endless stream of innovative ideas of his own," wrote Tim Street-Porter in *The Los Angeles House*. During this period he frequently collaborated with architect James Dolena.

"After World War II Haines opened a new office in Beverly Hills and Ted Graber became his partner. In post-war years, Haines quickly developed a new, more modern style," noted Street-Porter. This didn't mean that Haines and Graber couldn't still do period revival if they felt like it. In 1957 they scraped the Latin overtones off of a 1920s Spanish Colonial Revival house in Bel-Air by Roland Coate and decked it out in a full-on Hollywood Regency style straight out of the 1930s. The pair selected a more modern vocabulary for the pool pavilion. Haines died in 1973, but Graber continued the firm's work. In 1981 Graber was commissioned by Nancy Reagan to redecorate the White House.

Another protege of Elsie de Wolfe was Tony Duquette, a young artist who had been a store dresser for Bullock's Department Store and for Adrian, the fashion designer, at his Beverly Hills store. James Pendleton, whom Elsie de Wolfe had known from the start of his career as an antique dealer, saw Duquette's iconoclastic work at the Adrian Salon and liked it enough, wrote Jane Smith, to ask Duquette "to design a table centerpiece with figures representing the four continents. When it was finished he planned a large dinner part to show off his new acquisition."

"Lady Mendl was one of the guests and the next morning. . . . Elsie summoned Duquette to her presence and immediately announced, 'You must do a mueble.'" Once he understood exactly what a "mueble" was, Duquette took a black lacquer secretary and dolled it up with huge, glass faux emeralds, sculpted shells and a series of sprites on top. "Under Elsie's steady insistent patronage, Tony Duquette was often featured in the glossy magazines where decorating reputations were made, and became one of the great young successes of the local scene," wrote Smith.

Duquette went to work "in the promised land of the studios" in the 1940s. "You wouldn't believe the materials and the workshops they had then," in the studios, he recalled in a 1974 interview. The movieland finesse with make-believe enabled him to branch out to designing tapestries, costumes, jewelry, theater production and sundry objets d'art and curiosities.

Tony Duquette created this stage set like tableaux by applying bits of Victorian buildings to a former 1920s movie studio building. At Keith and Robertson in West Hollywood. The photo is c. 1980 and the ornament has since been removed.

The need for splendor in recent years has been neglected, Duquette declared in the interview: "There are no more carnivals, no more processions, nothing for people except the little box of television." It is the role of a creative person, as a magician, to create spectacles, mystery and magic, " . . . because the masses of people don't know how to do it anymore."

Personability and a talent for setting a mood are traits shared by actors and interior designers alike. As David Hockney observed, "There are other businesses like show business." Both the actor and the designer are selling themselves, in a sense. In the case of the actor it happens to be his or her appearance, personality and acting ability. The interior decorator has to have all of these qualities, as well as marketable taste and design expertise.

Tony Duquette summed up the idea of the decorator who is a celebrity in his own right by saying, "I'm not a decorator, I'm a creative force." In a similar vein designer William Haines was quoted as saying "Decorating is not a profession, it is an opinion." Many of the West Hollywood house remodelers I profiled in *Exterior Decoration* had started out as actors. Dean Reynolds, Jack

The now vanished grand salon of the Duquette studio, with its ceiling of egg cartons, lit by electric candles, photo c. 1980.

Stevens, Reg Allen and Terence Monk all dropped their given names in favor of their stage names.

Harold Greive already had a long career in art direction behind him when he opened one of the earliest designer's studios on Robertson Boulevard in 1927. Working his way up from prop boy he became Ralph Ingram's technical director for the *Four Horsemen of the Apocalypse* and the *Prisoner of Zenda*. He designed costumes for the principal actors in Fred Niblo's *Ben Hur* and worked on the original costumes and props for Douglas Fairbanks' *Thief of Baghdad*.

When Harold Greer, head of the costume department at Paramount, wanted to open up a courtier fashion shop on Hollywood Boulevard, he engaged Harold Greive to do the interiors. Once Greive found that the carpenters were copying his designs to peddle to other clients, he opened his own workshop. A celebrity clientele allowed him to branch out into interiors.

Experience in the ephemeral art of set design may have furthered the already strong tendency of some decorators to design buildings in an expedient, cosmetic and insubstantial manner. In Southern California interior decorators had many of the same freedoms that the set designers had. The mild climate allowed them to use the kinds of cheap materials that were often employed in sets. In fact, it was the profession of interior decoration that most successfully incorporated the attitudes and techniques of the movie industries in ways that became influential on popular architecture in Southern California.

When I interviewed design journalist Barbara Lennox in 1980, she told me an anecdote that illustrated the decorator's unconcern with permanence. "Now Reg Allen was great at effect. He had an $84,000 house up on Sunset Plaza, and in the bathroom he put marble, a crystal chandelier, and contact paper on the walls. I said, 'Reg, that'll peel off in six months' and he said, 'You know, I don't care, it won't be my house in six months.'"

There is no such thing as a simple, direct cause-and-effect with regard to movies and Los Angeles. Rather the two are involved in a continuous dialogue in which each shapes the other. For the Los Angeleno the movies create a possible alternative, fictive identity for their city, with glimmerings of movie artifice in the city's architecture and allied arts and an industry that is often part of the backdrop of everyday life. In movies from *Chinatown* to *L.A. Confidential*, and in its attraction of design talent to the city, Los Angeles has been a major character, a player with a career longer than any movie star or director.

how can i miss you
when you won't go away?

convention versus invention and the survival
of period revival in southern california

High art architects and their critics have become so fixated on making art out of architecture that they have forgotten how complex a discipline architecture really is. Their discussion places a high value on the innovation of new vocabularies and on abstract formal qualities. Architectural cognoscenti focus their attention narrowly on high-art work. Other segments of building production, which employ more populist and commonly understood vocabularies, such as period revival architecture, are ignored.

Making these grounds for judgment is a difficult but possible, and very necessary, task. Critics argue that architects are forced to define the world for themselves since the world is so confused. They can't express a social consensus since there isn't one abroad in society at large. Consequently they have to make it out of whole cloth. No social agreement, no responsibility—so the theory goes. Given the vacuum of modern society, architects are free to pursue their own concerns.

However, just because there is no universally accepted worldview doesn't mean that there are not sets of cosmological beliefs accepted by subsets of the public. Many well-defined subgroups within America have strongly held worldviews, from fundamentalist religious sects to Hells Angels and members of the Thousand Oaks PTA. And despite the apparent diversity of belief among subgroups within the American public, one seems to find a surprisingly great coherence around matters of architectural form and its symbolism—as proved by the success of consumerist architecture.

Works of architecture may begin as private statements of taste, but they inevitably become, to some degree, public artifacts that are part of everyone's daily life. You don't have to buy the kind of art found in motels and hang it over your living room couch as part of your everyday environment. Neither do you have to see motel paintings hung on museum walls next to avant garde art. However you do have to drive by the motel building, and it may be situated next door to a work of high art architecture.

For most modernist architects it has not been enough to master a set of forms or a system of composition. If any system of familiar references is apparent in their architecture, there are only two permissible explanations. One is that the references are not intentional and are side effects of satisfying some other consideration—such as a heavy snow load necessitating a pitched roof. The other permissible explanation is that an architect has invented a new

1207 N. Garfield Avenue, Pasadena 1990. This Mediterranean Revival police station by Robert Stern complements earlier buildings in Pasadena's civic center.

architectural vocabulary him or herself, in the manner of a genius such as Wright or Gehry, and therefore is not indebted to previous precedent.

The point of much contemporary high-art architecture is to launder everything out of a project except the abstract play of form. Only lesser mortals, incapable of existing on the thin-oxygen, high-altitude plain of distilled abstraction, fret over experiential qualities or relationships to site or other nearby buildings. They do not possess the synthetic and analytic skills of the true architect/artist, or so the dogma goes.

Plebians may concern themselves with the nuances of program, the daily and seasonal progress of sun and shade, parking requirements, handicap accessibility and the like. But the true architect is like the true artist. The architect of the highest caliber has only one thing on her or his mind: form. Broken, shattered, morphing, exploded, imploded form. For, after all, if architecture is a form of

A. J. Heinsbergen offices, 7415-21 Beverly Boulevard, Hollywood, 1927. Claude Beelman with A. B. Hein, details by Willard White. representing prewar period revival design in Los Angeles.

sculpture, an exercise in plasticity, why sully it with other, far more mundane concerns. Doing so can only dilute the sculptural purity and breach the finitude of the artistic endeavor by introducing subject material alien to the aesthetic.

In order to get this high-octane stuff really pure it has to be absolutely liberated from any hints of recognizable references outside the sculpture-pattern space-field itself. At its best, the meaning and the design process that the building held for its maker can only be derived from a lengthy accompanying text and would be completely indecipherable if judged only from self-evident visual information. Any system of form generation that involves selecting shapes at random and then overlapping, multiplying, randomly altering or distorting that initial shape vocabulary will do nicely.

The more closely an avant garde architect can come to treating their work as pure formal abstraction divorced from both structure and experience, the more prestige they have with their peers. The media, eagerly complicit, treats "avant garde" architects exactly as they would artists. Avant garde architects are encouraged to design buildings as though they were just walk-in sculpture, often ignoring even their experiential character, let alone the social and real world forces that are part of architecture.

John Chase's Spanish Colonial Revival Moreno house. Eagle Rock, 1990.

The dismissal of context, building typology and existing patterns of ordered urbanism in Southern California has encouraged local avant garde architects to behave as though these high-art perceptions were fact. These perceptions become an important determinant of design. Reinforcing degrees of agreement between buildings or districts has generally been a low priority with much recent architecture. Taking cues from a neighborhood or from a regional repertoire of building types to inform the design of a building is seen as a limitation on creativity.

These architects have the freedom to gratify individual whim and pursue a course of self-aggrandizement without the burden of responsibility that would be attached to a more complete description of their profession. It is not the devotion to or interest in formal or theoretical issues borrowed from the art world that is the problem. The problem is that the architect's freedom is often paid for by the loss of a larger consciousness of architecture's social role.

When I was at SCI-Arc (Southern California Institute of Architecture) I found that many instructors believed that studio classes in issues like special needs housing were actually harmful to the student—because they would interfere with the single-minded pursuit of abstract beauty.

New southern mansion, early 1980s. Metrairie, Louisiana, near New Orleans.

Battles to create categories of distinction in archecture are particularly fierce. There is an artificial opposition between the profound and the ordinary and a need to go outside architecture to borrow extraneous theorical justification. The introduction or consideration of sentiment is, of course, contemptible beyond words.

While this premise is theoretically liberating to the artist in his role as unfettered creator, it does have the practical disadvantage of creating environmental chaos and putting many architects in over their heads. Not only do they have to learn to speak a language, but they have to invent the language as well. Since the point of language is the creation of a framework of commonality to facilitate communication, full ownership of a new shape/form vocabulary by each individual architect creates a Tower of Babel situation.

Postmodernist architects encountered much the same difficulties. Their task was different. They had to find a way of distorting, parodying or otherwise ironically distancing themselves from the genre they have selected. The parody often has the effect of making their work brittle, silly and lacking in commitment. As the archness of postmodern irony and the antisocial abstraction of deconstruction have worn thin, we need to explore approaches that reinforce the environment rather than fragment it further. If we are ever to have a seg-

Neo-Georgian house, early 1980s. Metrairie, Louisiana.

ment of building production whose design intent can be clearly understood and appreciated by both the public and those inculcated in architectural culture, architectural cognoscenti will have to stop dismissing popular culture and values and find some common ground with the public.

Stepping beyond the cult of the architect-as-artist/personality and acknowledging and chronicling the vernacular that does exist in Southern California are first steps in that direction. If vernacular architecture can be judged and found lacking by the standards of formal purity of high-art architecture, then vernacular architecture also functions as a critique of high-art architecture and a call for it to communicate with a larger constituency.

In a contemporary consumer society many buildings have a primary or secondary function as consumerist architecture. Their relationship to consumer becomes one of the primary determinants of form. Just as both the detective novel and the essay are legitimate literary forms, so does architecture in its broadest sense allow for both the the high-art building and more populist work with a wider audience. The appearance of buildings in this latter category often serves to help sell the products or the services offered inside.

Thus, in a theme restaurant, the embodiment of a mood or set of associations ought to be and is the paramount concern. Just as a principal appeal of a western novel could be its romantic sense of escape, the principal appeal of a consumer-oriented building such as a shopping center could also be emotive or nostalgic—since architecture can be both a fine and an applied art.

If the provision of entertainment, symbolic recall, representation, hierarchies of building components and sequences of experience is a valid function of architecture, then the use of forms, details or patterns of composition evoking time or place other than contemporary America is quite appropriate. If such recall is an essential part of both fine and popular works of literature, then it also has a place in works of architecture intended to be similarly evocative. The success of a project in hitting this particular target and the coherency and appropriateness of its three-dimensional, material realization ought to be the principal criteria by which it is evaluated, and not its conformity to currently accepted rules of contemporary high-art architecture.

As Pierre Bourdieu wrote in *Distinction*, "Intellectuals could be said to believe in the representation—literature, theater, painting—more than in the things represented, whereas the people chiefly expect representations and the conventions which govern them to allow them to believe 'naively' in the things represented."

Thus it was inevitable that period revival architecture, with its clearly defined initial premises, has begun to appear more like a viable option and less like a cop-out. Revivalism continues to offer opportunities to work within an agreed-upon architectural vocabulary by extending and reinterpreting that tradition rather than by mocking it as Postmodernists do. Most importantly, it can create buildings whose design intent can be clearly understood and appreciated by the public.

Period revival architects were able to make the past their own without sacrificing the functional integrity of their buildings. Nearly all the forms and the symbolism that they employed are no less appropriate or anachronistic 50 years ago then they are today. The imagery of the American home in the 20th century has usually had some traditional connotations, even when these were mingled with modern forms, such as a wagon wheel and split-rail fence in front of a mobile home. The *gemütlichkeit* suburban life of backyard-barbecue-pool suburban life would not have always played well against an exclusive backdrop of corner windows and open, web-steel trusses.

Far from being the copyists that conventional wisdom assumes them to be, period revival architects often brought an informed sensibility to their source material, transforming it and making it their own. Each designer left an individual stamp on his or her work, just as each era revives the language of the past in its own way. As David Gebhard explained in his book *L.A. in the '30s*, the typical depression-era Southern California period revival houses had highly workable floor plans that allowed for easy access to the outdoors, convenient accommodation for the automobile and a logical circulation pattern. In this sense the Modernist house of the 1930s was not necessarily more functional than the period revival house of the same age rather it expressed the functions it was programmed to through different imagery. To the degree that both the period revival and the Modernist were framed the same way or warmed by the same brand of furnace, they were equally modern.

And, after all, period revival architecture has never completely died. It retreated from the front lines of architectural culture proper, but lived on in the worlds of popular architecture and interior design, among other places. There were even architects such as Wallace Neff, John Woolf, Kaspar Ehmcke and James Dolena who continued to practice it during the 1950s, '60s and '70s in Southern California. Therefore it doesn't completely qualify for a miraculous comeback from the dead, despite the new surge of interest in the subject. The situation brings to mind the musical question that Dan Hicks and his Hot Licks asked in the 1970s—*How Can I Miss You When You Won't Go Away*.

But as Tim Street-Porter has noted so eloquently in his book *The Los Angeles House*, while sophisticated period revival design was alive and well on the East Coast in the work of architects like Robert Stern and Allan Greenberg, the vast majority of recent period work in Southern California has been abominable— precisely because period revival architecture is viewed as an obscenity within local architectural schools and has such low status in the profession. "Opportunities for continuing a great regional tradition have been lost: the multitude of period-style houses built in Los Angeles in the 1970s and '80s have been invariably over-scaled, badly detailed, and poorly proportioned," wrote Street-Porter.

Period revival architecture will always be with us for the same reason that Santa doesn't get a new costume every Christmas. These styles simply carry too much baggage to jettison them. As a result it is safe to say that the production of vanguard architecture and the production of period revival architecture will remain too quite separate spheres of production, audiences, and ethos, fulfilling related but separate high-end market niches. Neither of them will be disappearing anytime soon. They are included as concrete proof of the varied nature of building production in Southern California both before and after World War II. These three achitects continued to design architecture with period revival references even during the 50s and 60s when modernism had a popular following, as witnessed by the construction of the stucco box apartments discussed in the first chapter.

Following are profiles, of varying length, of two period-revival architects who managed to work successfully in the genre, both before and after World War II: John Woolf, James Dolena, and a brief note on Wallace Neff.

john woolf

Nowhere is the outlaw status of California's postwar period revival relative to academia more evident than in the work of John Elgin Woolf. As the most inventive designer working within the Hollywood Regency, Georgian or Second Empire styles in the past 50 years, Woolf was regularly published in the popular press, in magazines such as *Vogue, Town and Country* and

Architectural Digest. He received no attention in professional or academic journals, however, because these journals defined their subject material in such a way as to automatically exclude him. Woolf's work did not conform to high-art standards of simplicity, abstraction or freedom from historical reference.

John Woolf's work was anathema to the generation of Modernist architects who began their careers after World War II, when his career was flourishing. To these architects, the forms employed by Woolf were debased symbols, empty of meaning and a target for mockery for their lack of connection to contemporary Southern California culture and to Modernists' notions of minimalist construction and flowing space. But while many architects disliked Woolf's work (to the degree that they were aware of it at all), interior decorators and status-conscious clients with traditional ideas about architecture had no such reservations.

Woolf adopted the Hollywood Regency vocabulary that was prevalent in Los Angeles at the time he arrived here in the 1930s, flavored it with recollections of Southern antebellum architecture and codified it into a formula that his firm practiced in a relatively consistent manner for over 40 years. In his almost exclusively domestic practice, Woolf emphasized the elements that were important to his clients: the entrance, the mansard roof, symmetry and privacy. He used eccentrically detailed elements with classical pedigrees, reproportioned and placed in new and often mannered relationships.

John Woolf's 1940 Chisholm house at 520 Beverly Drive in Beverly Hills led to a string of important larger commissions.

Shuttered windows and chest-high oval niches with a keystone at the bottom, acting as a base for an urn, were not original to Woolf, but they certainly owed much of their popularity among Southern California decorators to him. In many of his houses, Woolf created an axis that extended from the entry through the living room and across a pool, terminating in a pool pavilion. In a Woolf house, as in 1930s houses by Paul R. Williams and James Dolena, the axis might focus on either the living room or a polygonal reception area.

The 1942 Pendleton house, 1032 Beverly Price Beverly Hills, was the first of a series of larger residential commissions for Woolf. Legendary movie mogul Robert Evans was a later occupant of the house.

Born in Atlanta shortly before World War I, John Woolf was the son of university professors on both sides of the family. After obtaining his architectural degree from Georgia Tech in 1929, he spent several years working for the National Park Service. He came to Los Angeles in 1936 in the hope of getting a part in the movie *Gone with the Wind*. He didn't get the part, but, as a consolation, he later managed to meet more show business celebrities, as clients, than most actors ever do. His roster included well-known names from the entertainment industry and the society columns, such as Cary Grant, Lillian Gish, Mae West, John Wayne and Norton Simon. A passage in a *Palm Beach Life* article gives a sense of a representative Woolf Client. A Woolf-designed summer home in Palm Beach is a "'place to unwind, to realize peace and quiet' says the diminutive, vivacious Nina 'Puddin' Neal Dodge de Witz who divides her time between her Palm Beach Bay Club house, her condominium in New York City, her farm in Minnesota and the ranch in Colorado Springs."

Woolf's acquaintance with the famous was not a peripheral issue to his practice. Two well-known women aided him in launching his career: the pioneering American interior decorator Elsie de Wolfe, a.k.a. Lady Charles Mendl (who had been introduced to Woolf by George Cukor), and comedienne Fanny Brice. Brice commissioned the young designer to build a small Georgian Revival guesthouse. This building led to a number of other entertainment industry commissions including a Georgian remodel for Ira Gershwin and another for Manhattan socialite Hugh Chisholm. In 1940, Woolf remodeled Chisholm's small house at 520 Beverly Drive in Beverly Hills, adding a mansardlike roof and a front porch the length of the front facade. The porch, decked with wrought-iron trim, was inspired by the architecture of New Orlean's French Quarter.

Interior decorator James Pendleton saw the Chisholm house and asked Woolf to design his own house at 1032 Beverly Drive. It was this house that established Woolf's reputation as a designer. According to Tim Street-Porter in his book *The Los Angeles House*, "It was modeled on drawings of pavilions in Versailles, shown to the architect by Elsie de Wolfe." Much larger than the Chisholm house, it has the archly elegant facade characteristic of Woolf's work, and bears the eccentrically detailed elements inspired by neoclassical and Regency precedents that became his trademarks.

The Pendleton house has a three-bay configuration—with the central bay offset toward the front and containing a centrally placed entrance. The semi-circular entrance portico is supported by the slender, manneristic Regency colonnettes that delighted Woolf: There is a low, oval niche containing an urn on either side of the entrance and a single long, narrow window in each of the end bays. The house opens up to a pool at the rear. The relative blankness of the front facade, made stiffer and more boxy yet by the mansard roof, gives the impression of hauteur the decorators sought. The blank facade focuses attention on the delicate, capricious detail in a manner

The entrance hall of the 1956 Campbell Building on Melrose Place in West Hollywood by John Woolf has the appearance and the detailing of a movie set. Its volume is defined by the exterior walls of the apartments and offices, and it is connected to the outside through its large front doors and ellipsoidal skylight. Together with the plants at the base of the wall these features suggest an outdoor space. However the hall also has some of the features of an interior chandeliers using overhead and semicircular wrought-iron balconies that intrude into the space as though they were stair landings. On axis through the entrance to the apartment is a swimming pool.

similar to the 1930s work of Southern California architects George Vernon Russell and Douglas Honnold.

Woolf had a special knack for tiny follies that invited fantasy-tinged interpretation. Typically his pool pavilions combine a concavely curving, tentlike roof with an inwardly curving entrance and colonnettes attenuated to skeletal proportions. Producer Bob Evans bought the Pendleton house in the 1970s and turned the pool pavilion into a screening room.

During the 1940s Woolf played with the gable-ended silhouette of pre—Civil War Southeastern houses, French Quarter wrought-iron embellishment and the Mansard roof. Woolf employed the mansard roof far more than any other period-revival architect in Southern California during the 1940s and '50s. It was his use of the mansard and his deployment of piquant details against expanses of blank wall that captivated his fans, leading to the widespread imitation of his style among the Southern California designer demimonde of the 1960s.

The location of Woolf's office and apartment building on Melrose Place (number 8450) made it highly visible to interior decorators, who flocked to this part of town after World War II. This complex of buildings, constructed in three stages between 1946 and 1956 was itself a pioneering effort in the architecture of privacy for Southern California.

The studio office building that John Woolf designed and built for himself at 8450 Melrose Place in West Hollywood was widely admired and frequently emulated by decorators. This was the first building (1946) in which Woolf uses his Pullman door surround.

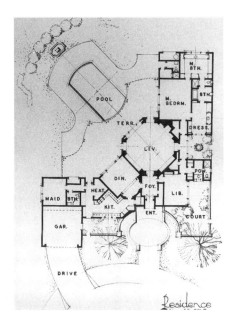

Woolf's 1958 Reynolds house at 200 North Rimpau, Hacock Park, was often reproduced by other designers and decorators in Los Angeles.

The floor plan of John Woolf's Reynold's house in the Hancock Park District of Los Angeles pivots around an octagonal living room.

This Woolf door in Beverly Hills is contemporaneous with the Reynolds house, 1959, built for Alphanzo Bell at 1207 Lexington. Drawing by John Woolf.

Leslie Armur's Moria house of 1974 at 3323 Floye Drive, Hollywood Hills, bears a striking resemblance to Woolf's Reynolds house.

3323 Dona Rosa Drive, Hollywood Hills, 1965. By and for E. W. Spinney. Woolf's 1958 Reynold's house redux. The Reynold's house was a favorite icon of 1950s and '60s decorator home builders.

The sheet metal mansard and the Woolf door as status signifier for a gourmet food shop in West Hollywood, c. 1961.
(Photo: Larry Limotti)

The entrance hall of the 1956 Campbell Building (one section of the Melrose complex) designed by Woolf, has the appearance and detailing of a movie set. Its volume is defined by the exterior walls of the apartments and offices. It is open to the outside through its large front doors and ellipsoidal skylight. Together with the landscaping at the base of the walls, these features suggest an outdoor space. However, the hall also has features of an interior. Chandeliers dangle overhead. Semicircular metal balconies intrude into the space as though they were projecting stair landings. On an axis from the entrance to the apartment unit is a pool. The tight spaces and relatively high density achieved in this complex presaged the town house and condominium types that came to dominate new construction in Southern California after 1970.

The most important contribution of Woolf's office building to the popular architectural vocabulary of Los Angeles was its entrance door, inspired by the door frame found on the exterior of a Pullman car, with its squared arch springing from the top of the impost. Woolf's door protruded above the roof in the same manner as those train car doors. Although his Pullman door is only one of Woolf's variations on the theme of entry—he also designed a pediment that poked above the roof and a baldachin-like portico—it was by far the most popular.

R. M. Schindler meets the Woolf doorway in this 1961 remodel of a former five unit bungalow court into a single family residence at 9020 Lloyd Place, designed by Dean Reynolds.

Its simple, continuous outline and its strong identity as an individual architectural element allowed the Woolf door to appear contemporary, while its association with period architecture and palace gates is equally unmistakable. Woolf often used the arch in the same compositional sense as it had originally been in France, as exemplified by the gates and doorways of 17th-century French architects such as Francois Mansart, whose maisons of 1642 to 1646 featured a gateway arch that pushes through the roof.

In doing so Woolf was part of a local tradition. Entrance bays articulated as projecting, semidetached pavilions with high, steep roofs and an exaggerated vertical emphasis have appeared regularly in Southern California architecture at least as far back as the 1920s. These buildings range from Rudolf Valentino's 1920s Falcon Lair and the 1927 Grauman's Chinese Theater by Meyer and Holler to small, contractor-designed houses such as the mock—Moorish

The Woolf doorway at the Deleray Apartment building, 900 Arroyo Drive in South Pasadena, 1962, by Robert Offenhauser.

The Regency at 740 Orange Grove Drive in Pasadena with a repeating Woolf doorway surround motif. Photo c. 1961 by Lawence Limotti.

K. Hyosoka's 1966 Mansionette apartments at 1764 Worth Sycamore demostrate the incorporation of the Woolf door into apartment design.

The 1968 Branson house at 7145 Pacific View Drive in the Hollywood hills.

A circa 1970 remodeling of 953 Orlando Avenue, West Hollywood.

Sprague house built by the Western Construction Company in 1920 or the 1938 neo-château Hattem house by A. G. Bailey. Other local precedents for the form include eyebrow dormers that gently break the roofline, which were used in residential Southern California architecture during the '30s and '40s.

But because of the importance of display in Southern California architecture after World War II, entrances have assumed a special importance. Due to contemporary desires for increased privacy, entrances are sometimes the only real articulation in a street facade. In a land in which domestic architecture often presents a blank front to the street and communicates only through its portals, it is not surprising that Woolf's entranceway symbols became so ubiquitous.

The Woolf arch is an emphatic punctuation mark. Its theatrically exaggerated height makes the door appear forbidding. Edith Wharton's aphorism applied perfectly to the Woolf entrance: "the main purpose of a door is to admit; its secondary purpose is to exclude."

In the Reynolds house of 1958 in Hancock Park, Woolf combined the arch with a tentlike mansard roof that pops up over the door. The Reynolds house was no sooner completed than copies of it, and then copies of the copies, began to appear all over Los Angeles. The tall Pullman door and the added height of the mansard gave the strongest possible emphasis to the entry. This partial mansard was economical as well, because only part of the roof had to be covered; the remainder of the roof could be flat and hidden by parapets.

A Woolf-style entrance quickly became a symbol of upper-middle-class sophistication, used in the same way as the words "decorator" or gourmet" to signify aspirations of wealth and education.

But by the end of the 1960s, the pop-up mansard could just as easily have been a symbol for cheesy and cheap. Mansards by the yard, in the form of plywood and batten knockoffs, appeared everywhere, from laundromats, liquor stores and fast-food stands to massive new apartment buildings.

John Woolf's most legendary feat, one that has received some degree of attention within the official culture of architecture, was the highly transgressive rehab of a house designed by Los Angeles architect Craig Ellwood. It was built as Case Study House No. 17 in 1955 as part of John Entenza's program of building Modern houses and popularizing them to the public with tours and publication in his *Arts and Architecture* magazine. While the the original client "had some doubtful moments about the house, and the manner in which it was to be furnished, such as the glass and steel and the hard beds and coconut chairs," John Woolf and his son Robert were not so shy about expressing their disinterest in the spartan interiors and immediately ripped them out.

They remodeled the house (purchased as a white elephant "fixer") in 1962 by opening up the center and adding Doric columns over the steel posts, "In order to give this beautifully made contemporaneous building a patina of age." *House Beautiful* magazine had no reservations about the results: "In the enchanted hour of dusk one might be reliving the past in a columned villa of Basae or among the temples of Paestum." To be fair to the breathless *House Beautiful* writer, the remodel did emphasize the neoclassicism of the building inherent in the original Miesian design. The "before" and "after" versions of the interior courtyard differ more in the style of detailing of their rooms than in their spatial composition.

John Woolf died in 1980 and his firm now operates under the direction his son Robert Koch Woolf, who was adopted by Woolf when Robert was an adult. The firm's work after 1970 lacked the sure touch and the knowing restraint of earlier designs.

Craig Ellwood's Case Study house #17, at 9554 Hidden Valley Road in Coldwater Canyon, in its original state as a temple of modernism. (Photo: Jason Hailey)

Case Study house #17 transformed beyond recognition in 1962 by John Woolf as a temple in the Hollywood Regency Revival style.

wallace neff

One of the signs that academia has finally embraced revivalism with the same enthusiasm that the public has long held for it is the spate of publishing on period revival architects such as Wallace, Neff and the Texas regionalist John Staub. The work displayed in Alson Clark's book on Neff offers an object lesson: it is not the choice of architectural vocabulary that guarantees a high level of design, but rather how that vocabulary is handled.

In his monograph on Neff, Alson Clark quotes Aymar Embury II, a distinguished East Coast architect and author writing in the 1920s. Embury praised architects of the time because he believed they were becoming more adept at adapting traditional elements to modern uses. East Coast period-revival architect William Adams Delano preferred to think of all of his work, however flavored by this or that style, as modern, because it was designed to suit contemporary needs and taste. Neff chose to call his work "Californian" to emphasize the primacy of the time and place of his buildings' construction over the time and place of their stylistic origins. In fact

A house at the scale of a Mission. The no longer extant Susanna Bryant Bixby house of 1927, by Wallace Neff, in Santa Ana Canyon. (Photo: Henry E. Huntington Library and Art Gallery)

Neff was most unhappy when forced to copy, as was the case with one commission, the Villa Sol d'Oro in Sierra Madre. The client required Neff to model in part after a building attributed to Michelangelo, the Villa Collazi near Florence.

Neff designed some 200-odd houses, most of them in period revival styles, and many of them for entertainment-industry celebrities Among them were vast spreads such as the Susanna Bixby Bryant ranch house of 1927 in Santa Ana Canyon. He equipped it with enough towers and arcades to humble any of the California missions.

Some of his buildings, such as the George O. Noble house of 1927, are as romantically overripe as Gloria Swanson's house in the movie Sunset Boulevard. Neff's now-demolished Harry Culver house of 1928 could have stood in for the decaying Spanish Colonial Revival house that plays a leading role in Robert Plunkett's satiric novel, *My Search for Warren G. Harding*. The Culver living room chandelier looked heavy enough to double as a wrecking ball, while the fireplace mantel could have passed for a baroque cathedral screen and the notched corbels supporting the gallery resembled the prows of a fleet of Viking boats.

Courtyard as living room, pool as hearth; the patio of the
Arthur K. Bourne house in Palm Springs, by Wallace Neff, 1933.
(Photo: Henry E. Huntington Library and Art Gallery)

Neff's architecture could be playful, and certain of these playful elements became his trademarks. One of them was an exterior staircase with a solid balustrade that stepped up in a series of setbacks. Sometimes he combined this stair with one or more columns resting against the wall. If there was more than one column, they would both have the same circumference but would vary in height because of the rise of the stair run. Neff was also fond of placing a column dead center in the gable end of a low-pitched roof, so that the column appears a piece of sculpture or an icon.

His tile roofs were often either very steep or very shallow—so shallow, in fact, that some of them could not be built and finished in the same manner

Henry F. Haldeman house, Holmby Hills, Los Angeles, 1939.
A light second-story portico on a substantial first-story base.
Neff's buildings often had the sense of having the upper story
barely tucked in under the eaves.
(Photo: Henry E. Huntington Library and Art Gallery)

now because they would not conform to present-day building codes. His fairy-tale-like play with scale sometimes makes his high roofs appear crushingly large, as they do in the Stanley W. Imerman house of 1936 in Beverly Hills. Some of the residences with low-pitched roofs have a heavy-lidded drowsiness, created by pushing windows or loggias tight against the eaves, as Neff did with his George Miller (1938) and Henry Haldeman (1939) houses. The exaggerated proportions of Neff's roofs were emphasized by his penchant for horizontality, which he expressed in a variety of quite dissimilar projects. Several of his buildings, such as the King Vidor house no. 2, have a front facade composed of a single, long, low-pitched gable end, similar to McKim Mead & White's shingle-style low house of 1886–87.

While some of Neff's buildings sprawled out into the green and gold California landscape, like the San Marino home of Arthur K. Bourne, others had plans that were basically formal and symmetrical, such as the M.L.H Walker house of 1923. Neff's easy Southern California familiarity with the outdoors found expression is his patio and courtyard spaces, which were sometimes planned as part of the entrance sequence. His Arthur K. Bourne house of 1933 at Palm Springs is a model of a desert oasis. Its courtyard has the festive yet dignified air of a Pompeian villa. Symmetrical colonnades with sturdy, Tootsie-Roll-like proportions flank the sparkle of the swimming pool

10615 Bellagio Road, Bel-Air, 1938. A traditional domestic vocabulary abstracted in Neff's George Miller house. It was later owned by Cary Grant and Barbara Hutton. Photo courtesy of the Henry E. Huntington Library and Art Gallery.

and its bordering bands of verdant lawn. Equally engaging is Neff's incorporation of a second-story mirador, a small lookout room and loggia for taking in the sweep of desert valley and mountains.

After the heyday of the 1920s and the difficult years of the Great Depression, Neff, like most other period-revival architects, did not get the same number or size of residential commissions that he had received before the war. He tried to keep up with changing public taste by modernizing his designs, but for the most part his Modern work was not as accomplished as his period-revival work. A few of his postwar buildings are downright embarrassing.

Neff was on surer ground with his more traditional postwar commissions. Some of these jobs continued to come his way in those years, given to him by clients who liked the look of his earlier work. His Eugene Allen house of 1968 was patterned after his Joan Bennett house of some 30 years earlier. Similarly, his Ralph Chandler house of 1963 gives the impression that it could easily be a Beaux Arts neoclassical product of 50 or 60 years earlier.

This post-World War II Beaux Arts house in Hancock Park, built in 1962 for Buckingham Homes, was designed by Wallace Neff.

Only at the rear facade is the true vintage of the house revealed—behind a serene screen of tall columns, the irregular shape of the house is baldly expressed. The higgledy-piggledy mismatch of regimented colonnade to rear facade can be interpreted as either ironic or as deliberately naive and awkward. It recalls similarly puzzling disjunctures in the work of James Dolena and John Woolf, Neff's fellow, post-World War II revivalists. While it may be tempting to label these lapses as precursors of postmodernism, it is equally likely that they were caused by last-minute client demand or by confusion about executing period-revival architecture at a time when agreement about the rules that govern it had broken down.

a brief note on james dolena

James Dolena is best known for his Georgian Revival, Federal and Hollywood Regency mansions of the 1930s, such as those for actor William Powell and actress Constance Bennett. The much-remodeled Farmers Market at Fairfax and Third in Los Angeles is probably his most prominently sited work. He joined with Robsjohn Gibbings to create the opulent Hilda Boldt Weber house in Bel-Air of 1936–38, later owned by hotel man

James Dolena's 1960 Virtue house at 216 Oakhurst Drive in Beverly Hills. Classicism reduced to the bare bones: symmetrical composition, a concave entrance and flanking Italian cypress.

The facade of James Dolena's Fred Prophet house in Beverly Hills probably dates from the mid 1950s anticipating the post modernism of the 1970s and '80s. (Photo: Henry E. Huntington Library and Art Gallery)

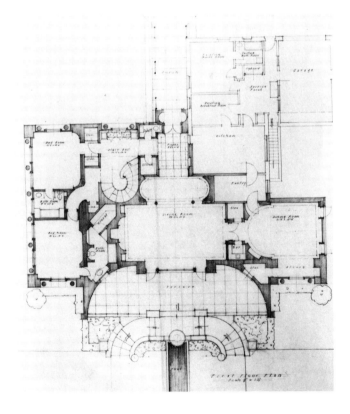

The ground-floor plan of Dolena's Prophet house also has affinities to '20s postmodern design in its playful geometry and use of thick walls to define space. (Photo: Henry E. Huntington Library and Art Gallery)

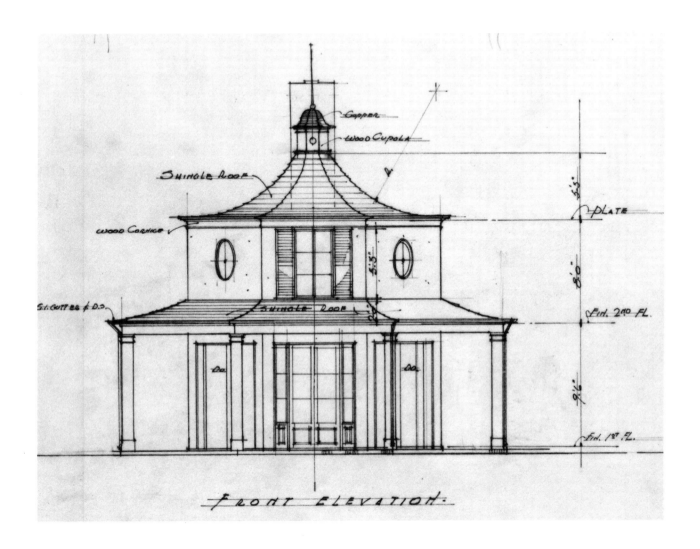

Labels on drawing: Copper · Wood Cupola · Shingle Roof · Wood Cornice · S.I. Gutter & D.S. · Do. · Do. · Shingle Roof · Plate · Fin. 2nd Fl. · Fin. 1st Fl.

FRONT ELEVATION.

Pavilion of the George Cukor residence, undated James Dolena.
(Photo: Henry E. Huntington Library and Art Gallery)

Conrad Hilton. Dolena's wryly elegant house for director George Cukor was a collaboration with decorating legend William Haines.

Dolena's work after World War II retained the use of blank walls and symmetry in both plan and facade. His use of isolated period details, such as columns and the Woolf doorway, against this kind of spare backdrop was close to the spirit of decorators' work, as in the 1960 Virtue house at 218 Oakhurst Drive in Beverly Hills. The Virtue house is a simple, three-bay symmetrical box with a gently curved, concave entry bay.

Dolena emigrated to the United States from Russia at age 17, graduated from the Chicago Art Institute in 1910 and began working on his own in California in 1929. He died in 1978. His drawings are housed at the Huntington Library in San Marino.

The Boldt-Weber house at 10644 Bellagio Road in Bel Air, 1936–38 is the largest of the Debonair Georgian, Regency, and Federal revival houses which established James Dolena as a fashionable domestic architect for the well to do in the 1930s. (Photo: Henry E. Huntington Library and Art Gallery)

knocking off the knock-offs

The last chapter discussed large period revival houses designed by architects for wealthy Souther Californians. This chapter profiles small developer-built bungalows from the 1920s that middle class Southern Californians remodeled, as part homage and part original invention, inspired by the large period revival houses. These remodels in turn influenced other genres of consumerist vernacular achitecture, such as apartment houses and storefronts.

> *What is so astonishing about anyone taking this remodel seriously is the attitude that absolutely anything can be transformed into architectural history.*
>
> —Reyner Banham, in a book review in the *London Times Literary Supplement* of *Exterior Decoration*, from which this essay is excerpted

The Swiss modernist architect Le Corbusier observed that a dream times one million equals chaos. In Los Angeles it is the millions of dreams of its citizens that make up the face of the city. If Southern California is often accused of having no public urban amenities in the traditional sense, it may be because they come disguised as private visions such as the Watts Towers, or at the very least, privately owned visions like City Walk, Forest Lawn and Disneyland.

West Hollywood is a small 1.9-square mile city nestled in between Hollywood and Beverly Hills, a section of Los Angeles where the contributions of private fantasy to the public realm come in the form of tiny stucco

8834 Rangely Avenue, West Hollywood. Benjamin and Betty Heiman's 1968 remodel of their house. Designed by Benjamin Heiman. This facade was removed in 1999.

8488 Carlton Way, West Hollywood Hills, c. 1946. The remodeled Frank L. Anderson house. It is the first published West Hollywood remodel that uses a screen wall placed in front of the street facade.for added privacy. Photo by Maynard Parker.

bungalows remodeled by interior decorators and decorator wannabes. The blanked-out exteriors of these miniature mansions became inside-out interiors: urns and finials were placed on rooftops like bibelots on a fireplace mantel; windows and panels of trellis were arranged as though they were pictures hung on a wall.

In the early 1950s a mania for transforming Spanish Colonial Revival mutts into French Regency pedigreed poodles swept West Hollywood. The Regency style craze of the Camelot years of the early 1960s saw the height of the box-in-the-old and tack-on-the-new movement; in its wake were left miles of garlands, a forest of pop-up mansards and enough carriage lamps to render the street lights redundant.

The decorator shops that grew up around Beverly Boulevard shortly after World War II attracted a colony of interior designers who worked in the neighborhood. Many of them would have loved to have owned a mansion in nearby ritzy neighborhoods like Brentwood, Beverly Hills or Hancock Park. But most couldn't afford to and made do with what they could. West Hollywood had been settled as the community of Sherman in 1895, built around a repair yard for the interurban street car lines. As a result many of the houses were built for residents with moderate incomes. Both lots and houses were small, a precedent that continued when the community saw its real period of growth in the mid-1920s as a bedroom community to surrounding cities.

Real estate speculation, aided by wild booms such as the bull market of 1975 to 1978, was a key motive in the remodeling fad. Speculators (including some gay couples who were returning from military service in World War II) would move from house to house, fixing each one up, selling it for a profit and then starting in on the next candidate. By the late 1970s houses that sold for $15,000 or less in the early 1950s were going for $180,000.

Despite the assumptions made by some observers that these decorator remodels are a campy in-joke, the little buildings reflect the anxieties produced by the city's many levels of wealth and status. With the exception of a few truly idiosyncratic buildings, the remodels are attempts to conform to accepted notions of upwardly mobile social standing, rather than to shock.

The typical remodeling project follows a relatively unvarying formula. Openings in the front of the house are closed off to screen out the street. Openings in the rear are enlarged to create spatial and visual flow between the indoors and outdoors. The kitchen and bathroom are modernized, light switches and door hardware are replaced and the master bedroom and living room are enlarged. Usually the exterior of the little houses become more formal to suit the social ambitions of their new owners, and more secluded to separate them from increasingly urban surroundings.

Expedience is everything in the remodels. The designers of the remodels, many of whom worked in the movie industry, never built if they could achieve the same effect by draping fabric and never ripped out a facade if they could cover over it or adapt it.

In the broadest sense, the West Hollywood remodel genre is an outgrowth of the Hollywood Regency style. The earliest remodels were in this style, and the idea of the remodels themselves was made possible by the style's appeal to the designers.

Few styles are more difficult to define than the Hollywood Regency. The Regency half of the name is itself confusing, as the affinities between the architecture of the English Regency period of the years 1790 to 1830 and the architecture of the Hollywood Regency style of the 1930s are limited. The Hollywood Regency is a revival of features drawn from the early 19th-century architectural styles of England, the United States and, to a lesser degree, France. The style strayed even further from English Regency during World War II and in the following years, when both architects and decorators gallicized it with the addition of a mansard roof.

Because the American Federal style and later the French Second Empire influences were as important as the English Regency precedents, it is more accurate to categorize the Hollywood Regency style as a descriptive term rather than as a literal revival of pre-Victorian 19th-century English architecture.

Even the English Regency style is ambiguous. It might be more correct to speak of a Regency era in English architecture than a single, well-defined Regency style. "Strictly speaking there is no Regency style. There was no universally accepted formula for design," wrote Douglas Pilcher in his 1940 book *The Regency Style: 1800–1830.* "There is, however, a tendency towards establishing an individual style which resulted from the balancing of these distinct points of view." Among these points of view was the belief that a building should suit the individual personality of its occupant. During the Regency era the cult of the Picturesque had a wide following. Derived from Romantic fiction, the Picturesque endowed the physical world, including

The interior of the Anderson house is styled in the modern Georgian Hollywood Regency style of the 1930s. Photo by Maynard Parker.

One of the ultimate sources for the Hollywood Regency style were English Regency era designs such as this pavilion by John Sloane published in his 1778 *Designs in Architecture.*

The back yard of 8984 Lloyd Place, West Hollywood, before glamorization struck. Photo by Harold Davis.

The same view of 8984 Lloyd Place after glamorization. Remodeled by Alden Thomsen, 1959. Photo by Harold Davis.

architecture, with the ability to inspire emotions such as awe, terror and enchantment. Regency architecture was eclectic, but may generally be characterized as a highly abstracted version of neoclassicism. Toward the end of the period, Gothic Revival became popular, as did exotic motifs from Islamic architecture, the Far East and India.

Wrought-iron balconies and entrances were widely used in Regency England, and exterior walls were frequently covered with a stucco finish. The neoclassic primary geometric forms, together with the attenuated wrought-iron trim and the smooth stucco walls, gave much Regency architecture qualities of insubstantiality and brittle elegance. Forms reminiscent of tents were employed in building form were common, and fabric was sometimes draped on interior walls to create tentlike rooms. The stucco walls, the use of French doors to link outside and inside, and the frequent employment of trellis and balcony were all features that made Regency styles attractive to California designers.

A 1939 issue of *Interior Decorator* credits a major exhibition of Regency furniture by Lenygon and Morant in London just after World War I for kindling interest in Regency furniture. In *The Glass of Fashion*, fashion designer Cecil Beaton credits the revival of the Regency style to the English playwright Edward Knoblock and its propagation to John Fowler and the socialite decorator Sybil Halsey.

By May of 1919, *Upholsterer and Interior Decorator* magazine could inform its readers that "both the Regency and the Louis XVI are meeting with renewed favor." This favor reached an "almost nauseating popularity," according to English decorator David Hicks. "In the late 1930s it had begun to be revived, and this was continued in the late 1940s," he wrote in *David Hicks on Interior Decoration*. Reproduction and reinterpretation of furniture by Regency designers such as Thomas Hope were much in demand in the United States just before World War II. The Regency influence in domestic architecture and home furnishings remained strong through the mid-1960s.

Regency details began to appear in Southern California in the 1920s, with buildings such as Marston, Maybury & Van Pelt's Dudley house in Pasadena of 1925–27. Regency elements were found on buildings in Georgian, Federal, and French Provincial manor house styles. During the 1930s Regency designs from architects across the nation, as well as from California, were published in national architectural magazines. But the

Regency style has been most closely identified with interior decorators, in Southern California and elsewhere. It was the decorator, as much as the architect, who helped popularize the stylistic code of the Regency as found in Southern California. This fondness of the decorators for Regency architecture is probably linked to the revival of Regency furniture and interior design in England and America between World War I and II.

The strongest reason for the popularity of Regency architecture in California during the 1930s was its compatibility with the American Colonial Revival style that dominated American residential architecture at the time. Colonial American architecture of the Federal period was an important influence on Southern California architecture in the 1920s and 1930s. Buildings such as the Ruges house, Columbia Falls, Maine, were widely reproduced in books and national periodicals. The Hollywood Regency adapted features from late Colonial Revival architecture, particularly from the early 19th century Federal architecture, which is the American counterpart of the English Regency period.

American architecture of the Federal period had a similar light, delicate appearance. The houses usually had very simple boxlike volumes, and flat or low-pitched roof lines. The boxy shapes might be varied by polygonal or curved bays. Some Federal period buildings have semicircular porches supported on slender columns. Federal architecture was generally more conservative than Regency architecture, simpler in form, lacking the dramatic black and white interiors and the sometimes exotic imagery of English architecture. Wood construction, employing clapboarded walls, was more frequently used in Federal, rather than Regency, architecture.

The Hollywood Regency stylistic mix of Regency, Georgian, Federal and, to a lesser degree, the French Provincial manor house revival styles were influenced by the emergence of the International style in the 1920s and 1930s. Several features of the International style affected the period styles: horizontality, strip and corner windows, pipelike poles, flat roofs and porthole windows.

There are also precedents for the Hollywood Regency style in the Spanish Colonial Revival style, which enjoyed great popularity in California during the 1920s. Elements that are related in the two styles are the isolation of ornament, blank walls and, in some examples, abstracted window placement. This trend toward smooth surfaces and unadorned walls was an

Many remodels privatized the front yard. In this West Hollywood house remodel by William Chappell and Paul Rich, the front yard is walled off from the street and linked by French doors to the interior. Remodeled by William Chappell and Paul Rich. Photo c.1981.

important ingredient in the Hollywood Regency style. This style was concocted by mixing modern and historically inspired elements with quintessential Southern California nonchalance. The style was a modernized version of Georgian/Regency/Federal/Second Empire architecture and was Southern California's own version of the Modern Georgian style popular nationally. The Hollywood Regency style was theatrical—its walls exaggeratedly blank, its columns impossibly thin. This architecture of glamour required a seemingly effortless balancing of the formal and the casual, as well as a knack for well-placed exaggeration and well-chosen omission. In short, the Hollywood Regency had much in common with the best of Southern California's sophisticated period-revival architecture of the 1920s and 1930s.

Primary forms were favored in Hollywood Regency architecture for the configuration of buildings. Walls were emphasized, rather than roofs, which were usually low-pitched or hidden behind a parapet wall. The building mass might be a single volume, or it might be broken into groupings of pavilions. Flattened or gently curving bays sometimes divided the facade. The detailing of Hollywood Regency buildings often had a flattened, two-dimensional quality, in order to match the sleekness of the wall surfaces. Hollywood Regency was the perfect architecture to represent the Hollywood that had brought "a world of silken underwear, exotic surroundings, and moral plasticity to the United States, through the medium of film," as William C. De Mille wrote in his 1939 book *Hollywood Saga*.

After World War II, the Hollywood Regency style was altered by the addition of the mansard roof. This roof, as originally popularized by the French architect Francois Mansart, was a steeply sloping, double-pitched roof enclosing a habitable upper story. Out of this modernized pastiche of English, American and occasionally French adaptations, the West Hollywood remodelers and Southern California interior decorators were fondest of those houses with specifically French references. The prototype for these houses as 1930s California homes with mansard roofs; tall, narrow window openings or French doors; and a symmetrical facade articulated as a set of pavilions or as one mansarded block. Buildings such as S. Charles Lee's Oldknow house of circa 1936, and George Vernon Russell and Douglas Honnold's alteration of a Topanga beach house of 1938–39 for director Anatole Litvak were precedents for the horizontal one-story mansarded houses of the 1950s and 1960s.

In the Litvak house a mansard roof has been placed over one section of the house, while adjoining sections are lower and the roofs are flat. This arrangement gives the impression that the mansard is sitting as a lid on the boxy body of the building, in the manner so prevalent in later years in the West Hollywood remodels. Without being inconsistent in his choice of architectural vocabulary, Honnold was able to use a period facade on the street and a beachfront facade at the back that suggested the European modernism of the 1920s. This independence of the two facades foretold the architectural tastes of the 1950s and 1960s in Southern California, where an otherwise standard tract-house design might have a mansard roof slapped on its facade as a false front.

By the end of the 1930s, one-story houses by architects such as Paul R. Williams, Ralph Flewelling and Roland Coate, Sr., combined high-hipped roofs set back from the walls with a symmetrical street facade. Concealed behind the facade was often a stretched-out, horizontal floor plan with long side wings extending to the rear. The layout of these houses was eclectic, combining the sprawling floor plans and horizontality of the California ranch house with more formal arrangements of axiality and symmetry in the public spaces. Wrought-iron Regency porticoes, or columned Federal porticoes, and a mixture of high French roof silhouettes and low Regency roofs show up in these houses. Their articulation as a series of pavilions was French in derivation. The houses beloved by the decorators were later versions of these 1930s models. The post-World War II houses had mansarded rather than hipped roofs.

These high, hipped roofs were generally used in Southern California buildings of the 1920s and '30s to suggest late medieval and renaissance chateaux. In the 1930s and '40s the mansard roof had been employed on a handful of houses such as Roland Coate's Niven house of 1939 in Beverly Hills or Jim Dolena's house of circa 1937 for actress Constance Bennett in Holmby Hills. In the Bennett house a hipped-roof central pavilion was flanked by projecting end wings, also with hipped roofs.

The popularity of the mansard roof for commercial structures in Southern California began just after World War II with buildings such as L. G. Scherer's Thatcher Medical Clinic (1948–49) in Pasadena, Paul R. Williams' Perino's Restaurant of 1948 in the mid-Wilshire district of Los

Angeles and Jack Woolf's office building on Melrose Place in West Hollywood. Right from the start of its widespread use in Los Angeles, the mansard was accepted as an indicator that a business catered to an upper-class or upper-middle-class clientele. Williams's free handling of the mansard at Perino's is significant because it is so similar to the manner in which the mansard would later be used. Its heyday came during the 1960s when it was often employed as a cheap and easily made false front for commercial strip architecture. The mansard roof was used as though its were carpeting, unrolled as a horizontal band to whatever length was desired. The canopy of Perino's appears as a dropped mansard. The broken pediment, or the front gable, is extruded as a roof form, and the circular window carries approximately the same compositional value as the neon Perino's sign.

The studio office building that John Woolf designed and built for himself at 8450 Melrose Place in 1946–47 was widely admired and frequently emulated by the decorators. This was the first building in which Woolf used his Pullman door surround and projecting extruded doorframe that rises just

8937 Ashcroft Avenue in West Hollywood, remodeled by Larry Limotti and Ross Worsley in 1961–62. The framing for the mansard roof goes up on the 1920s bungalow. Photo by Larry Limotti.

Roof framing complete at the Limotti-Worsley house. Photo by Larry Limotti.

above the roofline. The building was further added to in two installments. The
Mason Building at 8446 Melrose Place was built in 1950, and the Campbell
Building was built at 8436 Melrose Place in 1956. Woolf's use of this Pullman
door and pop-up mansard was immediately adopted by the decorators.

While Woolf was the most important architect for the decorators and the
West Hollywood remodelers, there were other architects they admired.
Buildings with period references by architects, such as Paul R. Williams
and Wallace Neff, have been models for the interior-decorator architectural
demimonde of Southern California, both in West Hollywood and elsewhere.
In their eyes, buildings by Jack Woolf and other society architects constitut-
ed a distinct, cohesive body of work, representing the discriminating taste of
the wealthiest and most famous residents of exclusive Los Angeles neighborhoods such as Bel Air and Holmby Hills.

Their reverent contemplation of the successful often took the form of a
grand tour of Los Angeles' plusher districts. Interior designer Larry Limotti,

Outside as inside. A back yard detail of the 1961 Limotti-Worsley
remodel, West Hollywood. Photo by Larry Limotti.

The completed remodel of the Limotti-Worsley house as it was in
1981. The landscape has since been altered.

who was responsible for several West Hollywood remodels, made just such a series of reconnaissance missions in the early 1960s. Among the buildings he photographed on these trips were Caspar Ehmcke's Bernstein house of 1954 in Bel Air, early 1960s Regency-style apartment houses in Pasadena, Jack Woolf's LeRoy house and the mansarded Brentwood Hamburger Hamlet. Limotti also included existing West Hollywood remodels among his subjects.

The influence of these studies is evident in the house that was Limotti's first design, built in conjunction with his partner, Ross Worsely. In the backyard of the house, the fence was adorned with urns corbeled forward on scroll-like brackets. The immediate precedent for this treatment could have been found in Limotti's photograph of a West Hollywood remodel by the Tishman Company for Eloise Hardt. In this 1961 remodel the facade was transformed into a billboard backdrop for urns and busts framed in recessed niches.

While Limotti's photograph album included shots of Regency-style apartments under construction, it is possible that the developers of these apartments were also photographing the West Hollywood remodels, and other buildings designed or influenced by decorators. Many of these developer-built apartment buildings of the early and mid-'60s resemble overscaled West Hollywood remodels. In the La Bon Vie apartments of 1963, the Pullman door has become a blank panel with a regulation plate-glass, aluminum-frame door stuck into one side. On either side of the door, three-story-high blank windows are suggested with applied trim. In K. Hyosaka's Mansionette apartments of 1966, the superscale clip-on and applique elements determine the character of the facade. The same motifs are found in Robert Duncan's Chateau Laurelle apartments of 1965 in Studio City.

The utilitarian stucco-box apartment house was perfected in the 1950s when its garnishings were modernistic. In the 1960s it became clear that with a few changes the dingbat stucco apartment could just as easily accept ersatz Regency ornament, which was itself replaced in a new wave of enthusiasm for Spanish Colonial Revival imagery at the end of the decade. By then the Regency's upper-class associations had been blurred by the use of mansards for everything from hamburger stands to laundromats. The Regency disappeared into the common pool of imagery drawn on by the developers and building designers responsible for Los Angeles' pop commercial architecture. By the late 1970s, a mansard roof was often finished in red Spanish tiles over a Tudor half-timbered wall.

Interior Limotti-Worsley house. Photo by Harold Davis.

525 Crescent Heights Boulevard in West Hollywood, prior to a regime of beautification. Photo by Larry Limotti.

In 1961–62 decorator Larry Limotti encased the 1920s cottage in a new shell. Photo by Larry Limotti.

Who says houses can't wear costume jewelry? The completed Limotti redo of 525 Crescent in 1962. Photo by Larry Limotti.

Possibly the only model ever made of a West Hollywood remodel is this one of furniture designer Herman Schlorman's 1961 remodel. Note the similarity of spirit to the Chateau Laurelle Apartments below.

The Chateau Laurelle, 4200 Laurel Canyon Boulevard, Studio city. Robert Duncan, 1965. The Chateau Laurelle is simply a West Hollywood house remodel in the Woolf style, blown up to super scale.

In an interview with the author in 1980, entertainer/interior designer Terence Monk, who was responsible for several West Hollywood and Beverly Hills remodels, commented on the changes that had occurred in his own remodels: "The interesting thing is, I've taken all those old Spanish houses and made them into something else—disguised them as a French townhouse or a chichi decorator-type thing. Now I'm dedicated to taking Spanish houses and making them more so." In the 1970s the mansard-roofed remodels seemed vulgar to the decorators. The fussiness and pretentiousness of the style marked an obsequious observance of social conventions that no longer existed in the same form.

By the late 1970s, the influences of minimalism, high-tech design and the contrasting fashion for rough-textured natural materials had replaced the imitation Second Empire references in the interiors of the remodels. The newer remodels were furnished in gray industrial carpeting, Levelor blinds and tall, potted cacti, rather than with chandeliers and black-and-white checkered floors.

By the time the disco era of the '70s arrived, the remodels had more to do with the East Coast revival of the 1920s modernism of Le Corbusier, as practiced by architects such as Richard Meier, Luis Barragan and Frank Gehry, than it did to the work of the Mansarts. The constant that has held for each era of miniature remodel has been the replacement of an outmoded or nondescript facade with a design that clearly conveyed that the occupant had made a conscious design choice to live life elegantly, by their own lights. Even if the results may not be to everyone's taste, surely the remodelers deserve credit for that all-American attempt to construct an identity by choosing among alternatives, to be self-made individuals by living behind a self-made facade. In West Hollywood, clothes alone do not make the man or woman. The house facade does.

PART THREE
LAS VEGAS

Las Vegas Boulevard South. Billboard-like advertising á la Times Square lends extra moxie to the traditionally important role given to signage in Las Vegas. At Gameworld V at the MGM Grand Hotel, the facade superscale signage reads effectively for motorists but also creates pedestrian interest by coming down to ground level.

las vegas: pirates!

volcanoes!

neon!

welcome to the capitol of non-glamour!

with Frances Anderton

a lucky draw

gambling makes it all possible: the all-you-can-eat buffets, the free, live band at the bar and the herculean wonders like the Mirage's flaming volcano lagoon. But as gambling tycoon Steve Wynn has noted, there are plenty of other places in the US where tourists can go to gamble besides Las Vegas. Visitors come here because Vegas is a legend. This is the place where you are supposed to wake up naked in a stranger's motel room, with a 10-daiquiri headache and no wallet. It performs the role that the carnival performs in other cultures, of defining itself by being everything you aren't normally allowed to be. Irresponsible. Hedonistic. Devil may care. Naughty as you dare.

When you think of Las Vegas you don't just think of gambling. You think of Elvis, Sinatra, Howard Hughes, the drug-crazed Hunter Thompson, showgirls and hookers, blinding neon and champagne-bubble twinkling lights. Las Vegas is the first place any self-respecting student of the built environment would go to in America to find white-hot visual excitement combined with the all-purpose moral license to enjoy it. For the public at large Vegas is synonymous with gambling, entertainment and casinos. Within the culture of art and architecture the casinos are a gold mine of pop references right up there with rock and roll and the movies.

During daylight hours the skyline of the city is dominated by the hulking presence of the hotel casinos. Most of the "older" casino-hotel towers are undistinguished late-modern dormitory-like blocks. (We've seen packages for generic brands of paper towels that have more design care invested in them than these hotel facades.) By night it is the fabled neon and flashing lights that signify Las Vegas to the world at large. The lights of the Stardust flicker, tickle, cascade and float, a burst of blue and magenta stars. The brilliant conical roofs of Excalibur beckon like Oz, bouncing candy-colored light into the the night sky.

The brutish twin Bally's towers fluoresce in a cobalt-blue glow. The vastness of the Caesar's hotel block and its attendant porte cochere, monstrous by day, turns seductive by night, radiating electric acid-pink and electric acid-green, an otherworldly fantasia. Las Vegas at night is not about your cerebral cortex, it's rather a love letter addressed directly to the primeval cortex of your brain. Like sweet taste or sweet music, our neurons crave colored light. The stimulation is too elemental to be denied. And the best part of all is that as on a theater stage, once an environment is all about the lights, what the lights are supported by and shining on doesn't make a lot of difference. Facades can be made cheaply or badly, but once nighttime rolls around, they will shine prettily nonetheless.

Joel D. Bergman for Bergman, Walls and Youngblood, Ltd. In the 1960s and '70s, abstraction ruled the roost for casino hotels. In the twenty-first century replication is king, as here at the 1999 Paris hotel-casino.

oasis to mirage

Las Vegas is located in the southern tip of the State of Nevada on flat, unyielding terrain surrounded by dramatic mountain ranges that separate it from the natural desert wonders of Death Valley, in California to the west, and the Grand Canyon, in Arizona to the east. Characterized by baking hot summers (110 degrees is normal) and windy winters, separated by short beautiful spells, it is an essentially hostile environment . It owes its initial habitation to the presence of water, in the shape of artesian wells, and its continued growth later to the presence of power, in the form of nearby Hoover Dam.

The city barely existed before the turn of the century. The area was inhabited by a series of Indian tribes, most recently the Southern Paiute Indians, then by Spanish explorers, who named it "Las Vegas," meaning "the meadows." It was later occupied by pioneers who, in 1865, transformed it into a wagon road for people working the nearby mines. In 1902 it was selected as a mid-route supply depot for the Los Angeles and Salt Lake Railroad, bringing the first of the many Mormon settlers who would subsequently invest in the city's future. Honest nongamblers with business heads, they account for 15 to 20 percent of the population, and along with the mobs, local banks and the teamsters, financed the gambling industry in the '40s, '50s and '60s. Their reputation for integrity and trustworthiness has been sterling. Howard Hughes selected only Mormons to be his caretakers in the 1960s, a period in which he invested heavily in Las Vegas.

In 1928, Uncle Sam stepped in, selecting Vegas as the site for that depression-time engineering marvel, the Hoover Dam (formerly Boulder Dam). During World War II Las Vegas became the location for the Nellis Air Force Base, a source of thousands of new residents. Nellis was a testbase for Thunderbirds, Stealth Fighters and bombers. In the 1950s, the U.S. military further expanded its presence in the area, selecting a site 50 miles north of Vegas for nuclear tests. These tests proved a boon, rather than a dampener, to the burgeoning tourist industry. Enterprising casino owners offered gambling guests the added thrill of atom bomb—viewing breakfasts and other spectacles.

The State of Nevada legalized gambling in 1931. Las Vegas' destiny fell into the hands of enterprising individuals and mobsters, personified by Benjamin "Bugsy" Siegel of "Murder, Inc.", who arrived from the East coast in the '40s and took over supervision of the Flamingo, which opened in 1947. The Flamingo initiated the trend for Beverly Hills Modern glamour in place of the rustic western imagery that had characterized the local resort architecture until then. This was the status quo until local purges of the criminal element in the '60s and deregulation in the '70s and '80s, gave rise to present-day Las Vegas, in which corporate-controlled casinos, of ever increasing scale, sell sanitized vice to an ever-increasing numbers of visitors, the preponderance of whom still appear to be middle-aged Middle Americans.

Its not as though the mob has disappeared without a trace. The current (1999) mayor of Las Vegas is Oscar Goodman, an attorney famous for representing mobster clients. An article on Goodman in the August 16, 1999 edi-

New York, New York. Gaskin and Bezanski, 1996. Pedestrian walkway elevated above the traffic mayhem of Las Vegas Boulevard South links the candy colored Sleeping Beauty's castle of Excalibur with Grant's Tomb and the rest of the New York, New York casino.

tion of *The New Yorker* quotes Goodman as saying that the only person who loved his job as much as himself was mobster Nicodemo Scarfo, "when he was pouring .22s into someone's head" while exclaiming "I love it! I love it!"

Las Vegas is a city that has catered largely to itinerant workers and gamblers, leaving a legacy of no-nonsense, serviceable residential and civic buildings, and virtually no traditional civic public domain. Tourism continues to swell. Twenty million visitors per year visit Las Vegas, and 30,000 new hotel rooms were under construction in 1995. Consequently the local population has jumped from 200,000 to nearly 1 million inhabitants in 20 years, producing dramatic physical changes in the scale of the gambling tourist center and the surrounding city itself.

The metropolitan area is trying to make a place for the arts at the same time as it is trying to keep pace with the traffic, gridlock, pollution, homelessness and other urban ills that such rapid success has created. The culture of high art architecture is taking on a greater importance in the city. Las Vegas is now spawning civic and cultural buildings, and, in the casino district itself, the gaming hotels, once defined by their neon spectaculars, have become in themselves spectacles.

The showgirl headdress Flamingo Hilton, 3555 Las Vegas Boulevard South. Sign by Heath & Co. 1975. An earlier generation of casino-hotels explored a seductive and joyful abstraction of light, color and form in their facades.

stacking the design odds

New sophistication and a continuing building boom not withstanding, it is still one of the least profitable cities in which to seek architecture that has any pizzazz at all—with the white-hot exception of the strip, Fremont Street and downtown. The sprawling city that services the tourist-oriented Strip and downtown Fremont Street simply do not feature in the tourist imagination, or for that matter in architectural and urban design critiques of the city. The explanation for this conundrum is that the visual excitement of Las Vegas is not derived primarily from its architecture, as observers from architects Robert Venturi and Denise Scott Brown to journalist and cultural critic Tom Wolfe have pointed out. Day or night, the character of the timeless world inside the Las Vegas casino is composed primarily of texture, pattern, color and theme—selected by interior designers and decorators.

Despite their apparent differences, casinos follow an essential formula.

The aim of a casino is simply to expose people to a maximum number of revenue-producing entities, namely opportunities to gamble, in as exciting a way as possible, and once attracted, to keep them spending as long as possible. The result is a shell of steel-frame and concrete panels thrown up at an astonishing speed with money spent on facade, spectacle, sign and interiors of varying degrees of splendor. Two-thousand-room hotels are built in a few months; it is rumored that Excalibur and the Luxor were built from a set of nine drawing sheets, just enough to get a permit. "Don't worry, we'll fix it on the rehab" is a standard response to any glitches in the design.

Low-ceiling casinos are jam-packed with gaming facilities. There are no windows, no clocks and the exits are obscured. Casinos are supposed to confuse and disorient you; they should separate you in time and space from your nine-to-five routine and the need to make your mortgage payment. You are meant to stumble about in them as long as possible and therefore keep gambling as long as possible. Instead of making your path from point A to point B clear, casinos make you travel past as many varieties of gaming opportunities and chances to drink alcohol as possible. Routes like the passage from the parking garage to the amusement park at the MGM Grand are confounding.

Now the fact that casino hotels are not architecture in the conventional sense doesn't mean that we don't love them to pieces nor does it mean that we think they are a worthless form of architecture lite. Rather we believe that the complicated hybrid building form of the casino/hotel/themed-attraction with its requirements for shops, dining and servicing for all the above is a highly demanding discipline in itself. It demands the talents of a highly skilled multidisciplinary team in order to pull off.

Ultimately the center-stage attraction in Las Vegas is show biz, not architecture. The magic and the medium of the hotel/casino/themed-attractions that is the economic lifeblood of Las Vegas is entertainment. The qualities that make it memorable and exciting are most likely to be contributed by lighting designers, show designers, landscape architects and interior designers and decorators. The character of the actual experience of being in, and looking at, the themed portions of the hotel/casino complexes is often determined by someone versed in arts and crafts more fluid, and less regimented, than the the discipline of architecture. If architecture is defined as a discipline wherein all the parts, each detail of organization, human activity, spatial experience, object-making and detailing, are integrated into an artic-

Caesars Palace entrance to forum shops. Architect Marnell Corrao Associates, interior design Dougall Design, 1966 to present. The only thing better than a triumphal arch is a string of arches, and the only thing better than that is a string of arches with a moving sidewalk. The pedestrian environment has become so important that casinos have created these elaborate paths from sidewalk to casino.

ulated whole, than the casinos could be defined as the triumph of theme over architectonic order.

Casino/hotels frequently jumble multiple conflicting themes, as at Luxor, or stop and start themed areas without thinking about the edges or the juxtapositions between battling modes of decor. For example, at Treasure Island clashing themes are cheek-by-jowl in the hallway where the coffee-shop-cozy theming and Cirque du Soliel—celestial theming intersect.

neon nights

Despite the shift toward spectacles involving performance as a marketing strategy, Las Vegas was, and continues to be, defined in the public mind by its neon. Neon light was discovered in England in the 19th century. A neon-lit sign was created in 1910 in Paris by Georges Claude; it was introduced into the West Coast of America, and subsequently into Las Vegas, in the early 20th century. As gambling exploded after legalization in 1931, Vegas went on to upstage other cities in exploiting the commercial potential of this pulsating, multicolored form of light.

Neon lighting derives its color range from two forms of gas, neon for the reds and warm colors, argon for the blues and cool colors. It depends for artistic effect on the type of gas, the color of the glass and the color of the powder coating on the inside of the tubes. The large signs used in Las Vegas are comprised of ornamental and informational components and consist miles of neon and thousands of light bulbs. They can cost many millions of dollars and utilize billions of watts of electricity.

In Las Vegas five sign-making companies have been responsible for the most prominent signs: Ad-Art Inc., Federal Sign, Heath and Co., Sign Systems Inc., and the oldest and largest, Mormon family-owned Young Electric Sign Company (YESCO). Over the years, these firms have been responsible for the most famous and influential neon-covered signs, pylons, fascias, entrance-ways and porte cocheres. These signs frequently upstage the often nondescript Las Vegas buildings they stand before. Commissions are won through competition; several agencies present design ideas to the client, and once an agency is selected, it functions as the designer, the fabricator or both.

As described in the primary text on the subject, *The Magic Sign* by Charles Barnard, sign-making is largely a collaborative effort. Its transitory commercial nature has kept the graphic artists whom Tom Wolfe referred to as "the designer-sculptor geniuses of Las Vegas" little known outside the trade of sign-making. However within the industry there are recognized masters of the art. These include YESCO's Charles Barnard; designer of Vegas Vickie; Marge Williams, of Federal Sign, creator of the Riviera; YESCO's Rudy Chrisotomo, designer of the Rio pylon; Paul Rodriguez, of Heath and Co., responsible for the Flamingo; YESCO's Dan Edwards, creator of Lucky the Clown; YESCO's Jack Larsen, Sr., maker of the Silver Slipper; Ad-Art's Paul Miller, designer of the 1967 Stardust pylon and YESCO's Kermit Wayne, creator of such classics as the Mint and the Stardust facade.

Fabricating a neon sign is, according to Steve Weeks, a representative of YESCO, a skill that requires a "time-honored apprenticeship," and one that will never be substituted by computer. While the craftsmanship of neon-fabrication may never become outmoded, neon itself is starting to find competition from other new technologies. Computerized digital lighting, for example, which sign-making companies are being hired to fabricate, is featured in the lighting spectaculars at the Fremont Street Experience.

As a result, many older, classic, signs have been torn down. Much of the unique commercial artistry of Las Vegas has already been destroyed. Until funding and a site are secured, discarded neon signs are maintained in the "Boneyard," a large open lot behind the YESCO's studio. Local preservationists, led by YESCO, are trying to save these signs. A Neon Museum, touted as "the final resting-place for old signs" is planned.

fremont street

Just as the archetypal Las Vegas Strip of the 1960s—with its towering, freestanding neon signs marking widely spaced casinos, seen across barren stretches of desert—has vanished so has Downtown's "Main Street," Fremont Street been irrevocably altered. Fremont Street is where gambling was born in Vegas. Incorporation of this district noted for saloons, gambling and prostitution came in 1901. The first legal casino, the Northern Club,

3300 Las Vegas Boulevard South. Joel Beroman (Atlantia Design). Design architect, the Jerde Partnership. Creative consultant, Olio Design, 1993. The pirate ship Hispaniola afloat in the Bucaneer Bay lagoon of Treasure Island is part of a Disney/Universal-style theme park attraction offered at no charge to the hordes of gawking pedestrians clogging the rope and plank sidewalk in this section of the strip.

opened at 15 East Fremont Street in 1931 following the legalization of gambling in Nevada. It went on to become the most famous avenue of blazing neon in the world.

Fremont Street is the home of the infamous Horseshoe casino, owned by father-and-son operators Jack and Benny Binion. The Horseshoe was famous for its showcase of $1 million bills, its record-breaking wagers and the world poker tournament. Near by is Jackie Gaughan's resilient Mexican-styled El Cortez, with its unadorned, smoke-filled, nicotine-stained interior, always jam-packed with locals who come to play for the lowest odds in town. The El Cortez displays a resistance to the current mania for healthy lifestyles, better ventilating systems, and upgraded theming, decor and entertainment.

Fremont Street was the canvas on which the largely anonymous genius sign designers, from such prominent local sign-making companies as Ad-Art and Young Electric Sign Company, honed their art and left their mark. That mark was often transitory, since Fremont Street is the epitome of a consumerist environment that thrives on novelty and change. Some of their handiwork remains, such as Vegas Victor and Vegas Vic, while others have vanished, such as the absolutely fabulous vibrating pink and green Mint, a now-extinguished '60s classic.

In recent years Fremont Street and the surrounding area has, like other big city Main Streets in the United States, such as Hollywood Boulevard, descended into economic decline and urban degeneration. Losing a large chunk of its customer base to the the more family-oriented Strip, Fremont Street had become, by the early '90s, a tawdry and crime-ridden neighborhood, passed through by tourists only by day and frequented largely by the homeless and die-hard gamblers.

But the downtown businesses and the city of Las Vegas had an economic incentive to revive Fremont Street. Fremont is in the City of Las Vegas while the Strip is in the county. Downtown's tax revenues are a vital source of income to the city. In a bid to stop the rot of downtown Las Vegas, a consortium of downtown casino operators entered into a public/private downtown revitalization enterprise. They considered numerous schemes, including Steve Wynn's wonderfully mad notion of canalizing Fremont Street and transforming it into a latter-day, neon Venice, before finally agreeing on a project that involves roofing over Fremont Street, enshrining the casinos and transforming it into a giant, controlled, pedestrianized urban entertainment experience.

The Fremont Street Experience was conceived by architect Jon Jerde, of the Jon Jerde Partnership, whose themed shopping and entertainment environments, such as Horton Plaza in San Diego and Citywalk in Los Angeles, have had stunning economic success. Completed in 1995, the Fremont Street Experience consists of a 90-foot-high space frame, a "celestial vault" that covers four blocks (1386 feet) and carries a "Sky Parade" and a digitized "light spectacular" designed by lighting luminary Jeremy Railton Associates and fabricated by YESCO. At a price of $70 million dollars, it transforms the street into a "foyer" for the Fremont Street casinos, which, collectively, have more gaming facilities and hotel rooms than any one casino on the Strip.

The space-frame canopy and its light shows dominate the existing storefronts, acting as a homogenizing and unifying element so that the street becomes one place instead of a series of individual events. The Fremont Street Experience has transformed the cacophony of the original Glitter Gulch into a single themed environment, more like a self-contained and privately controlled mall and less like a public street. Automobiles had to be banned once the space frame with its dazzling show images was put up since it would effectively stop traffic, causing pedestrians to stand in the street to look at it.

Down on the ground, the newly enclosed space competes for attention with street performers, kiosks, cafes, spectacles and the other attributes that are employed by the designers of American urban entertainment centers to counterfeit traditional urban street life. While it appears to have many of the characteristics of the themed casinos on the Strip with which it is competing, the Fremont Street Experience is intended not to attract families, but to serve instead as the "place where grown-ups come to play."

The strategy of the Fremont Street Experience is to unify the existing neon and blinking lights into a single mega-attraction that has the same power as a theme park. Aficionados of Fremont Street, concerned that the street is to be museumified within its celestial container, see this strategy as no complement but rather competition for the fabulous cascade of neon, once perfectly complemented by the dark night sky, and now subsumed into a blanket of surging light. Fremont Street is now controlled and managed, as part of the Fremont Street Experience, just as a shopping center has

3300 Las Vegas Boulevard South. Joel Bergman (Atlandia Design). Design architect, the Jerde Partnership. Creative consultant, Olio Design, 1993. Pirate carnage and pirate booty are part of an everyday stroll down the strip. A greedy skeleton at the Treasure Island lagoon.

an overall manager, to coordinate events promotion and the development of its identity.

The irony of Fremont Street is that the street had to be killed in order to be saved. Las Vegas is the epitome of the ever-changing hyperconsumerist environment where nothing lasts very long. Neon lights without economically viable casinos would not have much meaning. But even the most committed preservationists acknowledge that the Experience is a dramatic concept that may alleviate the degeneration of Downtown and even serve as a catalyst for a comprehensive revitalization of the Downtown area. The Fremont Street Experience represents the adaptation of a suburban model, the privatized shopping mall, to an urban situation. Project organizers are endeavoring to use the Experience to woo prestigious retailers into the area.

Yet unlike the suburban model, which sprouts forth from virgin territory, the Fremont Street Experience involved the purging of an existing area through a vigilant public safety and clean-up campaign, and the appropriation of surrounding land through eminent domain (compulsory government purchase), giving locals one month to vacate their residences. While the Fremont Street Company claims to be supporting the provision of affordable housing, the future of transplanted low-income families and homeless people is uncertain. The Fremont Street Experience is a stunning example of the chutzpah and optimism, as well as the cruel, raw capitalism, that has made Las Vegas. The Experience exhibits two traits that qualify as cardinal virtues in Las Vegas. One is sheer record-setting bigness and the other is sensory overload.

On the left bank of the Las Vegas strip, across the shimmering lagoon of the Bellagio Hotel, stands a replicated Eiffel Tower at the Paris casino. The only design dictum for the new cityscape of Las Vegas is that it must not look like Las Vegas.

the strip

At the beginning of World War II the casinos began to leapfrog downtown, opening on sites miles below the southern city limit. Thomas Hull's western-themed El Rancho Vegas motel, opened in 1941, was swiftly followed by a second hotel casino with western theming, the Last Frontier, located a mile south of El Rancho. Hotel/casinos proliferated on the Strip. It became the dominant public urban setting. It was the development site of choice for new hotels because of its vast expanses of land and ready accommodation of the endless parking lots that are required by the casinos and hotels. Casinos and hotels continued to grow in size, so that by the 1980s, room counts of 3000 no longer came as a surprise.

The most revolutionary of all these hotels was the Flamingo, a hotel started by Hollywood businessman and man-about-town Billy Wilkerson and completed by mobster Bugsy Siegel in 1946. Siegel was assassinated only a year after the opening of the hotel. His arrival marked the invasion of Las Vegas by Mafia-organized crime syndicates, which would control the casinos for decades to come. The Flamingo was designed by George Vernon Russell, a master of Hollywood elegance (and with Douglas Honnold, a prime practineer of the Hollywood Regency style that was hightlighted in the previous chapter) and well-known for buildings such as Ciro's nightclub on the Sunset Strip. The Flamingo helped create a Las Vegas that was synonymous with sophistication, a luxurious desert resort destination. This is the primal Vegas casino in the eyes of the true romantic who has come to Vegas to see mobsters, hookers, flashing neon lights and 24-hour hipsters at play. However, the real truth of the matter is that the Flamingo of yore is history.

Only the fabulous, pulsating cerise-and-orange Flamingo sign-work links the present complex to the mythological Las Vegas of the imagination. Designed by Raul Rodriguez of sign-makers Heath and Co. in 1976, the sign-work consists of porte cochere, corner element and a string of pink flamingos lining its fascia. And there is nary a more voluptuous and fleshy display of neon in all of Las Vegas, no other that so truly defines volume by its unfolding flame-like petals and twinkling, undulating bursts of light. Rodriguez' facade lives up to the fabulousness of the original Flamingo Hotel (remodeled several times) that inspired Tom Wolfe to declare: "Such colors! All the new electrochemical pastels of the Florida littoral: tangerine, broiling magenta, livid pink, incarnadine, fuchsia, demure, Congo ruby, methyl green, viridian, aquamarine, phenosafranine, incandescent orange, scarlet-fever purple, cyanic blue, tesselated bronze, hospital-fruit-basket orange."

Several generations of distinguished architects also made their mark on the Flamingo, now the Flamingo-Hilton, including the ever-so-suave Honnold and Russell during the 1940s, and Luckman and Pereira at their best in the 1950s, both well-known Los Angeles firms. The Flamingo, as designed by Luckman and Pereira in 1953, was the casino that brought the

3400 Las Vegas Boulevard South. Well established Vegas stars like Siegfried and Roy are a key element of casino-hotel complexes. This larger-than-life statuary tribute to showbiz at the Mirage is just one of many Las Vegas sidewalk attractions that offers prime photo opportunities.

The Venetian hotel-casino on the strip under construction in 1999, a Venice in no danger of sinking into the ocean. Designed by W.A.T.N.G. Inc.

abstract play of California Modernism to Vegas, upping the stylistic ante and introducing a new challenge of urbanity to the often rustic or more literal period revival theming that had characterized motels and casinos to date. The scale of their work was far too small to accommodate the demands of an ever-growing hotel casino, and all was swept away for a more pedestrian but larger complex.

It was the fabulous Caesars Palace, which Jay Sarno opened in 1966, that portended the future—a future of increasingly intense theming. Caesars Palace was an attraction itself with its gaudy, cheeky, Roman decor, costumed help and themed food and drink. In its current state Caesars Palace embodies the best of all of the golden eras of modern, big-time Vegas. How can you not love a place where, at one time, you could literally have the waitress peel you a grape? And, better still, it was all funded by Jimmy Hoffa's Teamster's Pension Fund. While Caesars casino/hotel complex looks like a women's prison in Tehran from outside by daylight, inside it is the ultimate Vegas casino—low, dark velvet ceilings hung with crystal prisms that convert the casino interiors into an endless chandelier-like fantasia. Hotelman Jay Sarno's Caesars was and is, in the best 1960s sense of the word, a camp masterpiece, a knowing parodic send-up of the impossibility of really theming a modern hotel on ancient classic lines. The irony is that spiritually, of all the Vegas Hotels, it probably really is the hotel that a licentious Roman of Imperial vintage would feel right at home in.

A vast and majestic double drive, lined by Italian cypresses on either side of a long pool punctuated by fountains, leads to a lurid, pointy-eared, tiered porte cochere, designed by Marnell Corrao Associates, with lighting and additional decor by YESCO, that seems to hover low, like a pink-lit invader from Planet Tacky. A giant pulsating dome, like some colony of polystyrene insect larvae from another planet, houses the Omnimax theater with its show recreating ancient Rome. Three, count 'em, three people-movers move you effortlessly into the casino. Caesars did this because they are so far back from the road and because the number of tourist pedestrians, and therefore the importance of luring them, has increased so dramatically over time.

While the cutest themed attraction in all Vegas is probably the floating Cleopatra's barge, added in 1970 (could Cleopatra's actual barge have been any more ornate?), the biggest news on the themed shopping front has been the Caesar's Forum shops. They mingle entertainment and consumerism as effectively as has ever been done to date. A trompe l'oeil sky with programmed lighting that simulates a transition from dawn to dusk, every hour on the hour, gives the shops their own atemporal time and space. Talking statues, created by EME Entertainment, Inc., function both as themed adornment and mechanical actors. Just in case you are under any illusions that this kind of show has any real content—it doesn't. The point is sheer showmanship, i.e., the pizzazz value of the statues getting up, prancing around and singing and dancing.

The downside to the Forum shops experience is the truly nasty and unconscionable Death March. Visitors to the Forum are marched right by an exit, which opens near the Strip. Yet while the Strip, welcomingly free from Roman theming, beckons tantalizingly, Roman armor-plated thugs heard you onto a nonfunctioning, nonmoving (on our visit) people-mover for a long, slow shuffle that forces you back through the casino to get to the street. Compelling you to go back through the casino is, of course, the goal of all right-thinking Vegas hotel owners.

Sarno's next casino, Circus Circus, opened two years later, taking the concept of linking gambling to entertainment attractions even further. It provided Circus performers in the gambling hall and a vast, pink glass dome full of amusement-park attractions.

Casino-hotel complexes often take over the design and landscaping of the public sidewalk along the strip. The result is an invigorating mismatch of totally uncoordinated individual efforts—this avenue of palms is only one block long.

There is very little credible architecture left from the 1950s and '60s. The c. 1962 building was originally constructed for Frontier Savings at 801 East Charleston Blvd.

This apartment hotel at the foot of the Stratosphere Tower is one of only a handful of buildings in the city in a commercial expressionistic modern vernacular.

The next major innovation on the Strip was the development of a resort acceptable to families and divorced from the old neon Mafia image of Vegas. This was the (literally) gold plated Mirage, conjured up by casino megaentrepreneur Steve Wynn. There is $540,0000 worth of gold dust on the windows to give it the allure of gold. (Too bad it makes the windows look as cheesy as gold-finished anodized aluminum.)

Wynn moved to Las Vegas in 1967 and acquired the Golden Nugget in Downtown 1972. He subsequently upgraded and stripped the Nugget of its neon, rendering it the only neon-free casino on Fremont Street. He is seen by many as the successor to the two primal Las Vegas visionaries, Benjamin "Bugsy" Siegel, creator of The Flamingo, and Jay Sarno, of Caesers and Circus Circus.

Wynn has melded the style of Bugsy Siegel's Vegas with the fantasy of Caesars and the mass appeal of Circus Circus. He has traded the neon, which, in his estimation, represents "Old Las Vegas," for spectacle, the tackiness for luxury, and, with help from a hand-picked team of architects, artists and show designers, is creating a series of high-quality themed casino resorts. The $650 million Mirage was his first deveopment, a Polynesian paradise in the middle of the high desert. The Mirage once sparked a renaissance in Las Vegas, that had become, by the '80s, a tawdry, jaded version of its former self. It also became the flagship for the family-oriented, themed casino/entertainment resorts that characterize the new Las Vegas.

The Y-plan international-style hotel (who says postmodernism oroiui deconstructivist smash and splinter has yet posed a threat to the dominance of modern blandness!) is trimmed with horizontal bands of gilded fenestration; its towers stick up into the sky like huge bars of white chocolate wrapped in gold paper. And there has been much effort expended in the lavish interior design by Roger Thomas of Atlandia design. But it is the Las Vegas elements—like the huge 20,000-gallon saltwater tank with its interior coral reef landscape—that make the hotel come alive. The flaming volcano outside, the 90-foot-high glass-covered atrium with opulent streams, waterfalls, orchids, real flowers and plants mixed with artificial ones, and a computerized misting system—now that's something to e-mail home about. The atrium and the volcano, and the lush landscaping of the Mirage in general, help create an atmosphere of genuinely over-the-top zany escapism—any theming the Tropicana ever tried as "The Island of Las Vegas" pales by comparison.

Show value and utility clearly separated. The MGM casino and its former lion mascot. Veldon Simpson was the architect for the billion dollar casino built in 1993.

The Mirage's volcano erupts every 15 minutes. A geyser of red-tinted steam erupts while scarlet flames run riot across the boiling waters of the lagoon, to the delight of the hundreds of gaping men, women and children that pack the street. The assembled throng in the road willingly risks death from the passing cars whose drivers do not yet appreciate that the car-oriented Strip is now, thanks to street shows like this, a pedestrian hang-out.

The volcano is the first in the Mirage's sequence of cleverly orchestrated, expensive attractions that draw out your arrival. By the time you've absorbed the tropical atrium, you've almost forgotten that you're being sucked into a casino. Once inside the casino proper, the dense foliage of the South Seas is replaced by a dense thicket of slot machines, in a typically low-ceiling, low-lit space. Conspicuously absent from the Mirage is a wall of neon. The Mirage, like that of other new casinos such as Luxor, has the kind of elaborate site development and themed attractions that make the role of signage in attracting visitors less important than it was in older casinos such as the Flamingo or the Stardust.

The Mirage does have a sign however, which bears the "first illuminated full-color photographic pictorial" of Siegfried and Roy, and an electronic message display (similar to those in sports centers and now mushrooming in Las Vegas). Designed by veteran sign designer Charles Barnard of Ad Art, with input from impressario Steve Wynn and architect Joel Bergman, the sign is strategically located for maximum visibility at the curve in the Strip (so near to the lagoon that its installation complicated the structural engineering). It is a colossal but simple, uninteresting, gold-and-white structure that, significantly, defers to the architecture, rather than dominating the building as the previous generation of signs would.

Wynn opened his next hotel, Treasure Island, in 1993. At Treasure Island he went one step beyond the traffic-stopping volcano at the Mirage. Here he entices gamblers into his otherwise hotel/casino complex, with a streetside spectacle on the Caribbean Sea. Once an hour, pirates aboard the Hispaniola and sailors aboard the British Frigate HMS Britannica duke it out in the Buccaneer Bay. The battle escalates until, amid explosions, flying stunt men and cannon fire, the full-size frigate disappears underwater, to the whoops and cheers of the thronging audience. It is an audience now ripe for the delights of a casino whose treasures few will win.

The finely wrought (in the Disney high-show-value scenographic style) 18th-century village nestled into the cliff face, the full-sized frigate and lagoon into which it is submerged, the hourly explosions and fires were the result of a collaborative effort. Wynn's in-house architects Atlandia Design worked with consultants Jon Jerde Partnership and show designers Olio Design, as well as an array of technical, pyrotechnic, theatrical and engineering experts.

While the project was being worked out, members of the design team dressed in full pirate regalia to get into the spirit of the Treasure Island concept. Wynn's hotel and casino exhibits an opulence and consistency of theme—from the gaudy, gold-plated bone chandeliers of Captain Morgan's Lounge/registration lobby to the Mutiny Bay entertainment center in an "ancient Moorish Castle," to the Treasure Island Buffet, Smuggling Cantina and Lookout Cafe.

Las Vegas city planners were initially baffled by Buccaneer Bay. So were cultural critics. They did not know how to characterize the show and the scenery, since it represented a new category of public outdoor activity. A spectacle rather than a sign, Buccaneer Bay represents the emergence of the show designer as the primary creator of meaning and iconography in Las Vegas. They now take up where sign designers have left off in defining the image of the city.

Now there was no question that gambling and entertainment had entered into a new synergistic relationship in Las Vegas. The message of the Mirage and Treasure Island was clear: the hotel/casino now needed to have a component of high-voltage themed entertainment in order to attract gamblers and guests. Entertainment could come in unexpected forms. Wynn's newest casino, Bellagio is celebrated for its multi-million dollar collection of Impressionist paintings (and a changing collection at that since the paintings are for sale.)

Increasingly, the new family-oriented destination resorts that have sprung up on the Strip, such as the Mirage, Luxor and Treasure Island, have a monumental presence of show attraction, landscaping and theming integrated into building form. Their presence is so powerful that the objects communicate across the landscape. They redefine urban space in the same way that the towering freestanding signs or the blazing neon of Fremont Street did in the 1950s and '6os.

There is no other American environment that you can enter without buying a ticket that is so much like being in a theme park. The Strip today essentially is a huge open-air urban theme park. However it is a theme park put together by a series of entrepreneurs acting independently, and not by a single corporate entity. It is lined with the kind of entertainment venues, clubs, restaurants and stores that would usually be built by a single entity and locked away behind the gates and boundaries of an individual theme park. The vitality that the Strip is now choking on is the thrilling anarchy of unrelated attractions crowing at each other. All of these wonders are set in an environment that is still, to some degree, part of the real world, traversed by taxis, fire trucks, ambulances, and delivery trucks. Unlike a theme park, its gutters are littered with crumpled ads for prostitutes and phone sex.

In Vegas the show on the Strip is out in the open, there for the taking. The Strip is part real city and part enclave, embedded in metropolitan Las Vegas as a semi-autonomous district. The large acreage required for hotel casinos and the internally focused development patterns of large casino complexes mean that the smaller streets rarely cut across the Strip. It can only be entered and exited at a few points without going through hotel/casino property. The combination of crowded traffic lanes and pedestrian activities make the Strip completely at odds with the character of the rest of the auto-dominated city.

The Strip is being rapidly built up to the point where traffic jams are an everyday occurrence. The Strip has become a hybrid automobile and pedestrian environment. Visitors now come to the Strip and leave their car in one of the enormous hotel/casino parking garages. Then they get out and walk a section of the Strip. Throngs of people immobilized by the dueling pirates of Treasure Island spill out in the roaring traffic of Las Vegas Boulevard. Las Vegas Boulevard is a bewildering hodge-podge without much coordinated planning. Sidewalks start and stop, narrow and widen. The Boulevard offers visitors to Las Vegas wildly differing relationships between buildings, auto space and privatized mass transit.

There is a mad assortment of kinds of access to the casino/hotels from the Boulevard at any given point along the Strip. Each casino/hotel is now obligated to provide special inducements and site planning, features such as people-movers or casinos built on the street frontage, to lure in the growing crowds of pedestrian visitors.

A patchwork of roadside walkways, moving sidewalks and monorails have begun to link casino/hotel complexes together. This circulation system has created a new pedestrian axis to rival that of the Strip itself, located at the rear of the casinos. There has been discussion of creating a monorail network between downtown and the airport passing through the Strip. The intersection of Tropicana and Las Vegas Boulevard (the Times Square of Las Vegas) is spanned by long bridges that seem like pieces of a theme park. Elevated and coordinated with the architecture of the casinos that receive the bridges, they become seamless parts of the transition from one casino to another. The bridges create the continuity of a journey through a shopping mall, without creating the oppressive sense of physical containment.

beyond the strip

Vegas is often seen as consisting of nothing but casinos, as though the maids, waiters, showgirls and gas station attendants vanish into a puff of smoke when they leave the glittering temples of gambling on the strip, and as if these service workers don't go back to a city where they have to go the supermarket and city hall. It's not surprising, given the sex appeal of the casinos and the drabness of non-Strip Vegas, outside of downtown. What has been somewhat neglected in the attention given by the architectural press to Las Vegas is the question of its urbanism, of the relationships between its constituent parts. The human and experiential aspects of living and working in Las Vegas have not been explored. The cost of uncontrolled and uncoordinated development, such as the routine channelization of Las Vegas arroyos and seasonal washes into concrete ditches, has not been assessed. The dominant attitude toward building and city planning in Las Vegas is one of expedience, whether that is the tradition of building with concrete blocks in simple volumes, or building large-slab casino towers.

An individual building itself simply consists of the least expensive enclosure of space that will keep the occasional rainstorm out and the always conditioned air inside. While casino architecture cleverly conceals its means of construction underneath a glittering, landscaped layer of illusion, the non-casino architecture makes no such pretense. Building in Las Vegas is austere. Even that mecca of Vegas attractions, the Liberace Museum, is casually tucked away in several storefronts of a banal mini-mall that could just as easily have housed a laundromat. Buildings are made mainly of stucco, metal and masonry—steel frame and concrete block or panel. They have a pragmatic quality that is perhaps appropriate to a city defined by self interest and don't-fence-me-in, boomtown, frontier-style private enterprise.

Non-strip, non-downtown Las Vegas is remarkable for the absence of older buildings with any discernible traditional architectural merit, as well as for any conventional urban streetscape animated by pedestrians. In its disregard for traditional urbanism and architectural niceties, Las Vegas is not unique, merely a clearer demonstration of American attitudes about building than most cities.

Until recently one-story, single-family homes made up the bulk of Las Vegas' housing stock. Much of Las Vegas still consists of mile upon mile of single-family houses dispersed over a grid of freeway-like streets that subdivide the town into mile-long superblocks. But even in a sprawling metropolitan area such as Las Vegas only 50 percent of its citizens now live in single-family houses. Seven percent live in detached mobile homes while another 40 percent live in apartments or condominium town houses. Traditional residential communities accessible to the general public, as well as to residents, have given way in recent years to walled bedroom

4211 West Sahara. Las Vegas has few icons that are not casino related. Babe's Italian Ices, erected in 1981 as the mascot of the small Liberty Square shopping center, is one of these casino-free landmarks.

communities on the fringes of the city, which cater to and reinforce the urban paranoia of security-conscious new residents. Many of them are master-planned communities, built around golf courses, artificial lakes, shops and schools.

Driving down the vast boulevards through these communities we passed row after row of walled offs backyards—no front doors, no front porches and no sense of communication between us and what we were driving through. Gated communities are as attractive to the wealthy homeowners who want to be physically separated from the rest of the city as they are to seniors who love the security and to young working families for whom jobs are readily available and property is affordable. The popularity of these fortified residential neighborhoods testifies to a pervasive urban paranoia and mutual distrust that characterizes Las Vegas—the Casinos are riddled with invisible high-security systems.

None of the features of local planned communities such as the Lakes are unique to Las Vegas; they can be found in many other American communities, particularly in Sunbelt cities such as San Diego and Palm Springs, as disucussed in the previous chapter on Mountainview. But it is safe to say that Las Vegas is among American cities with the highest proportion of their citizens living behind the walls of gated communities. It is a tradition that seems to have started with the construction of subdivisions of custom homes around the perimeter of private golf courses and has now become so widespread as to be universally accepted as the normal way that development in the Las Vegas Valley should occur wherever possible.

Until recently, Las Vegas beyond the Strip was architecturally undistinguished. There are few remaining examples of notable architectural work remaining that were built in Las Vegas during the 50-year period between the beginning of World War II and the end of the 1980s. But they do exist, as proved by DMJM's 1969 Las Vegas City Hall or Julius Gabriele's 1967 Las Vegas Country Club. Governmental work is executed by a dozen-odd local firms of which even the largest, Tate & Snyder, has a relatively small staff that includes 11 licensed architects.

Architects, particularly those involved with casino design, were known to work hard, play hard and live well (there are, allegedly, more millionaire architects in Vegas per capita than anywhere else) but to take little interest in broader issues. Historically Las Vegas architects have been known for

Book Mart & Steve's Buy and Sell Jewelry. 512, 510 Las Vegas Boulevard South. Ornament in Las Vegas during the 1950s and '60s was often supplied by the use of patterned concrete block.

being ruthlessly protective of their own turf, attempting to keep the cash cow of the casinos to themselves.

In recent years however, there are some signs of change. Today casinos, of ever increasing scale, are owned by large corporations, which sell well-scrubbed thrills and Disney-inspired family entertainment to ever-increasing numbers of visitors. Once the object of scorn for self-respecting "real" architects, now Las Vegas architects are the object of envy. Architects from outside are begging for a place at the table of lucrative theme architecture. Entertainment architecture has become the newest profit center for American architectural firms, and Las Vegas is a significant part of that boom.

As Las Vegas' population becomes larger and more settled, the desire for institutionalized forms of culture has grown. This is something that American cities generally feel the need to acquire as they come of age, as a badge of civic virtue. Historically there has been a public antipathy to taxes in Las Vegas, due in part to a Western dislike of government and in part to the huge subsidy that gambling provides as a public revenue source. But in recent years public monies have been spent on an ambitious library-building program, as well as on various street-improvement projects such as the $25 million landscaped median down the Strip. A huge sports stadium is planned for the downtown area, and high-tech mass-transit systems are under consideration.

Local magnates are donating construction funds for institutions, such as the University of Nevada at Las Vegas (UNLV), which is about to build itself, among other projects, a new architectural school, although they won't have the landmark design they could have had if they retained Barton Myers' powerful quadrangle design. The continued presence of an architectural school is bound to increase the involvement of the local architectural community in current debate and formal trends in American architecture as a whole. Outside architects have been hired for prestigious commissions, galvanizing the local firms into a greater emphasis on design. The architectural community is becoming more reflective of urban issues, having established a design awards program and having recently mounted the first symposium ever devoted to the architecture and urban design of Las Vegas.

Similarly, architects are trying to deal with environmental issues in a city notorious for thumbing its nose at any notion of conservation of resources. It has always represented the classic mid-20th century attitude that there could never be a limit to anything, so use all the natural resources you want. Vegas' solution to the merciless desert heat has been air-conditioning and plenty of it, and lots of water to make the desert go away. Casino architecture of past decades relates in no way to desert location except, sometimes, in its imagery, as in the Sahara, the Dunes and the Luxor. Contemporary noncasino architecture is rife with references to desert building, specifically that of a near desert neighbor, New Mexico, since the construction of the Las Vegas Library and Discovery Museum by Albuquerque-based Antoine Predock. A desert vocabulary, if not its climate-control systems, has become the rage.

Architects have taken the tradition of concrete-block construction in Las Vegas and adapted it into a building vocabulary of earthen forms: pyramids (inverted, truncated, flattened); cones; tiny square windows; smooth and textured sandstones, dry desert landscaping of crushed stones, red rocks and cacti. Given that Nevada is no more a home to the traditions of New Mexico that these measures evoke than it is to those of the Sahara, this is themed architecture of sorts but with a greater weight and presence than the monumental stage-sets that are the new Las Vegas.

The boneyard at Yesco Sign Company, 5119 Cameron Street. The cast-off relics of what Las Vegas is famous for in architectural cultural; big neon signs with plenty of moxie.

Antoine Predock's 1989 Las Vegas Library/Discover Children's Museum set the tone for austere fortress-like public buildings in Las Vegas often composed of a jumble of primary geometric forms.

viva las vegas vavoom

Ultimately, while most of Las Vegas is either relatively bland or utilitarian, the town can always be counted on to put on a good show in its entertainment zones. There will be lots more exuberant themed attractions, heavily elaborated hotel towers and gothic altars inset with video monitors.

The most logical place to which to compare Las Vegas is the resort city of Orlando, Florida, home of Disney World. Orlando is a series of themed parks and themed attractions, both large and small, created by the presence of Disney World. Orlando has nearly as many hotel rooms as the 90,000 some hotel rooms that Vegas had in 1995. In Orlando gleaming, late-modern resort towers located miles apart poke through the horizontal landscape of snake-and alligator-infested swamps. All the entertainment value, the show value, in each park is locked up inside. There is no relationship whatsoever of one theme park to another. There is no truly urban experience in Orlando to compare with the flashing symphony of chaotic lights and themes that is tourist Vegas.

In the final analysis, even a Vegas awash in T-shirt-and-shorts-wearing nuclear families still offers the adrenal rush of anarchy, greed, risk-taking and hedonism, truly uncontrolled. In addition it now offers the tumultous public encounters of a real city. Whatever Vegas has lost—both the bracing vulgarity and, to some degree, the elegance of earlier nightlife—it still has to put on a good show in order to persuade the public to fork over their gambling dollars. A true consumerist environment always develops by replacing the previous generation of consumerist delights with even more elaborate attractions. No matter how many other communities license gambling, they will always have to compare themselves to Las Vegas. The city that perfected the neon sign, the be-thonged cocktail waitress and the high-roller hotel suite is now perfecting the super-scale urban environment of open-air spectacle.

Vegas is not a city where buildings and site planning contribute to a coherent, organized whole. Going to the entertainment district of Vegas is like going to see a gladiator show or a battle between carnivorous dinosaurs. It is precisely the energy level of the conflict and the independent aims of the players that is so bracing. Fortunately so much money is being spent so fast by shameless private enterprise that the entertainment district of Vegas is safe from the deadening hand of conventional urban design and placebos such as sustainability and the New Urbanism.

PART FOUR
PERSONAL SPACE

Today's version of the now under construction pagoda.

a curmudgeon's guide to urban living

paranoia, pagoda, and pirate cave

I: suburban prologue

The end of the 80s and the beginning of the 90s: the riots, the recession the earthquake, and the further entrenchment of gang turf polarized Los Angeles into all or nothing—oppressed slum vs. privileged yuppieland. For me, living in Los Angeles meant fear of economic and personal survival, in the early 90s, after Southern California imaginations have been fed a TV news diet of media blurred shootings of all descriptions—from the Billionaire Boys club to a seven year old on the playground—there was a sense that the place might be out of control and uninhabitable

My childhood in post-World War II suburban Southern California environment promised order and safety. The household in tranquil suburban South Pasadena, in which I grew up, made the already protected environment, stiller, calmer, more protected than it already was. The gentle raining of the sprinklers on the dichondra lawn filtered through the drawn drapes and folded into the hum of the dishwasher and the air-conditioner. The biggest threat to health and safety was when the dishwasher broke. It was an

This memoir—wherein the author becomes progressively more fearful while creating his own personal urban hell—is included here to demonstrate how subjective notions of place and social identity become the world we inhabit.

affluent small town, a gracious—though racially, culturally, and economically segregated—environment, in which there was little consciousness that anyone could possibly have different values, or a different life situation than your own.

ask not for whom the sapote flies: silverlake

I bought a house on Ethelyne Avenue in Silverlake in 1987, five houses above Sunset. It was the last gasp of the real estate boom of the 1980s. I bought the house under the optimistic assumption that things would always get better, i.e. that any return on investment would be justified due to the continued rise in what were in reality already grossly inflated real estate prices. It was the first house that I could afford to buy on my own without the charming but dreaded continual presence of Lance, thanks to my job at Disney Imagineering.

The previous tenants of the house had been a punk rock band with a pet ferret, and a set of warrants out for their arrest. The popularity of that neighborhood as a home to immigrants from around the world has increased continually in recent years. On one side of my house on Ethelyne Ave. was Reynaldo, a red headed Cuban-born costume designer and his Vietnamese lover Max. On the other side was the slummy broken down set of buildings that the Vietnamese lover owned, as part of a real estate syndicate. That complex of buildings had started out as a single family house. In the early 1960s, the woman who had raised her family in that house, Mrs. Maxwell, built a duplex in the back, legally, and then bootlegged the division of the front house into four, gruesomely cramped, apartments. Her son, who was a gun nut, never said a word to any one. He lived up stairs in the old main house with his equally silent lover. Both men worked in the same gun shop.

The unit below the gun guys' unit was bad luck, too small, and therefore difficult to keep rented. Another gay couple lived there, at least one of whom was dying of AIDS and addicted to street drugs. There were repeated incidents of domestic violence that terrified the neighboring families and brought in the police. The units were only separated by a locked door, a door that shook each time a body was repeated slammed against it during a fight.

> The Ethelyne Avenue house was either a rotting hovel in a disintegrating neighborhood or a cottage in a miniature forest surrounded by the energy of an urban neighborhood—depending on my mood and the state of my fortunes.

Ramona' house next door on Ethelyne.

In the back duplex was the singing, fat lady, Ramona. Day and night she warbled the words to "New York New York", in paint-stripping Brooklynese, into her Mister Microphone home Karaoke unit. I had to go to the other sided of my house to loose the bass. She only left the house to walk her tiny streaked and stained poodle and attend acting auditions. I don't suppose there was much call for someone with that many facial warts.

The bone of contention between Ramona and I were the sapote trees that hung over her driveway. Sapote trees are a unique botanic phenomena, sort of a natural one man fruit kamikaze squad in tree form. Through some unholy collaboration between nature, and genetic selection by man, this tree manages to jettison hundreds of pounds of fruit on the ground, over a period of only a few weeks. Not just any fruit, but fruit that begins to rot as soon as it is separated from the stem. The sickly vegetative stench is at once unseemly and repugnant, sort of like lawn clippings mixed with Sweet N' Low. The yellow-green fruit sploshes and splatters when it hits the ground.

I have a certain affection for sapotes because of their formidable fecundity. Volunteers sprouted from sapote pits surrounded the house, springing up wherever the trees had hurled their fruit . Once established the intrepid sapote sapling needs no more maintenance than a pet rock. I rationalized their presence as a drought tolerant, sustainable flora that supported the burgeoning possum and squirrel population on my lot.

Damned if that Ramona didn't just hurl the sapotes that fell on her driveway back over the chain-link fence. I hurled them back if I found the splotches on the side of my house. But at least the Great Sapote War was a species of honest combat, in which the weapons enjoined were relatively harmless.

The next Great Battle of Ethelyne Avenue was far more lethal. It involved lawyers. Behind my house were two fences. Inbetween the fences was a thicket of golden bamboo festooned with rotting diapers, tin cans, and telephone books. The detritus had been tossed over the fence in long lost moments of extreme slovenliness. The bamboo was growing over the water heater. I had moved the heater out of the old laundry room in order to convert that room into my writing study. In my role of guardian of the public good, I decided that this potential trash hazard to the water heater should be removed. In hindsight, it is fortunate that I had surveyed the property. At that point I was still under the illusion that I was going to build on it. The survey showed a fence on my property, a fence on the neighbor's

I choose to create an adversarial mentality with my surroundings.

Sapote coming my way.

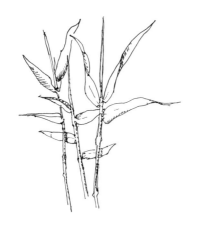

If the bamboo suit fits your notion of victim under siege then you must wear it.

property line and bamboo in between. I demolished my fence. I trimmed the bamboo.

The next thing I knew— while trying to compose myself after a difficult and troubling day, reclining on the piece of furniture I owned that came closest to resembling a real couch—a process server dropped a subpoena in my lap. It informed me that I had trespassed on my neighbors property. According to this document, I had uprooted and cut down his bamboo and lowered his property value by sixty thousand dollars. Thank God for homeowner's insurance. What was really going on, it turned out, was that my neighbor owned the oldest gay sex club in Silverlake . He didn't want the privacy of his backyard, and the Dionysian splendor of his hot tub and his Miller Lite stained glass porch light devalued by prying eyes. Little did he know I would have paid big money to avoid seeing that sagging butt of his plop into the fetid, churning water of his splintering hot tub.

The really weird thing about this was that when the suit came to court my neighbor produced his own survey, which pretty much exactly matched my survey. That crazy S.O.B. knew the bamboo was on my property all along. The judge came out to see the fence, took one look and dismissed the case on the spot.

Sometime after that I decided to give up on Ethelyne Avenue. The sapote-slinging lady's place had three times as many people living in it as it had when I first moved in. It had also acquired a flotilla of giant pickup trucks a quarter of an inch narrower than the driveway, trucks that had to be repositioned at all hours of day and night. The city had down-zoned my property although there was no warning when I went to the planning counter, and no notice in the mail since they take forever to update their property records. No more multiple units. Now that I wouldn't be building new units, the original house's flaws looked all the more lethal. The foundation had the appearance of having been made by a child out of a flour and water. The expansive clay soil shrank in the dry season—spiderweb cracks across the yard appeared overnight at the start of the long dry season. The jagged crevasses were actually wide enough to trip over.

The 90 year-old shingles on my house were curling and cupping like browning rose petals. They were barely able to hold the blistered scales of paint on them. Every week a few more shingles gave up the ghost, slipped out, and fell to the ground. Thanks to the great Southern California real estate bust of the early 90s the house was now worth tens of thousands of dollars less than the mortgage. It was all debt and no equity. At night I had to slow my car down to enter my driveway so that the sea of male teenagers hanging out in the middle of Ethelyne St. could grudgingly part. The local businesses that I liked, such as the Argentinean deli, the anarchist bookstore, and the good used clothing store all disappeared, to be replaced by 99¢ stores and video rental parlors.

I was mad at Lex next door for milking Mrs. Maxwell's old property on the other side of me for every dollar it was worth. Its condition was squalid, the rutted, dirty front yard strewn with cars and trash. When one of the tenants fired his gun into the sky at 2:00 in the morning that was it for Ethelyne. I left. I gave the house back to the bank. It was an even deal as far I was concerned. I left the house restored, and had fixed much of the damaged inflicted on its original 1906 cottage charm. When the bank auctioned Ethelyne off it ended up selling for $75,000 less than I paid for it.

The equity that I had built by fixing up houses and selling them with my friend Lance had already vanished. Nearby, the Virgil neighborhood that used to be good for a four dollar lunch at two different Japanese restaurants and a five dollar haircut from the near-blind Filipino Army barber, was now a drug neighborhood, rock around the clock for crack-hounds.

During the Rodney King riots I had watched as the Iranian merchants of the corner liquor store kicked and hurled back the burning detritus that was flung on the roof of their store. My friend Lance watched the fires and the looting of the riots from his seventh floor hospital room in Mc Arthur Park. He was in the final stages of cancer and AIDS. As Lance's I.V. sugar solution and oxygen tubes percolated, he could see a particularly industrious bargain shopper loading color TV after color TV onto a pick up truck. Emerging from the store with one more TV the bargain shopper was enraged to see an even more methodical shopper stealing the appliance laden truck. Lance was especially resourceful in taking entertainment wherever he could find it.

On my television screen during the riots was the shoe store where I bought my black canvas, gum soled, nine dollar shoes, and the stationary store where I bought my computer paper . As I watched as they were being devoured in apocalyptic flames. Also burned to the ground was the camera store that fixed my Yashica-mat $2\frac{1}{4}$ inch camera. The store where I bought my answering machine was being looted. The fires on TV were less than a mile away. I

> I saw my fortune as a reflection of my house and my neighborhood, personal doubts merged with a lack of faith in the city.

could smell them inside my house. This time the fine dispersion of dust, a mote-like ash, wasn't coming from a forest fire in the mountains

Later there was the earthquake. Along the route to the office building I was babysitting, World I era brick buildings had coughed up sections of their upper stories into the street. Inside my office quarters the upper section of brick wall that supported the trusses had separated from the rest of the wall, cracks ripped across the bricks

I was forty . The hedonism that used to work for a gay guy in a big city didn't cut it anymore, with or without the damping effects of AIDS. The pleasure had gone out of the local pleasure spots.

It was time to move, to some place quieter and further away from the center of the city.

There is always the illusion that it is the world and not ones reactions to it that is the true source of tranquility and well being.

ii: venice the menace

CASA LANCE

My father had died three years before, leaving me just enough money to get a mortgage on my friend Lance's house. The sale needed to happen while he was still alive to use the money. At the time, some of my graduate school classmates were opening up their own office space on the west side of town, near Venice. Sharing workspace with them, with their loping Irish wolfhounds and their kid running in and out, would be like being part of a family. I was leaving behind a disappearing gay neighborhood that no longer seemed safe for gay people. I didn't want move to another subcultural center just so I could be around people with the same sexual persuasion. Nor did I want to wind up as a token presence on someone else's exclusive turf, regardless of whether age, race, sexual orientation or educational and cultural background demarcated the territorial boundaries.

lance: his lot in life and ghost inhabitant of my house

Lance was, among other things, a socialite bon vivant, art dealer, telephone repairman and para-legal word processor. Most of him is now on the beach at Mykonos. A little bit of him is in a rock garden outside Edinburgh and part

Any lapse in efforts to sustain the life and memory of the dead becomes murder.

The deluxe fantasy edition of the gallery extension for Lance.
Drawing by Steve LaCap, Jackie McNaney and John Chase.

of him is fertilizing the timber bamboo he planted by the front gate. Cynthia, a woman who actually survived a business partnership with Lance (this is a little like surviving a flaming car wreck with a tanker full of propane gas) scattered his ashes at Mykonos. They had met as two American hippies traveling in India around 1970. Francoise did the honors in Edinburgh. She was a heiress with whom Lance had shared a friendship, and then later, a trouble-maker named Antoine. Antoine eventually got Francoise in so much trouble that her name was splashed across the pages of European tabloid newspapers. It took the Greek Minister of Justice to get her sprung from lock-up early. She has been reclusive ever since. Lance was lucky to get away scot free.

Lance grew up around wealthy Caucasian kids. It's easy to feel you are different from everyone else; in Lance's case the dissatisfaction crystallized around not being Caucasian and straight. He had baby blue colored contact lenses for ethnicity blurring and shock value long before I can remember any one else wearing colored contacts.

In the 1960s Asian kids who drove their Porsches to class at USC were unlikely to have many peers. Lance's boyfriends were never Asian, never black, rarely Latino. By the time I knew him they were always younger than Lance. The boyfriends were always an attempt for Lance to gain a surrogate identity, to attain by association the primal innocence that one could attribute to someone younger and less well educated. Lance usually described these guys to me as though he was talking about an especially sharp new puppy. I mocked him "Look how smart they are; they know almost all the letters of the alphabet, and they can usually tie their shoes without assistance." The problem is while you can be fascinated by your cocker spaniel, you can never actually be your cocker spaniel. The vicarious identities were a source of pleasure, but never entirely satisfied.

The lesson of Lance is that cultural identity is assumed not innate.

Lance was always a globe trotter, a chit-chatter, an inveterate visitor, legendary for his capacity for friendship. It is only appropriate that his ashes rest in several places with several different people. The world that Lance had inhabited when he still had money was foreign to me. I loved his stories. I had so little personal experience to relate to them that they seemed like fiction to me. (And, of course, some of it was indeed fiction.)

I am still very puzzled that Lance died. It is the only time I have ever seen some one stop living in front of me. Lance had AIDS and throat cancer. He ate through a stomach tube. He had gone in and out of a coma that weekend. But Lance was still Lance. Even in the twilight zone, he refused to have adult diapers forced on him. The Lance who had 13 pairs of Gucci loafers, all in shoe trees, stacked like firewood in his tiny closet, was not about to be caught dead in Depends.

On Lance's last day alive, a home health care worker and I had been dumping morphine sulphate down his feeding tube at 15 minute intervals, (inbetween the unrequited plays the sofa-sized home health care worker was making for me.) We had to stop because Lance's stomach was already full of morphine, just as though he had a full stomach from having a nice big Sunday dinner of pure morphine. I felt as though I had murdered him by priming the opiate pump. But the doctor's orders were clear: do not let this man return to consciousness so that he is conscious of the horror of his body choking himself to death.

And he did die by choking to death. Lance strained to sit up, his body blazed a deep crimson as he rose out of the bed, through Herculean effort, doped or not, struggling to stay alive as long as possible. Tendons lined his neck bursting through the flesh like steel cords He fell back to the bed. A wave of vile, sludgey phlegm slid forward out of his mouth, coating his lower lip. The phlegm was the pale green yellow color of glow-in-the-dark paint. It had the consistency of cake frosting.

Lance's flesh stiffened. He became waxy, still. I knew the Lance spirit had left him. All he had left behind on the bed was a congealing inanimate body. The smell of the morphine, and his dark-green, cedar-scented Rigaud candles saturated the room. (This cloying miasma settled into Lance's possessions. The smell went with them when I took those possessions to my house. I had that saccharin-sweet scent in my nostrils for months) Why, I wondered was Lance being carted off to the crematorium, and not myself? Had he done something especially bad (well, yes, actually quite a long list of bad things, but so had I.) Why was I alive, and why had the extraordinary friends of mine died of AIDS related causes—extraordinary people, such as artful preservation architect Peter Snell, macumba practicing Peter Lorre look-alike Roberto Scatena and the saintly, underground, legendary Peter Pan of architectural populism and transgression John Beach? And why were many more people I knew marked for possible premature death when I was not, when I was not any more deserving of long life than they were?

Going to Lance's apartment after his death was a disturbing yet exciting experience. His place was a treasure chest, filled with hidden bounty, long-kept secrets and desirable possessions—all of which I was now responsible for in my role as executor and beneficiary. Though I wanted to have the possessions and learn the secrets, it felt like a further violation of the dead. I had helped Lance remodel the little apartment just for him, one long, zinc-coated, steel shelf facing the ocean with two diagonal glass panels on either side, painted white on the back so that the glass would help reflect the ocean haze. I felt like I was looting his personal refuge.

In the small room were piles of medical bills, envelopes filled with hundred-dollar bills, pornography and a huge stash of prescription drugs, including Vikodin, Percodan, Morphine, Marinol and an assortment of injectable steroids. His closet was stuffed with expensive clothes and shoes. Although Lance was six inches shorter than I am, some of these clothes actually fit me, since they ranged in size from small to extra large. As Lance grew smaller and frailer the size of the articles of clothing he bought grew correspondingly larger.

I spent the money, I wear the clothes, and display Lance's possessions as part of the cannibalization process of ingesting the sum total of my friend's memory.

The Milton mandala.

The mystery was how could a life so fully inhabited not offer any insurance against premature death.

pegodaville

The house I own now, 416 Milton Avenue, both was and wasn't Lance's former house. Although he did own it he never lived here, because he could never afford to move out of the rent-controlled, beach-front apartment in Santa Monica. Lance loved the concept of owning property and having multiple residences, and the gouging rent he charged his tenants to live in Milton was always far more than the modest tab for his own one-room apartment.

By buying and living in Lance's house I prolong his existence.

Two neighborhood landmarks: Chiat/Day Building, 1984–91, Frank Gehry with binoculars by Claes Oldenburg and Coosje Van Bruggen; Jonothan Borofosky's Bum/Ballerina God, 1989.

416 Milton Avenue in Venice is located near two local landmarks: the Jonothan Borofsky clown with its four o'clock shadow and tutu, and the Giant Claes Oldenburg binoculars that are part of Frank Gehry's Chiat/Day headquarters building. Milton is the first walking street, north of Rose and east of Main. The house is 1913 vintage, remodeled in the 1950s. As found, it looked like a beat-up, stuccoed over Irving Gill (with a cornice on it like a flat Buster Keaton straw hat) that had fallen on hard times. When Lance and I first saw the dingy, spattered interior, it looked like a Wee Gee snapshot of a place where a recluse died and was partially devoured by his starving pet.

There is an illustration of 416 Milton that resembles a 1919 Department of Water and Power drawing that shows that additions that I designed that Lance proposed but could never afford. The addition facing you is a double-height gallery for his art collection, with a little tea drinking loft that overlooks the garden. Instead of the home gallery, I am making a Pagoda and a Pirate Cave for myself. Lance knew about the Pagoda before he died. He understood the idea immediately. The idea of the pagoda was not to create a one-to-one correspondence between structure and culture—although certain aspects of Chinese culture, such as herbal medicine, acupuncture or the uses of honor in family politics held a fascination for Lance at the end of his life. Seeing cultural references played with was an enormous source of pleasure for him. It simultaneously put him back in touch with certain aspects of his upbringing and liberated him from stereotypes about them at the same time.

The pagoda is no more Chinese, Polynesian, or Japanese than I am. It is about the celebration of American mythologizing of other cultures. These cultures are often fantasized by Americans as being less pragmatic, freer, more expressive or more integrated as a total culture than America. An example of this fictionalizing would be the Tiki apartment houses of the 1960s Southern California when tropical lagniappe could be rented by the month.

The Pagoda is the resort you invent because you need to go there. It is not a resort that actually exists and needs to be recreated or documented. The Pagoda has to be big and tall so that it's the most important thing in the house. It dominates and establishes a hierarchy of scale.

The formal point of my Pagoda is that intricate, frenetic or passionate density of polychrome ornament and partial spatial enclosures are strong enough gestures to make a place. The Pagoda is supposed to be tricked out

OCEAN PARK VILLAS

with enough brightly colored, ready-made nonarchitectural items, such as nylon climbing rope, strands strung with plastic kitchen sponges and beach balls, that it becomes altarlike. My pagoda is a pleasure barge, a treasury of attractive things that are readily available. The hubcap and the exposed colored light bulbs exist both as decorative elements, and as artifacts of everyday life. Many of the items are inexpensive and are usually consumed in a different way, so that this altar celebrates the potential of all objects, everyday or not, to both affirm their normal identity and to embody a larger world. The power of the objects themselves, the power of their being loaded in together with so many other objects, transforms them into a votive offering to the great, many-headed God of Color/Light/Form.

I made the decision to buy Milton in a completely illogical and intuitive manner. Lance was dying, he needed the money, the real estate market was

A thematic precedent for the pagoda in terms of beachyness & surfside living was this proposed version of the Lubowicki-Lanier designed condominiums at Sixth & Ocean park, Santa Monica, 1992. Lubowicki-Lanier were the original architects before they came to a parting of the ways with the client Jane Spiller. Drawing by Steve LaCap, Jackie McNaney and John Chase.

bad and by the time a realtor sold the house, in a bad real estate market, Lance would have been dead. The house was where it was, and Lance was in no condition to try to fix it. Only once I began to live in the house and take it apart, did I realize just how shaky a beach shack it actually was.

There are three basic challenges connected with my stewardship of 416 Milton. The first consists of facilities management and property management, putting in the physical improvements that make the building less likely to collapse in an earthquake, catch fire or leak. The second is the relationship between the cash I have and the cost of improvements that would create income-generating units (416 is legally zoned for occupancy as three units.) The third is making all of these improvements in a way that reflects my aesthetic preferences and serves as an example of my work.

The neighborhood is on a sand dune at the edge of old wetlands where the Los Angeles River once entered the Pacific Ocean. There are three blocks between Pacific and Main that are a little higher than the rest of the neighborhood. The sand happened to have been blown into a rise here at the time the neighborhood was developed. Desiccated 80-year-old dune reeds are still visible under my neighbor Sylvia's house. Part of my house has no foundation at all—the posts come down on a board placed lightly on the bare sand. Because the Venice bus terminal is two blocks away the house is always vibrating—little tremors that feel exactly like Northridge earthquake aftershocks. There still are moments when I wonder if having my bed shake every night is something I can live with.

Neither Lance nor I could have ever actually afforded to build the remodeled version of 416 Milton that I designed for him. And besides, 416 Milton sits at one end of the lot against the alley. Lance's gallery would have turned much of the yard space into internal contemplation space. I want to keep the space outside because the sun shines on it, the wind blows over it and you can smell the tar and seaweed of the beach. And for one hour every night, at four a.m., a lull in the bus schedule means that you actually hear ocean waves crashing on the shore—even though you have to really strain to hear it over the buzz of the bad security light transformer next door. Even as it is now, the yard, while bigger than a pocket handkerchief, is still only on a 30-by-100-foot lot, barely big enough to wander around in.

When I opened the walls at 416 Milton I found out that the termites hadn't left me nearly as much wood to hold up the house as I thought. Shoring up the insect-ravaged walls cost money. At the same time business dried up

Put simply, the house is a badly built habitation lightly placed on a sand dune subject to liquifaction should there be an earthquake.

at the office. I decided it was time to split up the top floor again, in order to try and reduce the bite that the mortgage took out of my wallet each month.

The strategy I pursued was to cut up and then pack the existing space down to the inch. One of my biggest anxieties about what I have done to the house is that I have spent all my money on things other than adding new space. In other words I will have set fire to money by spending it without thereby increasing the resale value of the house.

Probably as a product of leftover 1970s environmentalist thinking I got a certain compulsive pleasure out of fitting more human beings into Milton without increasing the footprint of enclosed space. (All human activity was bad in the 1970s because you were not supposed to leave any marks on the planet. Since, inevitably, all human activity does to some greater or lesser degree leave a mark, it's sort of a form of original sin.)

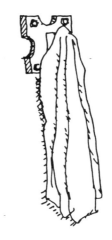

Pirate Cave towel hooks.

arranging the pirate cave

The first rearrangement of the space at 416 Milton, the Pirate Cave concept, came into being after Lance died. I had been trying unsuccessfully to live in the tiny front unit upstairs. When I bought it ,the building was essentially a one-bedroom flat over a two-car garage, a flat that had been divided into a bachelor and a single apartment in the mid-1950s. The single was actually a livable apartment, and had all the choicest rooms. The bachelor was hellish. When Lance owned the place our friend Gunther managed the building. Potential tenants came to look at the bachelor, liked it, moved in and then realized it was impossible to actually live in. The kitchen was too small to put a table in, and the bedroom had no closet. I tried living there, too. I just couldn't do it. It felt like a hard-luck crash pad, someplace where the compulsive gambler or the used-up drug addict would live.

I was worried that I wouldn't have enough space to have all my possessions out, something that is very important to me, since most of what I own is a memento mori either of my deceased parents or of Lance.

The only problem with expanding my share of the building, a part of this story I still feel bad about, is that the remainder of the top story was already occupied by a tenant, Mitzi, who had been living there when I moved in. Mitzi was happy

The primal Pirate Cave mirror and flames dancing on the P.C. cabinetry.

there. Mitzi sewed her clothing designs for a living and took care of the garden, planting bulbs and mowing the lawn in her gingham sun suit. Mitzi even invited me to her dinner parties. But ultimately I had to do the unthinkable.

I fired Mitzi as gardener. She had been receiving $70 a month off her rent, which she now had to pay as a rent increase. I also raised the new rent to the rent-control maximum, 3 percent plus 1 percent for each utility. That was it as far as Mitzi was concerned. She had loved the place, gardened up a storm, invited me to dinner and then I had turned around and raise the rent. So she moved out.

The first idea I had was to take the whole top floor and jerry-rig a 250-square-foot single out of the basement garage floor, because there was already an abandoned bathroom down there—so abandoned that it looked and reeked like something from *Tales of the Crypt*. The downstairs had obviously been lived in at different points in time—there was a hippie sponge painting from the '70s and layers of old linoleum from the 1930s and '40s. The downstairs was split level, and the ceiling was also interrupted oddly by the split level ceiling change upstairs. It had a sense of being hollowed out of the ground. So therefore I envisioned it as cave, a protected and sheltered refuge, where the bed is even more protected, in the most sequestered location with the least headroom, the only really private and secure location in the whole place.

The Pirate metaphor, part aesthetic and part modus operandi, came from expediency, from accepting whatever kooky conditions I found in situ. The talisman for the Pirate Cave is a roughly fashioned mirror that I found hanging in the abandoned bathroom. Its silvering is blistered and at each corner is an ace-of-spades design formed in wrought iron.

The Pirate Cave tactic is to use cheap materials and ready-made cabinetry—then obliterate it with ornament. (Although let's be honest, most of the time it is not materials that are the real expense, but the labor, so while it was the intent to do things cheaply, by the time I was through getting the medium density fiberboard panels sawn up to make the ornament I could have made other choices. The other inspiration was finding Lance's old skateboard wheels in the basement. Any contemporary Venice pirate would own a skateboard, and Lance loved all things skateboardian. In Venice, it is the gangs, the homeless people, and the oceanfront-walk crowd of beach revelers who set the aesthetic and fashion mood of the place. So jamming skateboard wheels onto melamine board doors as handles became the model for creating ornaments that literally have toothy sawn edges. Finally, flames came in

This was to be Gunther's new apartment/garage before the great real estate bust of 1990 and marriage bust up of 1994 sent him to the welcoming confines of the Pirate Cave. Drawing by Steve LaCap, Jackie McNancy and John Chase.

because the concept of cave implies Hell. 416 Milton is supposed to be heaven and hell, mausoleum and resort, heavy and light.

I like to draw flames because of their satisfying combination of curves and spikes. Flames are generally employed in popular culture, particularly hot rod culture, but they are not often found in architectural culture because of their dramatic and literal quality. The overall ornamental parti for the house is based on the shapes I doodle. I believe the unmediated subconscious mind should get the chance to have some say-so in how things look.

There are certain shapes and motifs that run through my doodling. My friend Travis has shown me examples of schizophrenic art, and the drawings done by patients who have deteriorated to the 50 percent gone stage look most like my doodles. I am hoping the resemblance is coincidental, rather than profound. Basically the doodle shapes are Rorshach blots, tea leaves, chicken entrails, starting points for divination. They are spirit guides, capable of multiple interpretation.

The open question with this house is whether or not such a basically unlovely and casually conceived habitation deserved to be fussed with to begin with. Perhaps the best thing that could have been done is simply paint everything white, in the absence of enough money to rip it down and start fresh.

A corner of the Cave.

While designing the Pirate Cave I realized that I was creating a place to live that was so small that no one would be able to live in it—which I did not want. But as the outlines of the place became visible, I found that a lot of people liked and understood the cave, including people I would not necessarily have expected to, such as Gunther's realtor cohorts, his cleaning woman and the cable TV installer. I could have rented it out many times over. As the project progressed the Cave became more and more a specific "custom" place in which there were designated locations for things. It became less generic and flexible. I stopped hedging my bets. I became more confident about building in things, such as benches that precluded moveable furniture arrangement. I allowed the space to become one space, with partially articulated subspaces created by removing internal windows and doors. I stopped worrying that the bed space was oppressively small and came to accept it as cozy.

Due to unexpected developments Gunther became both the resident and consummate denizen of the Pirate Cave. When his wife, his childhood sweetheart, kicked him out, the mortgage payments on the house that they owned in Hollywood became just another part of their marital debt load. Like my house on Ethelyne Avenue it was worth less than the mortgage. Gunther went bankrupt and dumped his house. Before his B-K judgment became final, the cave was his secret hideout-hole, his whereabouts unknown to creditors. In the cave, Gunther now lives out his new identity as beachside bohemian bachelor.

Gunther is a connoisseur of refinements and details. He has helped assemble furniture I designed. The place is furnished with just the right artifacts. The Cave is always kept in the immaculate order that truly small living places demand. Gunther believes that the Pirate Cave maintains the ideal lifestyle balance with his livelihood of realtor to let potential girlfriends know that he has a taste for eccentricity.

Once I got comfortable with the shapes in the cave I began to want to really go beyond what I done with them in the basement, to turn up the heat on the flames and make them vaporize in the upper story. I felt the most successful element in the Pirate Cave was the wardrobe because the whole thing was painted, saturated with color (unlike the kitchen where the cabinetry was part-white melamine) and the ornament was big. So, before I ran out of dough, I designed a whole set of itchy, crawly, scared-cat, claws-out chinoiserie in scroll-sawn MDF for my own unit, ornaments that relate to flames but are not actually flames. I still don't know when or if this is going to be realized.

In the final split-up version of the upstairs I divided the floor into two units. I got one more room than I had before, during the Mitzi era, the living room. The new unit was the only one left with a kitchen.

The up side was that the ever-reliable Richmond, a consort of my friend Amanda, would be the tenant in the back. What makes the triplex pleasant for me to live in with friends are the very things that would make it intolerable if I had strangers living here as tenants. Sharing the garage and sharing the yard with friends is totally different from encountering people you barely know there. Noises that would be disquieting or annoying seem

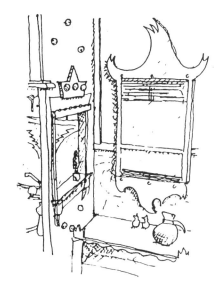

Mr. Flame, the Kustomized heater in the Pirate Cave.

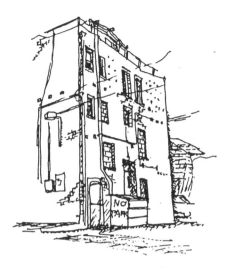

Tenement 911 glowers menacingly over the alley.

In Lance's eyes the proximity of Milton to the real-estate Shangra-La of Santa Monica three blocks to the North, and to the beach, made it a prized resort, rendering the question moot of its immediate urban setting.

comforting if you know who is making them. Between Richmond next door and Gunther below in the cave I feel like I am part of a crew, and feel psychologically stronger in the neighborhood, as if this colony of acquaintances is a little constituency in its own right. Given the volatility of the neighborhood, there is comfort in numbers.

THE NEIGHBORS

When Lance first bought this house in 1989 the old brick hotel next door was a drug supermarket. There wasn't a street drug brewed that you couldn't buy there. He never seemed to pay any attention to the building that I call Tenement 911. If he did he certainly never told me about it. Consequently, when I bought 416 Milton, I had no idea what kind of festering hellhole it was next to. At one of Gunther's barbecues I met a former Vice cop named Gordon. He claimed that in the 1960s Milton used to have the highest crime rate of any street in Venice. People shot and killed each other next door in Tenement 911, and in 1965 Gordon himself had shot and killed two drug dealers further down on Milton, at a coffee shop that was a notorious drug-dealing center. (According to Gordon the druggies shot first.)

In the 1920s Tenement 911 was a seaside hotel where tourists would stay while visiting the beach. It harks back to the era when it was harder to get around so that the resorts close to town were still destinations, when bucolic sectors of Los Angeles such as Sierra Madre and Laurel Canyon were seasonal resorts. The ground floor of the old hotel (its three stories on Electric Avenue and two and a half stories facing me) housed small stores.

Marian, who lives next door, tells me there were families living happily in the ground floor units of Tenement 911 in the 1950s when she was growing up on Milton. The building has been cleaned up a lot since its low point a few years ago, but it will never be an entirely normal place to live—though its seismic retrofitting may have a certain Road Warrior cachet, with beams, posts, and through-bolts crashing wildly through walls and windows. The ground floor spaces on Pacific are vacant, but not entirely enclosed, with long, open gaps in the storefronts, narrow enough to keep people out, but wide enough to see the shadowy, littered spaces within.

The building appears to have received its last coat of yellow paint at the same time mine did, at some point during the Truman presidency. Neighborhood scuttlebutt has it that the former owner of my house and the owner of

Tenement 911 (who has owned 911 since 1928) went in together on the rancid, margarine-yellow paint that covers both buildings. The bathrooms at 911 are down the hall, and the rent is cheap ($325 to $375). It attracts two categories of people. The first category of tenant has decided to check into this building as a way of checking out of society. They then go on to lose their jobs and any social mooring to the rest of the world they once possessed. The other category is total loners. I have never once seen these loners with a friend or relative. I would say that only about one-third of the tenants maintain a conventional level of connection to the world, in terms of activity and social interaction.

Following, is a list of some of the psychotic tenants next door, chez 911:

Tenant 1: The Ripper. Goes to Santa Monica Place, stabs an old lady, takes her purse and comes back to this apartment where he is arrested.

Tenant 2: Sparky. Habitually prances around naked while doing his laundry in the laundry room. He deliberately, not accidentally, sets fire to his apartment twice before being arrested for arson.

Tenant 3: Harry. The hairiest professional female impersonator I have ever seen. He bounced his car off my retaining wall and another tenant's car and then fled his collision in the Tenement 911 parking lot. The attempt to escape blame failed due to the large number of witnesses. During the subsequent interrogation by apartment manager Butch, Harry exhibited a confused demeanor that suggested the use of controlled substances.

Tenant 4: Louie. A short biker with full-body tattoos and a long ponytail. He dealt drugs out of the corner pay phone at Rose and Main. Tattoo Louie used to ask me for spare change for the phone, no matter how many times I told him no. He was whisked off by his doting mom and dad so that unfeeling policemen would not be able to make good on their arrest warrant for him. Louie had a penchant for short hookers with short hair. They came and went at all hours of the day and night. The metal security door on the alley clanged shut continuously (it was clearly audible in my bedroom), marking the arrival and departure of Louie's guests.

Tenant 5: Jimbo Jr. Jimbo surely holds the world record for number of times blasting the same damaged Doors tape, with a repeating section that Jim Morrison never envisaged, accompanied by his electric guitar, at four in the morning. Jimbo and his friend welcomed the entering graduate class at SCI-ARC during their visit to my house for a barbecue by pelting the students with wadded paper balls. Just good clean drunken fun.

The undeniable wholesomeness (regular jobs, friends, apparent freedom from substance abuse) of recent Tenement 911 residents makes me wonder if the dishonor roll of former residents wasn't something my own fears somehow willed into existence. I am sure I must have seemed equally psychotic to them.

Tenant 6: Carla. This 40-something night crawler can often be found at two in the morning sailing out in outfits that are a cross between streetwalker and gauzy, tie-dyed free spirit. Carla has lifted her blouse and flashed her wares at both my tenants, but not at me. I don't take it personally—I must not be her type. When loaded from the speed she buys from the corner drug dealer she meanders aimlessly around the Tenement 911 parking lot, her path like that of a slow billiards ball gently ricocheting off this and that invisible barrier. Sometimes she stares meditatively at her own window as though considering the mystery of the other self behind the curtains. A typical costume for this reverie is silver lamé floor-length gown and cowboy boots. Carla occupies a halfway point between the fully housed and employed and the street Gypsies who are her friends.

Tenant 7: Ed. The infamous Ed. A former plumber's helper who lost his job and started collecting cans in his bicycle basket which he cashes in for drug and booze money. Ed would collar perfect strangers wheeling their shopping carts down the alley and invite these new pals up to his room to "party" with him.

At different points during this period I would be driving around Los Angeles (sometimes in neighborhoods not that close to Venice) and see some of Ed's pals sailing down the sidewalks, shopping carts on parade. Since there is no intercom and no doorbell buzzer at Tenement 911, they would stand outside in the parking lot and yell for him at all hours, sometimes camping out in the parking lot until Ed eventually materialized. Getting Ed to show his face was often an extended process, requiring repeated shouted requests over a lengthy period time. I always thought the relationship between the alley denizens and Ed emphasized just how blurred the lines were between the housed and the homeless in Venice. Membership in one of those two groups was not necessarily permanent, nor did it prevent acquaintanceship with members of the other.

Contemplating my interactions with my neighbors reminds of the only quote from Bhudda that I know: "People in this world are prone to be selfish and unsympathetic; they do not know how to love and respect one another; they argue and quarrel over trifling affairs only to their own harm and suffering and life becomes but a dreary round of unhappiness." (*The Teaching of Bhudda*, p. 188. Bukkyo Dendo Kyokai, 1993, Tokyo.) (This book was a source of some bitterness to Lance since his brother Roman gave the book to him. Lance always felt that Roman had prevented Lance from getting his fair share of the family fortune. The origin of the book made him even madder. It is the kind of Bhudda Book that is left in hotel rooms along with the *Gideon Bible*. As far as Lance was concerned Real Presents (and most especially Real Death-Bed Presents) came in powder blue bags from Tiffany's, not in the form of travelers' leftover freebies.")

Catch-up, bless his heart.

in the dog house

Nothing caused as much friction with my neighbors as my dog. Oh, the trouble that innocent half Shepherd-half Golden Retriever puppy caused. Many of my friends get mad when I say this and claim that I have should have handled it differently. They claim that I using The Incident as a slimey excuse to forsake my responsibility as a dog parent. They think the fact that Catch-Up ate my mother's one silver bud vase and the passenger side door panel covering in my Nissan Sentra has more to do with his relocation than the neighborhood brawl.

Catch-up rarely barked. Instead he would whine or, as my neighbor has described it, "yodel." He slept with me, went to work me and, generally, as his trainer at Petville obedience school put it, was a high-contact dog. No puppy, least of all Catch-Up, is intended to be left alone. The one time I experimented with leaving Catch-Up in the yard, Gunther, the tenant in the Cave, had just moved in. Gunther went for his Saturday afternoon wake-up coffee. When he came back he was surrounded by a small mob of neighbors who felt that the dog should be whisked away by the Society for the Prevention of Cruelty to Animals for ever being left alone. After that visit from the lynch mob, if I had to leave Catch-Up alone I would lock him up inside. The windows were shut so that his pleading cries would not permeate the neighborhood in the same way. He tended to sound as though he was watching his mother and father being flayed alive and then fed into a meat grinder. It was heart-rending.

But locking him inside behind closed windows turned out not to be good enough.

The whole dog issue came to a head two weeks ago. Usually I go over to what we call Family Night Dinner with my officemates every Sunday night. This time Gunther was planning a barbecue. Some of his guests had canceled, he had extra food, and I wanted to show my officemates my cozy, newly improved surroundings.

The truth is I was a lousy dog parent. Parenthood was bound to end in trouble.

Armed and dangerous bunny statue purchased at Standard Brands Paint watches Norman's potentially lethal assault on the barbecuing Frederic.

So Gunther and I had Family Night at our place. We barbecued. Gunther's mother is Brazilian, and he has a monster macho host thing that generally involves serving lots of meat and plenty of booze. It always involves protestations of undying affection for the assembled throng. Having been recently booted out of his marriage has done nothing to tone down these predilections. Gunther supervised the billowing clouds of smoke, we drank, we talked. As I left to drive my office pals home Gunther was sitting contentedly, smoking his favorite Cohiba cigars with his friend Renzo, a stylish Italian scenic designer.

I put Catch-Up upstairs behind closed doors.

When I came back all hell had broken loose. Somebody, I couldn't figure out who, was yelling at Gunther through the chain link fence at the sideyard of the house, making unsuccessful attempts to climb over. The aggressor was in the yard of the house next door, where the perfectly gentle and unthreatening Marian, the neighborhood historian, lives with her family.

The guy in Marian's yard had just gone crazy. He was yelling, threatening the dog, me and Gunther with everything up to and including murder. At that point I was mad: my honor and my manhood were under attack, not to mention my pet-care standards. I rushed to the fence, grabbed the wire (hard enough to press pink and yellow welts into the palms of my hands), shoved my face up against the mesh and screamed (loud enough to strip my vocal cords) that I got the point and would take care of the situation. Just then I realized that he had a knife. (It turned out to be an old army souvenir, made of a special dense hardwood from Panama).

I was so angry and had so much adrenaline surging through my veins, that I was ready to have him stick me with the knife, just so that he could be arrested. But I didn't. Instead I made the better decision to go inside and calm down. The guy turned out to be Marian's brother Norman, who I had hardly ever seen outside. Apparently Norman is a cranky former volleyball champion turned heroin dealer who can't handle any stress (he just causes it). He's 55 and prematurely fragile, due to a recent triple-bypass operation.

Meanwhile Gunther had gone in and slipped his 40-caliber Sig Sauer semiautomatic loaded with illegal Black Talon bullets into his belt (Black Talons are illegal because their fragments cut the doctors' hands when they are working on people who have been shot, or so Gunther says. I don't find the gun or the illegal bullets funny, and I have asked Gunther, so far without success, if he could get rid of them.) The right thing for Gunther to do would have been for him to go inside when Norman first came out with the knife and call 911, rather than returning the hostility and egging Norman on.

Eventually Gunther went into his outlaw pal mode, acquired during the years when he managed a chain of seamy bars in the valley with his partner, Boris, before Boris quit to go into the meat-packing business. (One of their bars was the Fall Inn, located in a nondescript shopping center in Panorama City, out in the bleached northern flatlands of the San Fernando Valley. One afternoon a patron got up, walked out, robbed a bank across the street, walked back and sat down again. He was having whiskey shots with beer chasers at the bar when he was arrested.)

Gunther's angle of attack with Norman was "It's you and me against the world—just us fellow aggrieved and swashbuckling outlaws." As soon as I saw that passions had cooled, I came back out with my great-uncle Josiah's sword-in-a-cane. Then Norman and I compared his souvenir weapon with my souvenir weapon.

The day after The Incident, both Gunther and I were traumatized. I took Catch-Up straight to work in the morning. After work I dropped him off with my friend Gustavo, who knows and likes the dog. Within a week Gustavo had Catch-Up settled on a half acre in Hacienda Heights, with a family who had a Husky puppy the same age as Catch-Up. And while Catch-Up himself may be gone, there is still plenty of evidence of his presence, from the holes in the yard to the fleas in the house.

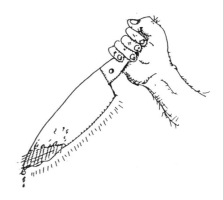

Artist's conception of weapon employed in mugging assault committed by Tenement 911 tenant.

paranoia on milton

So now there was no Catch-Up, and everything was copacetic. The next week, at five-thirty in the morning. I couldn't sleep. Suddenly the iron security door of the house next door opened. Norman stepped out, wearing boxer shorts, and stood in the alley waiting for someone. Shortly thereafter, a guy Norman's age or older appeared. "Scruffy" is skinny and drably dressed, with a beaten-down manner. I tentatively identify him as the best friend of Rainbow, a resident of Rose of Sharon manor across the alley from me. She

The balconies that put Rose of Sharon residents on such intimate terms with the alley.

Why was I choosing to focus on lowlife? Surely it is the unacknowledged Jerry Springer viewer within. Did I feel my own economic existence was so precarious that I would be subject to a fall?

is a perennial flower child, pieced together with steel plates and rods from a bad car accident, who seems pretty scrambled herself. Rainbow is always hailing me with news of various neighborhood evil doings, conspiracies and misdeeds, usually in versions that sound somewhat augmented and enhanced. I had no idea until after The Incident that she was a sometime confidante of the Whacked One. Scruffy himself is often to be found, muttering and sputtering, working on his battered truck, which sits, pieced together with rope and cardboard, in the Rose of Sharon garage. His most frequent method of entry to the vehicle is to crawl over the useless and permanently lashed-together driver's-side door.

Scruffy immediately handed Norman something tiny and white. It looked like the little pieces of rock cocaine on episodes of "Cops." Or it could have been something else entirely and I was just constructing the whole thing out of paranoia. But I think that's why Norman is so whacked out; he maybe not only be a former drug dealer, but a current crackhead.

Norman and his pal had a long argument at top volume (top volume on Norman's side, at least; his friend maintained a low William Burroughs rumble), which seemed to involve how long this guy could keep sleeping in Norman's battered VW bus in the driveway. Norman alternately threatened to throw his pal out on the spot, and warned him that he has to be out of there in two days.

There was much discussion of a guy named Madison. Could it be the same Madison who used to be a friend of my friend Gustavo's before Madison went bad, I wondered? How many guys named Madison were there in Venice, after all? Jeremey, a former friend of Gustavo, drove by Madison just this week—a Madison who was homeless, shirtless and filthy, sprawled lasciviously on a bus bench. He was groping his crotch and beaming a Satanic grin at passersby on Santa Monica Boulevard in Hollywood. His libido was so chemically amped that he did not even recognize Jeremey and gave him the big come on, as though Jeremey were a perfect stranger, a fresh prospect.

After the lover who had watched over Madison died, he was never the same. Since there was no one to take care of him he let drugs take over, while he went on autopilot. His friends, his house, and his employability as a mechanic all evaporated long ago. The unsettling aspect of the possible Madison connection was that it meant I was not completely separate from the chaos around me. It was a moment that caused me to ask, do I live in an impersonal big city, or do

I live in an agglomeration of smaller pieces of socially and geographically defined worlds in which there are unpredictable elements of congruency and synchronicity, both bad and good. I hated the thought that I could not pick and choose how I fit in, that I was inevitably tied to an endless chain of human misery and evil, however tenuous the connection.

It occurred to me that there are times when life on Milton is aggravating my native paranoia.

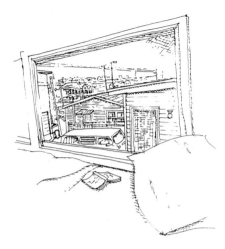

My neighbor Norman's house and the alley seen through my bedroom window.

CITY LIFE ON MILTON

I haven't mentioned the "normal" neighbors, including the Catch-Up fans, since, by and large, we haven't interacted with each other. The exception is my friend Sylvia who lives across the street with her husband and baby. I have known her for almost 20 years, went to UCLA architecture school with her and relish my conversations with her because of her highly analytic mind. When I look out my window, the idea of baby Mike in his crib soothes me. I think of him lying there in his cot, blissfully free of adult cares such as mortgage payments, hard drive crashes and the Christian right.

But Sylvia would be out of this neighborhood in a flash if she thought she could sell her house for anything close to what she and her husband paid for it. The neighborhood makes her crazy. It starts with the karmic history of her cottage.

The previous owner of her house was a wealthy gay guy. He resolved his conflict with the neighbors by firebombing them. The entire neighborhood was evacuated while a SWAT team stormed the cottage to capture the mad bomber. When Sylvia was restoring the cottage the same neighbors who had been firebombed panicked when they saw gypsum board dust on the sidewalk. They called the hazardous materials police, claiming that Sylvia was strafing the neighborhood with deadly asbestos dust. Only a thousand dollars and another haz-mat team later, was Sylvia cleared of any toxic waste skullduggery. And while I have had my dog problems, Sylvia has had a cat conundrum. Expressing concern about marauding cats bothering her elderly feline instantly won her hysterical accusations of cat poisoning from high-strung neighbors.

At the moment Sylvia is trying hard to remain calm. The house next door to her (not the fire-bombed house, but the other one) has been given back to the bank since the mortgage debt was $250,000 more than it was worth. A changing group of single males, mostly young, white and stinking drunk, have been crawling in and out of the windows for the past three weeks, filling the front yard with trash and peeing outside in liberal enough quantities to be palpable walking by on Milton. One Sunday night I walked around the corner of the house, coming from the alley, just as Sylvia was running into Gunther's open door with her baby. She was screaming at the top of her lungs. One of the derelicts next door had walked right into her living room.

In one sense, Sylvia's encounter was perfectly predictable. This neighborhood is close to social services for homeless people and the tolerant milieu of the beach boardwalk. It is plainly turf where the dispossessed belong. Sooner or later everybody has some of dealings with everyone else. The avoidance of disturbing or challenging people, and the exaggerated fear of them, further impoverish urban life, as many observers, such as William F. Whyte, Mike Davis and Stephen Flusty, among others, have noted. The city is a lab in which it is possible to conquer the fear of the unknown and the uncontrolled. Consequently it is essential that the city belong to different groups. But this diversity makes a degree of conflict and tension inevitable, and it means that many people would just as soon check out of the laboratory.

In his book *The Uses of Disorder*, published in 1970, Richard Sennett compares a mature and civilized urban environment to the process of personal growth that occurs during adolescence: "experiencing the friction of differences and conflict makes men personally aware of the milieu around their own lives; the need is for men to recognize conflicts, not to try to purify them away in a solidarity myth, in order to survive. A social forum that encourages the move into adulthood thus first depends on making sure there is no escape from situations of confrontation and conflict. The city can provide a unique meeting ground for these encounters."

Density, diversity and propinquity are valued in the culture of urban design and architecture. At the same time individual Americans, including Southern Californians, are often focused on what provides the most convenience and amenity for themselves. For 50 years after the real estate boom of 1887, many immigrants to Southern California came from rural and small town environments. They were suspicious of cities. Even today in Southern California the more space you have in-between you and other people, the better your living environment is perceived to

> Maybe some of the children of affluent American suburbia just can't handle the connectivity to all aspects of life—good and bad—that cities offer.

be. The more control you have over who passes through your immediate environment, the more responsible you are perceived to be in providing for your family.

For many commuters, three hours on the freeway is not too long if they believe that the commute places them beyond the dangers of the city. At all costs they want to avoid Sylvia's experience of smelling urine from the neighboring repossessed house, and seeing strangers crawl in and out of boarded-up windows next door.

The value placed on household autonomy and control is so great that this hatred of density has impelled greater Los Angeles to reach beyond the San Gabriel mountains, out into the series of desert valleys that stretches toward the Arizona border. Sylvia was not up to learning more about her fellow human beings by having her living room turn into an agora of conflict, a classroom of cultural differences.

A week after the intruder incident I was standing outside in my yard, going over the plans for the pagoda ornamentation program with Richmond, when I heard someone scream, "You are scaring me." A short preppie-looking youth in a fraternity T-shirt bolted out of the front door of the abandoned house and scooted across the parking lot of Tenement 911 with three cops in hot pursuit. The cops let him go with a warning.

The irony of Venice the Menace is that the menace, in good urban fashion, is bound up with promise. I may hate living among a shifting community of strangers and a cacophony of sirens, car alarms and and shouted midnight alley conversations. But that proximity is also what makes it possible for me to be near so many things I love. From the Milton house I can walk to the beach, to the thriving boardwalk with its amazingly diverse crowd or to the conspicuous consumption of Main Street. The comfort of commerce and recreation, on largely traditional urban terms, is available to me on all sides: a flood of skaters, bicyclists, joggers, bodybuilders, shoppers, strollers and members of the neighborhood synagogue on their way to services.

That's actually why I wanted to live here, a place that was many different peoples' turf, with its liveliness and eccentricity. I wanted to build something that was celebratory, that did not say "house" in the usual modern or period revival vocabularies, but which expressed my particularly unconscious aesthetic mindset—love of ornament, horror *vacuii* and the piling up of individually attractive pieces to make a larger collective.

negotiating venice

The irony is that I came to Venice because I thought this was the one place where I could get away with it. Old hippies-never-die-they-just-end-up-in-Venice; old-time beatnik Venice where there was cheesecloth over the windows of the abandoned stores on the boardwalk, concealing the drunken poets within, and a coffeehouse with a bathtub on the floor (Gunther's father remembers Venice this way from a visit in 1955); Jim Morrison's Venice; Charles Bukowski's Venice; cover of 1980 *Domus* magazine filled with Venice architects Venice. Well there is no place you can ever please everyone, or assume that everyone is going to be happy with your actions. I called attention to myself by building something in a neighborhood where no one has built much for awhile. I introduced a pet into a community of dogless apartment dwellers. In a yard visible to hundred of eyes I hang out, wander around and talk to my friends, so that all aspects of my identity are on display, including being gay. All of these things eat away at my degree of domestic privacy and the ability to act autonomously that I might otherwise have had. I remembered beach and artist; I forgot homeless, hurting and packed-to-the-gills urban warren of too-tiny apartments and too few parking spaces.

As a result of my interaction with the neighborhood, my feelings about my house have changed in two respects. First of all, I have found that I need as much privacy as I can get by means of landscape. I regret this. I like being able to look at and talk to people walking by on the walking street that fronts the southern edge of my house. I have generally always enjoyed ignoring the fact that my house has no backyard whatsoever. I use my front yard as though it were a conventionally enclosed suburban backyard. But in fact it is exposed to the walking street on one side and has only a veil of chain link fence between it and the parking lot of Tenement 911. I feel obliged to plant out my surroundings with a DMZ of timber bamboo because it makes me, and anything kooky I do, less visible, and therefore less likely to be a target of any conflict, conflict which will interfere with my ability to feel comfortable and make a home here.

The rest of the landscaping is yet to be figured out. Gunther is supposed to get his own private space, with a fence made out of plywood surfboards and a hedge of cannas and bananas so that he may keep his blinds open and barbecue in private splendor. The remainder of the space is also to be divided up not, necessarily by hedges or fences, but divided nonetheless into other programmed spaces for specific functions such as storing tools (since Gunther's unit used to act as the tool shed), providing shade in summer, cutting flowers or watching TV outside in the summer.

Second, I have been so strongly affected by paying attention to the dysfunctional aspects of the neighborhood and my dysfunctional neighbors that I have poisoned my soul (if I hear one more can-collector smashing cans outside at two in the morning!) and I now need to make peace with my surroundings. There is no real danger to my person, only to my personality. Neighborhood conflict is merely an at-home object lesson in the uncontrollability of the larger universe.

Part of me wishes I never had to leave the perfectly protected world of South Pasadena, and part of me thinks that's all I would have needed for the waters to close over me. Right now, its very clear to me that, even while I marvel at how inspiring and how upsetting this spot on the planet is for me, I do need the provocative and disquieting lessons the place has to teach.

afterword

This essay was written, in many respects, to be as subjective as possible. I was worried at the time I wrote it, and since one of the versions of this appeared in the *Architecture of Fear* (edited by Nan Ellin) the point was to focus on fear. Any subjective view only holds its form for a certain time and is edited from a larger and more contradictory set of attitudes and memories. This was an essay about the emotional construction of place, at a certain point in my life in 1995.

Here's what has happened in the five years since I wrote the essay: Tenement 911 has been painted, the bad security light that buzzed louder than an entire power station has been removed and the tenement is so defanged that even young girls live there now—all thanks to the clever management policies of wily manager Butch. The abandoned house next to Sylvia got laboriously tarted up and was rented for criminally high rates to two young, female ABC-TV vice presidents. Gunther astonished me by studying so hard that he broke into the fast-track combination Master's and

Bachelor's degree program at UCLA and later was accepted to Yale law school. Richmond has been replaced by weight-lifting trainer George and his 19-year-old girlfriend Rachel in the back. George trains both Gunther and me at Arnold Schwartzenegger's World Gym around the corner. My Pagoda itself still has no landscaping and more incriminating than that, none of the much-vaunted decoration on the outside is up. I have a government job, doing work that I believe in. Apparently there is life after paranoia.

trashy space,
trashy people
and trashy behavior

The true language of cities deals with relationships rather than free-standing objects.

—Grady Clay, *How to Read the American City*

trash at the office

Where there is trash, there is life, rotten though it may be. One weekend I arrived at the offices I share with friends to find that a sociopathic therapist had made a major deposit in our dumpster. It was all too easy to reconstruct the trail of sorrow this Casanova had trodden. Among his psychojunk were letters from the female clients he had romanced and slept with. You could see why they would have been especially vengeful from the other supporting evidence he had left behind. There was a huge, almost competently done water color of a benevolent New Agey angel, radiating healing and forgiveness.

This simultaneously healing and wounding counselor had also left behind a stack of dubious self-help books: babbling tomes on putting the sexual magic back into your marriage, manuals detailing how many scoops of ice cream to give to your inner child. Part of me felt that a call to the State licensing board was in order. Another part of me worried that this therapist was a veritable Chernobyl of bad karma. I did not want so much as one scintilla of it rubbing off on me.

It seemed wiser to let the orphaned evidence be hauled off to the bucol-ic, oak-tree-studded canyon at the edge of the San Fernando Valley that our waste disposal firm is despoiling by filling with trash. At any rate, I was sure one of the many outraged women (shockingly, the letters were from not one or two patients but many, many patients) had surely taken matters into her own hands. One could only hope that Mr. Wonderful would soon be selling shoes or peddling insurance in another state, no longer able to pass out love joneses like Halloween candy. At any rate, trash showed itself as a supple medium for the recording of human behavior.

Since nearly all possessions ultimately end up as trash, the trash universe is virtually infinite as a topic. Rather than take on the whole dumpster, so to speak, I am going to confine my remarks to trash as geographical marker, trash as barter and livelihood and trash as symbol. These are my trash terri-tories of choice.

I strongly suspect my evil neighbor two doors down of abandoning and then torching his skeletal Christmas tree in the alley just to annoy everyone.

Trash is disorder personified; it offers horrific proof that wanted possessions are all potential changelings, that even the most benign objects and activities have a fecal underbelly. A lush landscape becomes lawn clippings, a feast becomes bones, a cupidlike infant produces soiled Pampers.

trash at home

To control trash is to strike a symbolic blow at entropy. I learned this from my parents early in life. From my mother I learned that having candlesticks that matched the place settings meant one had conquered all. From my father I learned the fine points of trash management. Pop selected all of his pleasures and his worries carefully. They tended to be capable of being addressed through direct action, whether that was purchasing the pickled pigs feet he loved or getting up early to meet the trash men. The trash men, as I understood them in my childhood, were part of the army of black and brown service workers who swarmed to white, upper-middle-class suburbs in Southern California to renew the gloss on utopia, ensuring that floors shone, that beds had fresh linen, that lawns were properly fertilized. When I was a child I hated the fact that Pop would question the inevitability and completeness of these arrangements, privileged arrangements that I was eager to take for granted as base conditions for existence.

If a trash pickup looked dicey to Pop, if he knew full well, in his stewardship of 1410 Milan Avenue, that the trash exceeded the capacities of the ranks of metal and vinyl containers in the service yard, he would squirrel away the overflow until the time was right. Part of the problem was the unending flow of suburban agricultural product, the mountains of clippings generated by the expanses of lawn, hedge and leaf-dropping trees. Before the era of recycling clippings, the suburbs were farms growing a crop harvested strictly for trash. Even before they reached the cans, these pyramids of lawn clippings would start to heat up, fired up by decomposition.

At the end of his life his concern with order increased. Pop asked for very little of the world; for him, self-interest came down to a concern that *you* be happy. It was a matter of honor, however, that bills be paid and obligations discharged. I would sometimes arrive at my father's house to find it awash

Tenement 911 rear door vignette after a December rain.

in tangled paper trails of decades of bills, tax filings and personal papers. He would spread these across the living room in much the same way that my mother, in the middle of an uncontrollable manic-depressive high, had earlier covered the living room with pictures of my sister and myself at all ages.

If the household interior was out of control at least the trash could be controlled the universe. Having kept a particularly vigilant eye on the contents of the trash, Pop would spend days in advance fretting about the strategy for its removal. This strategy usually involved my father materializing at just the right moment with the correct folding green for the garbage men.

trash and i

My father's obsession with the choreography of trash removal annoyed me to no end. From my perspective, it was clearly not a fit subject with which a grown man should concern himself. Naturally that meant that I soon found myself just as compulsive on the subject as he was, if not more so. At some point in my thirties, I developed the nervous tic of kicking crushed cigarette wrappers and crumpled beer cans into the gutter. To this day it takes a certain amount of will power for me to walk past a tempting pile of old newspapers laying on the sidewalk and not give them a good swift boot. It is humbling to realize that in some primitive, and apparently quite extensive, part of my brain, I somehow think I am making the world a better place with each carefully aimed kick. Walking away from a garbage kick, the ur-mammal within is persuading me that now that I have made my offering, the majestic, slow-moving street-sweeper gods will come in the dead of night to sweep away the detritus and purify the site. It also stems, in part, from the fascination I had as a kid, throwing papers, leaves and bugs in a streaming gutter during a good, hard winter rain and watching them rush off on their storm-drain journey to the ocean.

trashy neighborhoods one: echo park

Once, as an adult, while I was babysitting a cavernous, old brick building in the nether zone of Sunset Boulevard that lies between Silverlake and Echo Park, I nearly got busted for kicking trash in the gutter. That building was a little like an armed frontier fort against the dispossessed of the inner city who passed through on their trek from the druggy depths of McArthur Park to the equally tough streets of downtown Hollywood. The parking lot, the bushes behind the building and the planter next to the building on Sunset all had their habitues. For awhile the homeless were discreetly living in the upper reaches of the unused loft and raiding the office refrigerator at night, while in the planter outside, a porky guy with long, spiky locks would bang out his own version of "Just like a Woman" on guitar. His version, "Just like a Pig," included a spellbinding chorus of oinks.

As caretaker of someone else's building, I felt it was my duty to dust off the debris from the planter. So I was ticked off when the neighborhood watermelon vender moved his site of operations in front of the building. Satisfied clients left rinds galore on the sidewalk and planter. My approach to starting an open dialogue between reasonable people was to kick those rinds (the larger ones had to be shoveled by hand) into the gutter while cursing vigorously. One day, while in mid-curse and mid-kick I was halted by a motorcycle cop who swooped around the corner. I had to haul every last rind out of the gutter while the vendor watched. Humiliating.

Cast your bread upon the asphalt: / Wonder no more: / Rather pigeon feed.

The motorcycle cop was a regular visitor to our parking lot, where, because our building created a blind corner, he could lie in wait. He'd zoom right past the super-dirty boozer who was habitually flat on his back next to the dumpster.

I have been known to climb into a dumpster. At my old office in Silverlake, I often seemed to have filed some vitally important piece of paper in the waste basket. Invariably, upon recovery, it would have become tangled up with the true detritus. Unsolicited donations regularly left the dumpster awash in an unappetizing mix of beer bottles, gutted limes and bloody dental casts.

I would scramble from the commodious recesses of the dumpster fuming because of these deposits, contributed by the neighborhood dentists and by the Latino bar across the street. The bar featured high-heeled, micro-mini-encased B-girls and a curbside roach-coach vending carnitas and tacos as its twin attractions. But all attempts to bring the Silverlake dumpster miscreants to justice were in vain.

trashy neighborhoods two: silverlake

I took the daily tides of the trash ecosystem even more personally when I moved into my house on Ethelyne Street in Silverlake. Every day a new deposit of flotsam and jetsam would wash up from the flow of auto and pedestrian traffic. One day it would be the endless strands of broken cassette tapes, the next day the unwanted portions of multiple McDonald's Happy Meals. Each day brought with it a new sunrise, a new edition of the morning paper and a new scattering of bottles, cans and candy wrappers. Sometimes there were surprises, like the almost functioning engine left over from a curbside car repair, or the discarded "Lifelike Sex Toy" large enough to deserve a liability disclaimer. Unless I went out there each day to litter-pick, the front yard would end up looking like Woodstock the morning after.

When I bought the house, the yard still bore the last signs of the neighborhood's former identity as a locus for the party times of the late '70s and the early '80s that had receded in the face of the onslaught of AIDS. The former gay bar around the corner had become an AIDS service center. The notorious S/M bar at the bottom of Ethylene was now a neighborhood Latino church. I probably cleared a gallon bucket's worth of little, amber-brown bottles from the front yard, bottles that had been filled with amyl nitrate inhalant and used as aphrodisiacs for plein air frolicking. It made me wonder if there used to be a whole lot more bushes in the front yard.

trashy neighborhoods three: venice

Once I moved to Venice I was no longer the King of Trash. That title, on my new block, clearly belongs to Butch, a white-bearded former coal miner with most, but not all, of the teeth with which he was born. Butch rules the roost as manager of the building next door, whose dumpster I have an excellent view of from my dining room window. I have watched Butch finesse the trash to a fare-thee-well. The man is not above climbing into the bin and jumping up and down on the trash to squash it flat enough for the dumpster lid to close.

He always narrows his eyes when he curses the local fish restaurant, whose workers keep sneaking their reeking offal into the container. Twice daily, when Butch takes his supervisory constitutional around the block with his wife's vicious little Chihuahua, the dumpster lid is lifted and the contents are inspected for suspect, nontenement material. Woe betide the one who appropriates space for alien trash in that dumpster. Butch's management policy for the dumpster is, first, to immediately return the foreign items to their presumed owner (I know from personal experience that he doesn't always guess correctly, since he has mistakenly assumed that I was the felon in question more than once) and second, to ferret out any possible items of value that he himself or his tenants might need. There are times when Butch nabs the recyclable items out of the bin, though whether he sorts them to supplement his beer fund or simply to prevent alleyites from profiting from the loot I have not yet established.

It's natural for anyone who lives, as I do now, on an alley in Venice to be obsessed with trash. The alleys of Venice are a 24-hour open-air market for the deposit, the sorting, the trading in and the removal of refuse. Those who have fallen on hard times know that the alleys of Venice are paved with soda pop bottles and cardboard. These transactions are fostered by legislation designed to encourage recycling. Cans, bottles and paper products bring cash when traded in—not very much cash, but just enough help with the needs of the homeless and the poor, and often just enough to buy more booze or more drugs. Some trash can raiders specialize only in slips of paper with credit card account numbers, valuable data that can be fenced on Oceanfront Walk.

Trash-trading thrives here more so than most other places in Southern California because of the famous live-and-let-live attitudes of Venetians and the shelter offered by the beach. The sand here gives displaced people somewhere to live with more dignity and style than is possible in many other neighborhoods in Los Angeles. Day and night the rumble of shopping carts and the jingle-jangle of the tin cans they contain is heard in Milton Court alley, located between my building and the Rose of Sharon Manor on Rose Avenue.

The Rose of Sharon Manor is a two-story, covered-parking vintage 1974 building in a developer schlock—Mediterranean style. The stylistic overlay consists of a "Spanish lace" stucco finish, like the left-over epoxy when you take up linoleum, and a few clay tiles, throw in some aluminum slider windows and call it a day. Loathsome. Located to the north of my building it has a great view across Milton Court into my bedroom.

Tonight at seven o'clock, in the open garage of the Manor 25 feet from my house, four bedrolls will appear. The people who sleep on them will probably be the fifth or sixth generation of transient residents in the garage space since I moved here two years ago.

The drawing card for any back-alley forager is its trash containers. The tenement next door has a capacious dumpster while the Manor just has trash cans. The dumpster is the foraging receptacle of choice for alleyites since its size makes going through a large volume of trash easier. Dumpsters hold greater promise of larger and varied treasures than do mere trash cans. On the other hand, the Manor has the advantage of a roof over its trash cans in the form of covered, head-in parking. For the alleyites, this parking area has been the spot to take a leak, hang out, argue, drink, do drugs, change clothes and sleep at night. Lodging comes in the form of a two-and-a-half-foot wide, six-foot high concrete platform at the back of the garage. It is just low enough to allow clearance between a snoozing guest and the car bumpers that extend into the space. The longest term nighttime denizen of the garage was a broken-looking women with long dark hair, who swept up after herself every morning.

If I ever needed a reminder that not everyone has access to shelter who needs or wants it, all I had to do was to listen for her hacking, tubercular cough. Many of the homeless are out on the street mentally ill or alcohol and drug addicted thanks to cutbacks in California's social services. The Manor management (consisting of an elderly woman and her elderly Dalmatian, along with the personnel of the bootleg repair service that the landlord runs out of the basement) tends to leave the homeless alone.

At one point a homeless man was living in one of the left-over storage spaces under the stairs at my house until I put my stuff in the space and padlocked the door. At the time I had no idea I was sharing the house with him.

For about a year another homeless man, a mean drunk who accosted passersby and swore at them, lived in a derelict cottage that sits at the corner

The two conquering vehicles of alleydom: the dumpster and the shopping cart.

of Little Center Street and Milton Court, on the other side of my neighbor's driveway. Mean Drunk's speciality was to stand in the middle of Ocean Avenue and stick his arm out so that passing cars would have to move out of the way. Butch saw him get hit once. The accident broke Mean Drunk's arm. The motorist freaked out, but the impassive Butch sent him on his way, explaining to the guy that he was not responsible for the fact that old M D. liked to play a high-stakes game of chicken by lunging at passing cars.

Later M.D.'s cottage was taken over by someone I call Prince Val, a former dweller of the tenement. Butch arranged a special low-rent deal between Val and the landlord. Since the house was filled with junk Prince V. solved the problem by dumping it, load by load in various locations. Piles of it would appear overnight in the public parking lot at the corner, in front of his old tenement or stuffed into my garbage cans.

One of the low points in alley trashology was when Val put his Christmas tree out in the alley and set it on fire.

The alley has a human ecology of its own. Any vacuum is quickly filled. The current occupants of the garage happen to be meticulous. They arrive and depart at set hours. They have no shopping carts, and they do not leave large piles of possessions behind when they are not there. Nor do they have large crowds of hangers-on. For all practical purposes the garage might as well be a hotel room with a printed set of rules and a check-out time posted on the door. They limit their signs of occupation and their transgressions of private space in order not to jeopardize their right to continued night stays.

All of the alley nomads have not been such assiduous charm-school scholars, however. One scary, extra-tall guy (I would swear seven feet, easy) used to beat the crap out of his girlfriend in the alley, and, yes, we did call the cops when he did that. Many garage inmates brought in trash to sort from other places and ripped open and tossed out the contents of the assembled ranks of trash cans, thereby creating a cozy trash nest for themselves. As a sleep aid some of the inmates would partake of a little nightcap, shooting up, without always bothering to remove the syringe from their arms, before drifting off to slumberland.

The alley recyclers are there for economic reasons. The alley space functions as public space in the truest sense of the word—no one is excluded. The homeless who sleep in the garage across from me are just as much residents of the alley as I for whatever time they remain there, since for the nights they sleep there they are no less clear about where they are sleeping or what space they are inhabiting than I. Like sea gulls trailing a fishing ship, the garbage sorters fill the alley in greatest numbers just before the arrival of the city trash trucks on Tuesday mornings because the pickings are best then. At its high-water mark, the public space of the alley spreads to the parking lot of the tenement next door.

At other hours, on other days, the alley becomes the purview of beachgoers roller-blading, bicycling or walking, taking a shortcut to the beach. This use of space is determined by the weather: the hotter and sunnier the day, the greater the numbers of surf-seekers. At still other times the combination janitorial staff and hot appliance-repair business takes possession of the area.

During some periods, the alley has been dominated by rent-paying tenants of the Rose of Sharon Manor across the alley, in the short-lived honeymoon period of their initial occupancy. For a few weeks the happy new Manorites, flush with pride at their success in having scored beachside digs, brave the inhospitable alley environment. Against all reason and common sense, they actually use their balconies, water their plants and talk on the phone outdoors.

I give them six months, maximum, before they give up and move, leaving the blank sliding-glass doors and white-box interiors of their apartments behind. The alley always wins.

official trash

In my alley as elsewhere in this vast metropolis, the effects can be felt of the City of Los Angeles' elaborate, officially sanctioned recycling program. The program comes complete with specially engineered but temperamental garbage trucks that occasionally come apart and kill hapless motorists, trash bins to fit the trucks and little plastic recycling containers for the more precious cargoes of metal and glass. Each of the garbage cans is individually numbered, a marvel of obsessive bureaucratic thinking.

Crack cocaine may be sold with impunity on the streets of Los Angeles, and vast disparities may exist in educational, social and professional opportunity between different neighborhoods and demographic groups. Yet somewhere the bureaucratic geniuses who came up with this brazenly utopian idea are contentedly counting their numbered trash cans being flung into the dumpster trucks, like sheep jumping a rail, as they settle into a deep, happy slumber.

In a sense, being issued pedigreed trash cans seems entirely un-American. It's as though Los Angelenos couldn't be trusted with their personal and household hygiene and had to be issued official toilet brushes, dental floss and clean underwear. By requiring that the trash cans be placed in the street, the trashnocrats have eliminated tens of thousands of parking spaces at one fell swoop, altering the delicate parking ecosystem in neighborhoods across the city without the slightest thought to where the cars displaced by the officially placed containers are supposed to go.

The new trash cans are made of a soulless, black-brown plastic, their stylistic inspiration perhaps the Ford Taurus, as though they had been sculpted to symbolize low wind-resistance, meant to be envisioned speeding fast enough to break the sound barrier. The regimented rows of regulation-issue garbage cans lack the sangfroid of the traditional rubbish containers they have replaced. It is difficult to imagine properly unkempt alley cats sitting on top of them yowling at the full moon. If you've seen one official City of Los Angeles—issue trash can, you've seen them all.

In real life much of this elaborate civic infrastructure designed to accommodate trash is simply ignored. Recycling in Venice is not done by the city. There is nothing left to recycle by the time the city trucks arrive. The bright-yellow, plastic recycling bins have been scoured clean by squadrons of can, and bottle pickers. The recycling program is exemplary of the ways in which government officials and the public increasingly demand a perfect world that will not harm anyone in any conceivable way under any conceivable scenario. It is a perfection so demanding of ordinary citizens in the pursuit of ordinary tasks that most of us simply ignore the perfect rules altogether. Thus the political bureaucracy of trash and the barter economy of trash coexist, side by side.

the economy of trash

The trash of Venice is a medium of exchange between income groups. It acts as a privatized form of welfare. More often than not, Venetians who have decided that the time has come to part ways with a garment lay it down gently on top of a trash container. They may even go to considerable effort to display their offerings enticingly, freshly laundered, folded and pressed. Once upon a time these cast-off garments might have been ferried to a thrift store, but my neighbor now believes that she is being a good Samaritan when she places these offerings on top of my trash can. To me, this placing of charitable offerings is a breach of my territorial rights and a subsidy of the alternative alley economy that I do not appreciate. Hurling her offerings into the depths of my trash can gives me a momentary sense of control.

When a housed alleyite neatly lines up a row of empty bottles against a wall or carefully folds a newly laundered but worn blanket on top of, but not in, the garbage can he or she becomes part of a transaction in which something that no longer has value to one economic class becomes valuable all over again to another economic class. The excess or unwanted remnants of the housed alleyitesbecome the life blood of the nomadic alleyites. It is a currency exchange created by a slight geographical repositioning of the currency in question: i.e., rubbish and castoffs. Transference outside the cell wall of the dwelling releases this currency into the veins of the alley economy.

As the sun sets over the Pacific just below the palm tree a cheerful, whistling alleyite rummages through a dumpster.

From time to time, alleyites attempt to find new uses for found objects. One midwinter day, at dusk, I arrived home to find an alley gypsy intently refashioning a large, periwinkle-blue ceramic vase. He was pounding the vase on the tarmac, methodically knocking off fragments of its lip. As he worked he would stop and hold up the vase to appraise its progress. When he was through removing the lip, he began to rotate the vase on the pavement, attempting to grind off the now vestigial remains of the lip. He must have judged the final product a failure, for he left it sitting there in the tenement parking lot.

the territory of trash

The deposit of trash is a territorial power grab. If someone leaves trash in a location he or she lays claim to that location in the same way that an animal does by leaving its scent along a trail. If someone throws a bottle over my fence just after he or she has polished off the last of a Brew 102 or bottle of Ripple, that person has made a claim on my yard. By the time there are substantial amounts of wrappers, newspapers and other debris swirling around my yard I have begun to lose control of that territory.

At one point, when the tenement harbored its party-eartiest crew, there was not much difference between the trash crop I had to contend with in Silverlake and the harvest I was finding on my doorstep at the beach. Party ringleader Ed would chain his bike and those of his friends through my chain-link fence so that the handlebars stuck about six inches, into my walkway at the border of my property. This and the trash that spilled out of Ed's basket and blew under the fence onto what I will charitably call my lawn—made me mad.

One day, when I was in a bad mood, I snapped. I walked next door, grabbed the bike and shook it as hard as I could, so that all of the crushed cans fell out. I shouted up at his window, "Don't chain your Goddamn bike through the fence!" What really made me mad is that he had clipped a hole the size of a cantaloupe through the chain link in order to put the chain through. Chain link has been a sore point with me dating back to my Ethelyne Avenue house. Its chain link fence eventually fell over because the neighborhood kids played on it so much and the neighbors' cars ran into it so often.

Trash is a visible record of occupation in the alley, where greater garbage-can pilfering and greater numbers of homeless leave behind greater amounts of trash, as well as a predictor of the activity level in the near future by the alley gypsies. The presence or absence of large amounts of trash is a clear sign of what kind of social order is prevailing at that time. The moments when the alley seems an urban dystopia, adrift in overturned cans and overflowing shopping carts, are precisely the moments when the gypsy alleyite population grows largest and most active.

Along the alley, house and yard are recognized by all as zones of privatized domesticity. Placing items in the alley transforms them from off-limits, as part of the household, to fair game for the alley public at large. The edges where private space meets the alley are sometimes defined by small architectural elements—a set of two or three steps, a stub of half-height wall or an overhanging balcony.

But these boundaries are situational. An unlocked yard with no trash cans is likely to remain untouched by outsiders for years at a time, even if it holds a relatively transportable item of some minimal value, such as a Big Wheels tricycle. Placement of a trash can within that yard changes the equation, making it far more likely that alley nomads will violate the privatized space, compelled by the need to sift through the trash for recyclable prizes. Any space that functions as an adjunct part of the alley because of the presence of trash may become de facto public space.

Because the alley space is not officially defined, surveilled or regulated, illegal activities inevitably occur there. Sometimes the alley space is used as a latrine, sometimes not. There are waves of public drug use, and then the drug use dies down. During the tail end of the tenement's wild times, the space of the alley became a kind of annex to the building. There have been instances of theft in the alley, especially from the trucks of workmen who have tool chests or bicycles locked to them. The alley's asphalt paving is often dusted with the emerald crumbs of auto windows shattered from break-ins.

There were a few times over a period of several months when I would bound down the steps from my house to the alley to find a virtual convention of shopping carts. A selection of purloined and salvaged wares would be laid out in front of my garage door surrounded by a crowd of appraising alleyites, the alley counterpart of a gaggle of suburban shoppers comparing notes at a yard sale.

The two categories of residents, alleyites and non-alleyites, are not mutually exclusive. In the space of the alley, mediation between economic castes and between legal and illegal activities occur. There are housed recyclers, homeless recyclers and homeless who do not recycle. Of the homeless some are drug addicts and some are not. Of the drug addicts some are homeless and some are not. Individuals fall into different categories at different times in their lives. Venice is not a place where boundaries are always clear, where categories are set in stone.

Sometimes the gypsies carouse with the tenement dwellers in the alley; at other times they sleep with the tenement dwellers in their rooms. There are also fleeting networks of association among the people who live in the houses and apartments that face the alley—associations that sometimes include the alley gypsies.

The alley space is not a static topography so much as it is an social tidal zone, in which those with less privilege and less legal and financial buttress for their right to be there float through more quickly than those who have more assurance in these matters.

In that liquid rhythm of the alley as shifting private/public space, trash is one of the elements that mark the narrative history and uses of the space. In that sense trash isn't really "thrown away" so much as transformed in its role. Like it or not, the discards continue to have value as determinants of behavior and symbols of territorial occupation.

**Westside Pavilion, 10800 West Pico Boulevard, Ranch Park,
Los Angeles, 1985.** Jerde Partnership, Sussman Prejza signage
and color palette. For Westfield Holdings Ltd. of Australia. Each
generation of the shopping mall building type introduced new
demands of size, imagery and accommodation of program.
Packaging the mall in a way that communicated the attraction of
the goods and the shopping experience within is required for high-
end developments.

the typology of building production

*The requirements of professional empire building apart, the demand
that all buildings should become works of architecture (or the reverse) is
strictly offensive to common sense.*

—Colin Rowe and Fred Koetter, *Collage City*

*Nearly all items in human landscapes reflect culture in some way.
There are almost no exceptions. Furthermore, most items in the human
landscape are no more and no less important than other items—in
terms of their role as clues to culture.*

—Pierce Lewis. "Axioms for Reading the Landscape"

how do those of us inculcated in architectural culture coexist with the
world around us, which largely ignores the values and rules of high-art architecture? What is the relationship most of us have to the actual built environment around us? How do the buildings that we see from the freeway, the
developer housing, the blank-faced speculative office buildings and the shop-

ping malls get designed? How do they effect the quality of our lives? Those are primary questions at the turn of the century.

Building production is a term for the sum total of the built response to human needs. A building-production typology is the roll call of categories of buildings, land uses and activity types that answer the needs of a community. It is the complete listing of additions to the man-made physical world, understood not only in terms of appearance, but in terms of purpose: why individual buildings came into being and the role each plays as part of a consumerist society.

Not all buildings address the full range of architectural concerns. Some buildings may be about revealing the means of their construction, and others about the masterly handling of light and space. Still others may be concerned with beautiful ornamentation or with ingenious methods of prefabrication. Architecture, in its broadest sense, allows for both the high-art building as well as for more populist work with a wider audience. In the system of building production one is not judged as being better than the

Changes in style and building form often occur simultaneously in the development of a building type. Residential packaging evolves in pre- and post-1980 Houston. Pop mansard on the left c. 1970s and early 1900s traditional on the right.

other; both are subject to judgment according to their own ground rules. The ability to communicate to the public, to symbolize, embody and create emotions and experiences, has largely fallen to consumerist architecture—most populist architecture could be judged as consumerist architecture, architecture that must perform, must contribute to the experience of patronizing the building, in order to function economically.

The notion of type is primary to the study of the built environment. Building type can be defined as a set of programmatic and morphological attributes that are shared by a set of buildings. In order to constitute a type, a group of buildings must share enough programmatic determinants of form that each one effectively calls up and represents all the others. The notion of type, in a sense, depends on a program with such specific needs that it puts its stamp on each building of its kind. Building types such as grain elevators and water towers are products of their storage functions. Theaters (even movie theaters, before the advent of the multiplex cinema) are marked by the tower of their proscenium and by their projecting marquees.

Architectural culture tends to overvalue the importance of the individual architect in determining the nature and design of buildings and to underplay all other factors. The notion of type has the virtue of emphasizing the forces of creation that buildings have in common, of finding links across time and space. In addition, the notion of type allows buildings to be seen as a hybrid of style, program, economics and construction practices. It takes into consideration the economic incentives for the building's construction, the method of its construction and use for which it is intended. Only then is the role of the architect considered.

As Pierce F. Lewis wrote: "The fact that all items are equally important emphatically does not mean that they are equally easy to study and understand . . . Sometimes the commonest things are the hardest to study . . . "

The most common elements of what Lewis calls the cultural landscape and what I call building production—motels, tilt-slab warehouses, shopping malls, parking structures and parking lots, ice vending machines and concrete-block warehouses—are the most difficult to see because they present the problem of never having been encountered for the first time, and certainly never in a reified, honorific or even especially focused way. They are so ubiquitous that they present a conflict between the role every designer has as an inhabitant of the world, using and accepting that world as he or she finds it, and the role of the designer as changer of the world, imposing upon it some degree of new order.

A typology of building production elaborates the roster of types, listing what representatively houses the activities found in American towns in the present. It describes and analyzes these building types, types that often remain outside architectural culture, from car washes to tract housing; from hybrid hotel/casino/entertainment attraction complexes to self-storage facilities, mobile home parks and speculative office parks. It also includes structures that exist without official permission, such as shelters built by the homeless and buildings that have been modified without benefit of permit, such as garages converted into extra dwelling units. Some land uses may not

Alfa Ital car garage, Silverlake, Rowena Avenue and Rokeby Street, is an example of a utilitarian building, a category of building production in which there is no attempt to incorporate any symbolic or cultural content because any attempt to do so would not produce additional revenue for the building. Its form is governed by the demands of its building type.

be represented by a building type, such as the temporary special event night-club or the garment workshop.

It is important to categorize the sum total of recent building-production types. Because most architectural history and criticism is devoted to high-art architectural production, the backdrop of overall building production within which this architectural production is set, the larger physical environment, does not receive attention sufficient to its predominance. When this broader built environment does receive attention, it is often in a trivializing or patronizing fashion that indicates a lack of interest in attempting to understand the factors that bring the non-high-art sectors of building production into being.

It is simply impossible to avoid having a relationship to the world around you. In the United States, at the turn of the millennium that world includes shopping malls, fast food, auto-dominated environments and segments of architectural production that involve popularly understood iconography.

As Ian Chambers explained in *Popular Culture: The Metropolitan Experience*, "The previous authority of culture, once respectfully designated with a capital C, no longer has an exclusive hold on meaning. 'High culture' becomes just one more subculture, one more option, in our midst." He continues, "Today, the metaphysical separation between idea and material, between original and derivative, production and reproduction, taste and commerce, culture and industry has collapsed. The struggle over 'Culture' may still be staged—at least in the universities, learned journals, art galleries, official cultural agencies, 'serious' literature, cinema, journalism and television, between these assumed oppositions. But popular culture has bypassed the question. It is popular culture—its tastes, practices and aesthetics—that today dominates the urban scene, offering sense where traditional culture can usually only see nonsense."

Architects and designers need to know about the context in which they build, and about the companion structures outside of conventional high-art architectural practice, including those not generated by the rulesof, or for the typical clients of, high-art architecture. Planners and urban designers also need to understand the actual fabric that makes up the built environment in the United States. Historic preservationists need to have a sense of the overall character of building production if they are to assign significance to individual buildings as exemplary of a formerly common building type that is now becoming rare through the rapid pace of commercial obsolescence.

In contemporary American society, cultural meaning is largely created through consumerism, through the means of consumption and production. High-art architecture tends to be honorific and possesses a hierarchical value system that honors places and situations associated with money, power, prestige, fame and conventional architectural culture. This latter culture ranks architects by aesthetic creativity, commodifying those at the top of the profession. The issues on the table are the architect's ability to master space, structure, light, programmatic organization and the making of objects. This architecture requires a great deal of effort, a scale of effort that most people either simply can't afford or don't want to pay for even if they could.

Architects and designers are products of the cultures of architecture and design. Their values, beliefs and preferences tend to direct their awareness quite naturally to the sector of building production that most validates these cultures. As a result, most architects are trained to focus on certain building types, such as the museum, the private "custom" home and the government office, as being more important than other building types, such as concrete-block automotive repair shops or corner minimalls. Consequently the built environment is selectively understood in terms of the ability of architectural culture to meet its own aesthetic standards, rather than in terms of the different roles that individual building types play, or what makes up the actual fabric of American communities.

This book focuses on building types that often remain outside architectural culture because of cultural viewpoint and or financial limitations. Building types such as the freestanding doughnut shop or the roadside convenience store are part of people's everyday lives. Land uses such as the homeless occupation of public space and street vending are expressive parts of the city. Structures such as the residential subdivision and speculative office buildings form the fabric of contemporary America. None of these have received sufficient critical attention from the point of view of typological study, nor have the economic factors that bring them into existence been are sufficiently studied. Users of the as-built environment, such as warehouse-supermarket consumers, laundromat users, the employees at tilt-slab warehouses and the residents and caretakers of single-story post-World War II nursing homes should have the building types that they use on a daily basis considered a legitimate part of the built landscape, not because of aesthetic merit, but because these building types are integral parts of daily life and American culture.

For example, why not consider residential building types—such as traditional, center-hall tenements; mobile homes; garden apartments; courtyard apartments; high-rise apartments; row houses; town houses; detached single-family houses duplexes and triplexes—and classify them according to factors such as provision of parking, site-plan building form and footprint;

Modern office towers such as these in downtown Los Angeles are often so general in their design that their primary identity is that of representing a building type.

unit floor plan; relationship to the outdoors; morphology; economic strata
and level of amenity; relationship to the automobile; lack of parking; surface
parking; exposed, tuck-under, ground-level building parking; semisubter-
ranean, subterranean or multilevel subterranean. In many cases, style is
the final element of the typological classification—as in the popular ranch
house or the Tiki-garden apartment house.

An example of this kind of analysis is Richard Longstreth's study of
department stores and retail centers in *City Center to Regional Mall*.
Similarly, the department store can be considered as a set of types according
to its location in a conventional downtown, a strip center, an unenclosed
shopping center, an enclosed shopping center or an urban entertainment
district; its floor plan, number of stories and amount and placement of window and display areas; and its relationship to the automobile. For a movie
theater, the same issues of relationship to site, such as location in a mall or
on a conventional street, and relationship to the automobile would also
apply, along with other factors such as the building's original identity as a
single-screen house or multiplex, the scale of the mythic overlay attempted,
the presence or lack of a symbolic tower, the expression of the backstage and
the incorporation of other uses (such as stores) into the theater building or
the incorporation of the theater into another building (such as an office).

Ultimately, studying this typology illuminates the changing character of
the American landscape and creates a better understanding of its constituent
parts. The goal of a typology is to clarify the relationship that exists between
individual citizens and the culture of American consumerism.

There is still much to be discovered about the role building types and land
uses play in the contemporary American community. For example, the
recently published "Preserving the Recent Past" conference proceedings
edited by Deborah Slaton and Rebecca Shiffer points toward an unfilled
need for clearly established criteria for judging, observing and classifying the
architecture of the recent past. Other applications include planning, especially in rethinking categories of land-use zoning; architectural history, particularly vernacular history; and the teaching of design in architectural
schools, as an aid in understanding actual urban context.

I have already posited various categories of building production, with
their relationship to consumerism as the ordering principle. The next step
is to develop a system of classification for building production that encom-

passes the full range of contemporary building types by their function and economic purpose as well.

The creation of a fully fleshed-out typology of building production must be based on field observation and the use of primary sources. It is better to sort through the as-found built environment to find sites, and then research them, than to proceed from sites of previously determined historical or architectural interest and then to research them on a site-by-site basis.

In the long run, a typology of building production is intended to illuminate the contemporary urban landscape in a way that is redemptive, one that allows for creative reinterpretation on the part of individual designers, architects and citizens, so that we can react to consumer culture and appropriate it rather than just being passive consumers of it—or being overpowered by it.

The Mayfair Market, 8330 Santa Monica Boulevard, West Hollywood, is an example of a once common but now vanishing building type, the glass-fronted modernistic 1960s supermarket. There is no preservation constituency for these markets. Ron Cleveland, Leach Cleveland Assoc., 1966, for the Arden Group. It was remodeled in a Mediterranean Revival style in 1999.

duty and the beast

the representative and the lovable
in the preservation of the recent past

If you keep an animal around as a pet you generally do so for one of two reasons. Either you think it's cute and friendly or you feel it represents something important about the universe, a life force that transcends and complements human identity. Similarly, preservationists want to keep a building around for one of two reasons. Some preservationists cherry-pick individual buildings or entire districts from the past that they think are the most accomplished, the most closely associated with celebrity power or cultural meaning, or have innate value as finely crafted material artifacts. Historic preservation is often employed as a way of preserving the most highly evolved, highly accomplished material record of human accomplishment. Others value buildings that are considered to embody a transcendent and enduring memory that accurately conveys a sense of what life used to be like.

If a broad enough representation of buildings from the past are preserved, they will effectively transmit historical information to the present, or so the argument runs. However, in order to be an accurate record of the past, the buildings preserved must represent a cross-section of uses by a cross-section of economic, social and ethnic groups. So it is one thing to think of what to preserve in a 19th-century Hawaiian fishing village, and quite another to make the decision to preserve the landmarks of the exurban past. In the first example, there will be probably be widespread political agreement on preserving the different types of buildings that made up the town, because of their small scale and their value as aesthetic objects. Much more problematic is the decision about how to handle the preservation of a suburban town's first minimall. Thinking of what will be worth preserving in the immediate present and immediate past is a good exercise for sensitizing ourselves to the values we actually bring to historic preservation. It is obviously politically more feasible to preserve monuments of the celebrated and the wealthy. Large, impressive buildings with elaborate craftsmanship and fine materials provide accessible, vicarious "Lifestyles of the Rich and Famous" *Architectural Digest* entertainment value. Given the choice between a tour of preserved San Joaquin Valley migrant labor camps and one of ranch houses of the same valley, most people would get on the land-baron bus. After all if one is going to time travel, why be poor and powerless when you can be rich and powerful? Reformers like Dolores Hadyen have been invaluable in creating a broader and more accurate understanding of site specific history. However, insisting that people eschew relics of the ruling class in favor of sites of social strife, class conflict and progress in workers' rights is a little like translating the advice of nutritionists into a campaign against red meat and candy. There is typically a conflict between what is representative of a historical period or way of life and what is most attractive both to the general public and to preservationists.

There is an additional conflict when it comes to preserving consumerist architecture. The pace of change in consumer culture means that consumers long outlive buildings. Most consumerist buildings have no hope of making it to monument status because they die such an early death. The shopping center that is bulldozed at 25 years never makes it to a hundred. In Los Angeles, building types like the 1950s coffee shop and the glass-fronted Modernistic supermarket of the 1960s are already rapidly vanishing.

As if it were not hard enough to preserve buildings that have a clear aesthetic appeal, like the '50s coffee shops, it is even more difficult to preserve the kind of commercial in-fill structures that were also built at this time. Consequently, it will be difficult to reconstruct the 1950s and 1960s from the built environment. To do so will probably require the aid of museum exhibits, books and videos. And even if some buildings are individually preserved, they won't manage to represent the building production of the era, because a building's meaning is inevitably distorted by being pulled out of context. Ultimately, the most that can be hoped for, and this often quite enough, is that a building can reveal something about itself—about its manner of fabrication, the uses for which it was built and the manner in which it was inhabited.

Only a limited range of buildings will be salvaged from the recent past because inevitably some preservationists will conflate historic and typological significance with nostalgia and formal aesthetics in evaluating this architecture. Neither the identity of a building as a cultural or sociological artifact nor its significance in economic terms plays nearly as great a role in the likelihood of a building's preservation as its charm as a physical artifact. Historic preservation mediates between the preservation of history and the recording of everyday life and the needs of a fast-paced consumer economy that thrives on novelty and planned obsolescence. It is time to acknowledge the historical importance of the ordinary, the representative, as well as the extraordinary, the landmark. Deciding whether or not to preserve ordinary buildings is a separate, political decision from that of simply acknowledging their status as historical artifact.

In a consumer society the means of production, advertising, distribution and marketing of goods have a life of their own. Just as mechanization invariably drives out less mechanized means of production, commercially advertised and marketed commodities drive out commodities that are neither advertised nor marketed. This happens not because of some conspiracy, but rather because these forces set new benchmarks of profitability or productivity that competitors must equal or fall by the wayside. Similarly, newer products and services drive out older products and services, frequently making the services that certain buildings housed obsolete. Consumerist buildings are products of change, proof of change. Attempting to preserve a commercial building without the activity that it originally housed becomes nearly impossible when consumer businesses are part of a complete package of signage, interiors and symbolic appurtenances that must be changed nearly as often as a diaper on a new-born baby.

In most towns there is no possibility of preserving the last pre-fab metal gas station from the 1930s, let alone the first one-story convalescent home in town from the 1950s, or the first tilt-slab warehouse from the 1960s. If billboards are eliminated, no one is likely to mount a campaign to save the first one. If the last of a series of concrete-block electric-transformer stations from the days of a suburb's first major expansion are to be ripped down, no one is likely to protest. So the preservation of the recent past will always be laundered—a beauty contest rather than a contest of meaning or typicality.

The only way to be clear about the process is to admit right off the bat that it is impossible to physically preserve a representative swath of contemporary consumer culture. Such a position puts one in the politically untenable position of asking to save immediate consumerist relics, as Richard Longstreth argued in his celebrated October 1993 "Forum of the Society of Architectural Historians Committee on Preservation. "

However illustrative of economic and social trends or of the history of a building types a building may be, it is impossible to practice historic preservation in the conventional sense with consumerist architecture. It occupies too much valuable real estate and represents too high a level of capital investment to preserve merely because it will help constitute a complete record of a time and place. And, in fact, given just how nasty much post-World War II building production has been, who would want to retain the first slump-stone post office in a community, or the first sprawling horizontal-plan high school, unless there were additional layers of historic significance or aesthetic merit. Ronald Lee Fleming sums up the argument for restraint in preserving the recent past.

> What about the increased plethora of mass-produced items, from sheets of asphalt on that invasive parking lot in a 1930s neighborhood shopping center to the stand of telephone poles around the village green, to the thousands of Holiday Inn signs (designed by the chairman's wife) or the McDonald's and Burger Kings that increasingly bracket the most culturally and historically interesting part of our cities? Whether such artifacts are evidence of our early infatuation with outdoor electric lighting or telephonic communication, or vital documentation of the strategy of corporate commodification of special districts (or theme parks in current argot), doesn't the sheer plethora of their numbers on the landscape tells us something about making choices? After restoring the first surviving McDonald's with the huge golden arches (already done by the corporation, thank you) or enshrining a Holiday Inn sign in the Smithsonian (as the Venturis did in the 1970s), do we really need to keep every iteration of the corporate visual rip-off of the American landscape as a memorial to our failure to do effective land use planning that would keep our centers vital and our countryside visible?

There are many cases in which it could readily be established that a building was the last of its type remaining, or one of the first of its type constructed. To claim that the first building in a town to be isolated from other buildings by a parking lot is not historic is ridiculous. It just happens not to be the kind of history of which most people are particularly fond.

At this point it might be useful to turn to the world of conventional architectural criticism to contrast the grounds by which it values buildings against the grounds adopted by fans of roadside and consumerist architecture.

The small multiple storefront minimall, Koreatown, mid-1980s. A building type often considered too prosaic, too ubiquitous and too ugly to consider to have any of its earliest examples eligible for preservation.

Within the conventional culture of architecture, merit is determined in much the same way that merit might be determined for a work of art—by evaluating its vocabulary of forms, its articulation, level of detail, massing, materials, colors and so on. In the study of architectural history much credit has been given for the creation of new vocabularies of architecture, for the creation of sets of rules that have a complex or demanding internal consistency. If one were to make a conventional definition of high-art architecture it would be as follows: architecture that has a low degree of literal reference to non-Modern architecture as it is conventionally understood, a rigorous abstraction that may involve the subjugation of structure to a formal abstraction or the actual exposure of structure, that emphasizes the abstract play of form.

Then there is the rest of building production. My argument is that selecting between systems of formal abstraction is not the dominant force in the gen-

Car wash, Hollywood, built c. 1960s. There has been at least one preservation battle over a car wash in Los Angeles, but car washes generally are of a building type that is not always included on the preservation roll call.

eration of form for the bulk of building production. The bulk of building production is economically determined, and one of the most important factors is
its involvement in the integrated process of production/marketing/advertising
consumption. In this sense we are considering the building as a product, as a
commodity, and we are considering the building itself as an integral part of the
marketing, consumer provoking image making whole economy.

We are therefore considering building production in a different light
from that in which it is conventionally considered within the culture of architecture. The building production we are considering has been designed
from the point of view of what its user will think of it, how a consumer will
react to it and how she or he will behave in relation to it. Unlike high art
architecture, these buildings are not necessarily designed to express indi-
viduality or generate the maximum amount of formal innovation.

In this sense we are considering architecture *very* differently from art, as a
multidisciplinary, multimodal intersection of the demands of everyday life, the
economic needs of a consumer society and a building's actual experiential
function and identity. Members of a common building type share common
functional needs: these become as important in determining form as outright
formal distinctions. This is a complicated way of saying that we are judging
architecture as an applied art; architecture as it is received and as it is conceived.
This is a way of saying architecture as a form of social and economic exchange.

A new set of rules for building production must help judge a building within the internal value system of consumerist architecture and its users.

These rules would place less emphasis on formalism and a greater
emphasis on the ability of the work of architecture to be accessible to its public. They would ask: Does it inspire emotions? a sense of familiarity? of
adventure? Does it allow the user to participate in comprehensible experience, such as a trip to the moon or a ride in a covered wagon? How effectively
does the building serve its function? For example, if it's a retail building, how
effectively does it move the merchandise? These rules would place a value on
the degree to which a building helps its user make sense of both the building and the community in which the building is located.

Outside of the realm of high-art architecture, these rules would allow us
to judge a building on its own terms. For example, a building type like the
stucco box apartments of the 1950s had certain well-defined graphic and
morphological features. Does the stucco box in question make good use of

its courtyard for the individual units? Do its window surrounds and surface stucco treatments make an effective graphic composition?

Finally, for these rules, one would adopt the same broad definition of merit that one would for any building, even high-art ones. This would include: sequence of spaces, experiential qualities, use of light and maximization of carefully thought-out amenities for the users in terms of balancing, budget, building code, program and site.

A common motivation for many people to involve themselves in the study of roadside commercial or populist architecture is the desire on the part of individual observers to deal with the relationship of this building production to their own personal history as a record of their own lives and experiences. Younger preservationists who are the children of consumer culture, who have grown up in an era when mass-media culture was in full force, harbor affection for influences that shaped them. For them, making distinctions about what is good and bad or distinguishing between different levels of architectural production is seen as unbearably arcane, and outdated, as the calling card or the typewriter. There is an out-and-out reveling in the lack of distinction, in the omnivorous insistence that all distinctions of categorical merit have been breached and obliterated. There is a joy in bringing an equivalent level of analysis to all levels of cultural production, regardless of the complexity of the effort or the sophistication that went into it.

With this determinedly enthusiastic approach, even meaningful distinction and categories of building production are blurred.

What is lost in this valuation is the important relationship of the artifact to its makers and users. The work of trained architects and more properly vernacular work ends up being lumped together merely because they both have the same amount of moxie, oomph and sex appeal in the mind of the observer. The fact that the architect is working inside the traditions and conventions of architectural culture and the building designer without architectural training working outside them is ignored—as is building type, the building technology of the times, changes in building codes such as parking requirements and changes in patterns of daily life.

Just as commercial vernacular architecture has builders and designers like any other category of building production, so does it have a set of reasons to exist—economic, social and functional, not merely aesthetic. Before a building from the recent past can even be evaluated for preservation, it also needs to be placed within the full spectrum of building production, a task that is not as self-evident as it might seem.

Following is a list of criterion for evaluating recent everyday building production.

1. Is the building designed by an architect who had full control over the design? In that case the building may not even be commercial vernacular; it may instead simply be part of a deviant high-art tradition that shares the expressionism and directness of consumerist architecture. In that case the building actually belongs to a neglected part of the conventional study of architecture.

2. Who called the shots? Was the building designed by an architect under duress from a strong-minded client who conceived of his or her building in a vernacular way? Or was the building designed either by someone who did not have the conventional design-training of an architect or by an architect choosing not to play by those rules? Any of these situations could result in a building being categorized as commercial vernacular.

Finally, having issued exhaustive warnings about the dangers of aestheticism, I will propose a system of aesthetic characteristics that might make a non-high-art building valuable and thereby eligible for preservation. Buildings that have not been canonically anointed may be valued because:

1. They bend shape and meld the conventional rules in ways that give a pleasant frisson of violation and naughtiness to those observers who have cultivated an awareness of these rules.

2. They are so lovably inept in their handling of rules of composition, massing, detailing or formal references that they inspire fondness, of the same patronizing type that is inspired by watching a monkey attempt to play the piano. They constitute a form of architectural ignorance. They are notable for their blithe disregard of the usual care in detailing and complexity of composition that a trained architect would invest in the same building.

3. Their economy of means is so great that they consistently substitute a graphic solution for a conventional, holistic, architectonic one.

4. The building is a aesthetic success on its own terms.

Ultimately, a dualism that says consumerist architecture has more power to communicate with the public and high-art architecture represents a higher level of intentionality and training is unsatisfactory. Rather, both are products of a set of design determinants and must be judged on that basis. Preserving the recent past should be a two-step process in which a building is first evaluated for aesthetic, historical and typological merit, all considered within the system of building production. Only after that evaluation has been favorably made can the separate process be undertaken of deciding whether or not to preserve the building. That is an entirely political decision that must take into account the popularity, quality and aesthetic character of the building and its ability to accommodate new, economically viable uses that will not obliterate the traits that deemed it worthy of preservation.

you are what you buy

the consumerist imperative in american building production

building production

The best way to know what a building is and what a building means is to understand the forces that brought it into being. The concept of "building production" is an organizing system based on the idea of economic output and on physical facts, rather than on the hierarchical aesthetic priorities of architecture.

Conventional architectural criticism asks, What is best? Consumerist architectural criticism asks, Why is that there?

Classifying the built environment as building production is not a perfect approach for every structure out there. It is merely a tool for looking at buildings by means of a system of appraisal that is weighted differently than that conventionally used in the culture of architecture.

In classifying buildings by intent I have devised five very broad categories: Vanguard, Corporate/Institutional, Consumerist, Utilitarian and Personal Fantasy. This essay is largely concerned with Consumerist architecture but I have included definitions of all of the other categories, below, in order to clarify what Consumerist architecture is, and is not.

consumerist categories of building production

To differing degrees, the economic success of these three categories of building production depends on the designer's success in creating an image that reinforces marketability, whether of the space itself or of the products or services it houses.

VANGUARD

DEFINITION: Buildings that are presented as art.

FUNCTION: To serve as test cases for the development of new formal vocabularies and uses of materials. Vanguard buildings fulfill the need of the person buying or using them to patronize a name-brand architect, to get a distinctive product and to have their sense of aesthetic sophistication and discernment validated. This category of building production sets itself apart by being opposed to commonplace attitudes about architectural type, iconography and style.

CHARACTERISTICS: A priority is placed on the architectonic relationship of the parts of the building to the whole, and the coining of a system of abstraction that subsumes the identity and functions of the building.

EXAMPLES: Open the pages of any architectural magazine.

CORPORATE/INSTITUTIONAL

DEFINITION: The work of large offices designing large projects for large firms or government entities.

FUNCTION: These buildings package large, flexible, neutral spaces in styled containers.

CHARACTERISTICS: Blankness, impersonality, in human scale and a tendency, especially in Late Modern projects, to design buildings at the level of the object as a whole, as a packaged sculptural object.

EXAMPLES: Government buildings, office parks and towers.

CONSUMERIST

DEFINITION: Buildings that are extensions of the products they sell inside.

FUNCTION: These buildings sell the products associated with them and either complete or augment the experience of acquiring these products. Consumer buildings frequently borrow images from times, places and activities other than those occurring at their site.

EXAMPLES: The mansarded condominium that uses the mansard to convey social status, the Tiki apartment house whose mock Polynesian features symbolize escape to a tropical island, the theme restaurant in the style of a Spanish hacienda, that symbolizes the food served within.

non consumerist categories of building production

The economic success of these categories of building production does not depend on the ability to create a marketable image.

UTILITARIAN

DEFINITION: Buildings that are engineered rather than conceived of as architectural design, that consist only of those components absolutely necessary for the building to perform its functions.

FUNCTION: To provide a physical plant for the production of goods, services or other utilitarian functions.

CHARACTERISTICS: The form of the building, which conceals the activities within, is determined largely by economic expediency. It may simply be a shell or these activities may partially or wholly determine the form of the design.

EXAMPLES: There are two major kinds of utilitarian building: straightforward building, such as concrete-block garages or metal self-storage sheds, and buildings with complex technological functions that must be expressed in their form, such as oil refineries, dams, grain elevators and bridges.

PERSONAL FANTASY

DEFINITION: Buildings commissioned, built or designed by their owners for their own pleasure.

CHARACTERISTICS: These buildings are the direct expression of personal fantasy in architectural form, a variant of Folk Art. They may or may not follow conventional rules of architectural composition or organization and are as likely to borrow from vernacular building practices as from architectural history. They are credited for reasons of personal fulfillment and expression, rather than for participation in a consumer economy.

EXAMPLES: The Watts Towers, Grandma Prisbey's Bottle Village.

Post-1933 new Chinatown between Broadway, Hill and Yale, north of College Street, downtown Los Angeles. This 1938 section of Chinatown, like the hispanic-themed Olvera Street, is one of the precursors of the themed shopping mall/urban entertainment center. The architecture of Chinatown is an integral part of the experience that attracts consumers. The theming of the architecture stimulates sales of the similarly themed merchandise.

consumerism

I have classified buildings according to their relationship to consumerism, since in a "free market" economy, consumerism is the single most important social and economic organizing force. The distinguishing characteristic of "consumerist" building production is that its relationship to the consumer is a central concern in determining the appearance of the building. Consumerist architecture is consciously crafted to inducing consumption. In some cases consumerist architecture is its own product. This is true for the single-family house, the largest consumer purchase that most people ever make.

What distinguishes contemporary consumerist architecture from earlier forms is that it is conceived of as imagery, as a form of marketing-based environmental psychology. Theme environments such as Disneyland are planned to play upon the emotions of their users. The unity of conception found in earlier vernacular architecture between a building's program and its imagery breaks down in today's consumerist architecture.

In broad terms, all contemporary architectural practice in the United States can be viewed as a consumerist enterprise, as Stephen Kiernan has shown in *The Architecture of Plenty*. According to Kiernan, this production has consumerist characteristics, such as being "conceptually if not materially expendable," and employing the marketing concept of "augmented" qualities beyond mere utility. Contemporary architecture, he says, shows evidence of four formal traits: packaging, style, special features and brand names, all of which can be manipulated to establish an identifiable position for a product within the marketplace.

Architects themselves have been turned into famous people in order to make them more fitting objects of publicity. The only thing that satisfies the media appetite for promotional copy is a personality. Witness the infamous Michael Graves' Dexter shoe ads or designer Brian Murphy's ads for the Gap. The media ranks architects as more and less fashionable. A name architect give the consumer a secure "opinion base" and permission to like the work. Likewise the most consumable architecture is that which has been most widely publicized.

Private houses are published over and over again because people can imagine living in them. Everyone understands what a house is and what it is like to live in one. Houses have the additional advantage of allowing architects more creative freedom than other categories of building. Many architects go on to superstar status from an initial base of published residential work. As Sharon Zukin has pointed out, the large scale and high profile of major developments require the participation of architects who are already superstars in order to answer "the desire by major corporations in the services to recoup value from long-term large-scale investments in product development."

Consumerist architecture operates like any other form of marketing and advertising. The labeling of a building is as important or more important than the actual character of its design. Stephen Kiernan has compared these buildings qua containers to consumer packaging: "A package has three marketing functions: to be visible; to be found (by differentiating it from other products through form, style, color, and texture) and to be legible (by conveying information about its contents through graphics and details)."

Fast-food architecture, for example, is carefully calibrated to appeal to potential customers, and the choice of the correct imagery can make or break a business. According to market strategy, the consumer needs to believe that there is a conceptual difference between restaurant A and restaurant B. This product differentiation can be accomplished by altering the menu or changing the wall coverings and type of seating, for example, so that the appearance of the exterior matches the character of the food and service offered inside. Taco Bell restaurants located in areas outside of the Southwest are designed to appear Hispanic, but not too Hispanic. In actuality, they are rather straightforward buildings with a few superficial Hispanic touches.

The precision necessary in the design of consumerist architecture can be seen in the chain of Friendly's restaurants. In one incarnation the building design set up customer expectations inconsistent with the food and service available inside—it resembled a small New England branch bank. Phillip Langdon noted in *Orange Roofs Golden Arches* that "People attracted by the meticulously detailed exterior were disappointed to find that they had to sit at counter stools choosing among hamburger sandwiches, ice cream and other common fare." In order for the chain to succeed, Friendly's had to make its exterior simpler, more informal and more suburban.

There are two levels of involvement by architecture in the process of consumption: primary and secondary. In the category of primary level design a building may be styled like a tube of lipstick or a sports car, to be consumed as

Although the **Bear Tree** has much in common with the category of personal fantasy buildings constructed to satisfy an individual dream, it actually belongs in the category of consumer buildings because it was designed to sell teddy bears, the product it houses, through the use of storybook imagery. Bea de Armond, Jason and Michelle Walker, Anaheim, 1982–83.

Bunker Hill steps, Fifth Street between Flower and Grand, Lawrence Halprin. On this site the city of Los Angeles and the community redevelopment agency allowed the last residential hotel that still remained out of the entire now-vanished Bunker Hill neighborhood to be torn down to further intensify the golden ghettoization of downtown's west side. Because late modernist corporate architecture is so completely devoid of any reference to social/experiential or even functional communication or expression, it becomes necessary to provide elements of relief such as these stairs. In the frantic confusion of trying to be the Spanish steps, a babbling brook and a set of Charles Moore–ish knick-knacks, the Bunker Hill steps point out how difficult it is for these enclaves of amenities to make up for everything that is lacking in their corporate surroundings.

an object in its own right. It may be designed both to sell itself, and to enhance the experience of consuming the product associated with the building.

Primary consumer buildings, from themed resort hotels to themed gambling casinos, must offer a complex, intense experiential package so that their public spaces, as well as their facades, convey a special ambience. They carry a broader range of representational meaning than does, say, corporate architecture. Consider the bewildering variety of ethnic and theme restaurants now endemic across the United States, with motifs borrowed from virtually any geographical locale or time period. One of the crazes of the 1980s was recreating diners from the 1930s, '40s, and '50s, such as Johnny Rocket's on Melrose Avenue in Los Angeles. More long-standing is the tradition of South Seas exoticism in restaurants such as the late and lamented Kelbo's in West Los Angeles, with its flaming blue drinks and multiple Tiki gods.

Secondary-order consumerist buildings such as industrial parks and government structures, are designed to be independent of the goods and services being offered by the businesses they house. These structures are treated as styled containers with neutral, drywall, hung-ceiling interiors. The speculative office building has become the cheapest possible envelope for the amount of space it surrounds. Most of its budget is devoted to the provision of required services. Many of the spaces inside, such as interior hallways, lack distinguishing characteristics both because of rigid development restraints and because the plan must present the fewest obstacles to any interior alterations.

In a second order consumerist building the appearance of the building represents the status of the tenants but does not directly affect their experience of the building in the same way as a themed resort hotel for example. They are meant to appear prestigious so their imagery tends to be confined to a display of wealth consonant with the institutional identity of the client. They may make a slight bow to fashion, to allow both client and architecture to appear up-to-date.

Buildings that house consumerism are not automatically consumerist, since that requires the need, motivation and intent to make the building part of the advertising, marketing and retailing experience. The architecture of a Wal-Mart, for example, is a far less significant factor in their success than store planning—the location and presentation of merchandise. The discount shopper cares primarily about getting his or her microwave oven at the lowest possible markup above the wholesale price. The shopper may not care whether K-MART is physically integrated into a set of local institutions around a civic plaza.

This discount philosophy reflects the increased informality of modern life and contemporary building. The public at large dresses with less respect to ceremony and a greater interest in convenience than in the past (with the caveat that clothes still convey social status, only now that status is tied to a designer label). Thus the usher vanished from the movie house at the same time that hats disappeared from the heads of the moviegoers and the gilt cupids were stripped from its walls. In the past a movie theater was expected to be a spectacle in its own right. By the 1970s it had become nothing more than a warehouse for movies.

The attitude that most buildings need only exist to serve a function, and not as objects of any great interest in themselves, was aided by advances in building technology and legitimized by orthodox Modernism drained of its earlier ideological basis. The prefabricated panel replaces the masonry block; the single sheet of glass replaces multiple panes. Now walls of glass can be epoxied to the surface of a building without the need for even so much as a mullion. Late Modernism has celebrated the machine's capacity for producing repetition and blankness by creating buildings that are articulated neither by ornament nor by the materials from which they are made. The America of blank-concrete, tilt-slab warehouses and identical franchise buildings feeds the public's desire for a substitute reality.

Two Rodeo Shopping Center, Willshire Boulevard and Rodeo Drive, Beverly Hills, 1990. Kaplan McLaughlin Diaz, associate architect, Brand and Allen. The current high-water mark of themed environments is a privatized "public" street on a man-made slope.

tourism

The growth of tourism and the acceptance of the concept of leisure time have also contributed to the rise of consumerist architecture. The precursor of the modern consumer was the tourist, who saw the environment as a series of cultures and places to be enjoyed as literary or artistic experiences, but which one did not have to inhabit. Many of the contradictions of consumerist architecture can be explained via metaphor. Tourism combines two contradictory but linked impulses. It, is on the one hand, an attempt to experience the unfamiliar and the unknown. But since this encounter with the exotic can be unsettling, tourism also produces the desire for familiar comforts, as any traveler knows. Foreign places call for an antidote to their foreignness: a watered-down version of a strange land that is easier to assimilate than the real thing.

we go shopping

Basic to the concept of consumerist architecture is the idea that the experience of one's surroundings—and more particularly, the experience of shopping or being entertained—is enhanced when presented in

The decidedly utilitarian rear wall of Two Rodeo fronts on an alley.

terms other borrowed from elsewhere rather than what is expected. Theming fits with shopping since both are ways of augmenting the shoppers identity, as each purchase of good is also a purchase of an augmented identity.

The power of shopping as a compulsion, and as an escape, is certainly not an entirely benign phenomenon. Shopping in a modern consumer society encourages the quantification of the world in superficial, simplistic and materialistic terms. In a totally consumerist society, individuals would only be judged by the cost and programmed associations of their clothes and possessions.

But is it really the architect's role to squash the Imelda Marcos within? Must the architect somehow instruct the shopper that he or she really does

Church of the Living God, 112 N. Arizona Avenue, Maravilla, East Los Angeles, 1984. The congregation of Casa de Dios designed the church with the aid of draftsman Jesus Nolasco. The scoring of the stucco to imitate masonry construction and the tall spiral columns have iconic significance, labeling the building as special because its elements are so officially splendid that they separate it from the secular world.

Pinnacle Peak Village Plaza, 8711 East Pinnacle Peak Drive, Scottsdale, Ariz., 1975. Dick Davis and Associates, architect, for Jerry Nelson. The purpose of the ersatz mission pictured in the background is entirely secular. Shopping provides draw to give locals a place to go as an alternative to listening to the drone of the TV and the air conditioner.

Stein Building, 13323 Washington Boulevard, Culver City. Thomas Layman, architect. Bill Stein, owner and interior architect. 1984. This Los Angeles "spec" office building has the typical inconsistencies of pop revivalist architecture. The inconsistencies between the domestic 19th century vocabulary and the contemporary office functions it performs are simply ignored.

not need another new pair of Hush Puppies? Perhaps the most an architect can do is try to harness the commonly shared interest in shopping in the service of creating public places that people really want to use, places that relate shopping back to a larger public and civic identity.

Indeed, shopping can be a form of consuming in a purely devotional sense, a subjugation before objects to which one attributes magical, transformational powers. Thus, shopping is a form of religion as well as a form of recreation. It is a way of taking on substitute identities, of transcending the self, of acting out hidden parts of oneself by purchasing artifacts that symbolize these alter egos. It is both a commercial and a act. The individual shopper joins with the countless others to participate in a joint ritual. Shopping dissolves ego boundaries.

In the 1980s a shopper who stepped into a clothing store fitted out in then-chic decor experienced vicarious excitement by receiving the reflected glow of modern technology.

The shopper, through his or her act, participates in a larger worldview, a cosmology of television and magazines. Through advertising and marketing, we as consumers are able to experience goods and services twice, instead of just once. The experience of anticipation becomes as important as the experience of acquisition. Once we have purchased the object, memories of our consumer-anticipation reinforce and validate our ownership. A message delivered long and loud enough by advertising and marketing takes on great credibility.

In 1990 the *Wall Street Journal* reported the influence of advertising on "Tonja Ward, a 21-year-old in Harlem. She watches eight hours of TV a day. After viewing a Roy Rogers ad that touted a new chicken sandwich, she asked her boyfriend to buy her the sandwich downtown, since there was no Roy Rogers nearby. A McDonald's ad made her feel she 'had to have' its double cheeseburger; a subsequent Roy Rogers ad for its double cheeseburger produced the same yearning. She also went to Kentucky Fried Chicken tempted by its 'corn mania' promotion."

Jordan Pacheco, a member of Chicago's Imperial gang, explained the status of fast food in the same article. "Everybody is tired of their mother's food—rice and beans over and over. I wanted to live the life of a man. Fast food gets you status and respect."

the shopping mall

Crucial in the development of consumerist architecture has been the United States' progressive adaptation to the auto. The auto has brought into being the growth of the single-purpose enclave, best illustrated by the evolution of the shopping mall. The commercial strips of the teens and '20s gave rise in the 1930s to corner markets and convenience centers with small parking lots facing the street. These were followed by shopping centers, anchored by department stores or supermarkets, in the 1940s and 1950s. In the 1960s and 1970s the shopping center was supplanted, to a large degree, by the enclosed, multilevel suburban shopping mall. Today the shopping mall has claimed the heart of the American city, occupying much the same role as European shopping arcades, such as Milan's Galleria Vittorio Emanuele II, and often replacing conventional downtown retail districts.

Marble arch townhouse apartment complex, Westheimer at Merilee, Houston. Photo 1985. Even if its plywood is popping at the seams there is no mistaking the architectural intent of this portico. It is supposed to be a major event, making anyone who passes underneath feel important.

The shopping mall is popular because it gathers a large volume of goods in one place, offering convenience and economies of scale. As shopping centers evolved they broadened their original single purpose use to include banking, restaurants and movies all in the same complex. The idea of the auto-isolated enclave also blurred as shopping centers were built as infill in urban areas and as streets in existing cities such as Santa Monica's 3rd St. Promenade were developed managed and marketed as open-air malls. Consumers may shop, bank, eat and watch movies all in the same complex.

In the "World in a Shopping Mall" in Michael Sorkin's anthology *Variations on a Theme Park*, Margaret Crawford describes the economic underpinnings of the shopping mall:

> The malling of America in less than twenty years was accomplished by honing standard real-estate, financing, and marketing techniques into predictive formulas. Generated initially by risk-free investments demanded by pension funds and insurance companies (sources of the enormous amounts of capital necessary to finance malls) the malling process quickly became self-perpetuating, as developers duplicated successful strategies. Specialized consultants developed techniques of demographic and market research, refined their environmental and architectural analysis, and produced econometric and locational models. Mall architect Victor Gruen proposed an ideal matrix for mall-building that combined the expertise of real-estate brokers, financial and marketing analysts, economists, merchandising experts, architects, engineers, transportations planners, landscape architects and interior designers—each drawing on the latest academic and commercial methodologies.

The various predictable mixes are fine-tuned to the ethnic composition, income levels, and changing tastes of a particular shopping area. Indexes such as VALS (the Values and Life Styles program produced by the Stanford Research Institute), correlate objective measures such as age, income, and family composition with subjective indicators as value systems, leisure preferences, and cultural backgrounds to analyze trade areas.

Among the categories of consumers that Crawford cites are Brooks Brothers—wearing outer-directed *achievers*; younger, status-conscious *emulators*; struggling, poor *sustainers*; and middle-class, conforming *belonging* shoppers.

The need for the shopping mall and for consumerist architecture has been fostered by the growing dominance of the machine in daily life. Large-scale systems of production and distribution have become more important

1607 Lucile, Silverlake, c. late 1970s. A modest but effective way-out west, full antlers—on personal fantasy achieved through the most minimal of means. Educated design professionals are usually trained out of being able to do this.

than the social mechanism of shared civic life and human interaction. Buying a newspaper from a familiar salesperson at a corner stand, for example, creates the possibility for social exchange; buying the same newspaper from a vending machine does not. Consumerist environments supply this missing element of human contact.

american architecture and urbanism

Expediency characterizes American architecture. Land planning in the United States tends to solve one problem at a time without taking into consideration the side effects. The superhighway that guts a town center, or the low-income housing development that institutionalizes a ghetto, are typical examples of this approach to problem solving.

American land use is far less controlled than European land use by the planning and zoning efforts of local governments. In America, almost everything is for sale at the right price, whether it is a vineyard or a church building. Profit determines what goes where. The entertaining variety of new American townscapes is the result of the collective acts of real estate developers and corporations, the result of expediency and real estate as commodity more than planning.

The post-World War II generation of consumerist architecture has been shaped by a reaction against the street. As J.B. Jackson, writes. "This development is typically a self-contained complex with its own surrounding buffer zone, its own orientation, its own pattern of movement." Such complexes are isolated from the rest of the city and turn inward on themselves. We do not pass by the facades of mall stores in passing through the city, as we might the storefronts in a conventional retail distinct. Ceded to the motorist rather than the pedestrian, the street is no longer a pleasant place to stroll, window-shop or see old acquaintances. These self-contained complexes, really encapsulated pedestrian wildernesses, are inevitably fertile spawning grounds for the creation of consumerist architecture. Here the shopper must be seduced to linger and programmed to consume.

Nowhere is the absence of historic context, and the freedom to build almost anything, more extreme than in Houston, Texas. Private deed covenant is the only zoning this wide-open city has ever had . Its first development restriction,

Houston apartment house styled to resemble the Alamo.
Photo 1985.

Callender's Restaurant, 5773 Wilshire Boulevard, Los Angeles, 1985. Jim Adams, architect, for Marie Callender's pie stores. Marie Callender hurls pie at the pace of clean lined modernist 1948 Prudential Building by Wurdemana and Becket. The owners of Callendar's knew that no one would pass through the button-down portals of an international style office building to wolf down baked goods so they frosted the facade of the Prudential Building with plaster and used brick.

Office building, 19805 Wilshire Boulevard and Crescent Drive, Beverly Hills. Much late modern corporate architecture is simply cosmetic packaging of interchangeable space through manipulation of various curtain wall materials.

a minimal setback ordinance, was not passed until 1982. In Houston there is almost no public life, in the classical sense as defined by Hannah Arendt's book, *The Human Condition*. Even Houston's downtown has minimal street life—a system of underground tunnels, linking its office towers, segregates its office-worker population. Some neighborhoods, such as the Post Oak/Galleria area, do approach conventional notions of urban density. But a hierarchical notion of place is foreign to the city; high-rise towers may erupt in neighborhoods of two-story houses or in areas just beginning to be developed.

Architect and visionary Rem Koolhaas writes about Manhattan as "Delirious New York," in his 1978 book of the same name. To Koolhaas, Manhattan is a landscape of possibility, where human aspiration can find expression at fever pitch. In Manhattan it is the propinquity, the piling up of the shared lives of millions of people, that makes the city vital. In Houston it is the simultaneous importance, the equivalence and the every-developer-for-himself quality, of the open terrain that gives the city vitality.

One of the most insightful commentaries on the nature of American commercial vernacular architecture has been made by Peter Papademetriou. He notes that in developing cities of the American Sunbelt, the traditional hierarchy of building *type* has been replaced by a hierarchy of building *style*, of copies and reinterpretations of a wide variety of architectural prototypes. In the dispersed, suburban space of the Sunbelt, it is the symbolic messages and stylistic allegiances of buildings that create whatever larger network of meaning that the landscape has to offer. These references could be to almost anything: from Mies van der Rohe to 19th-century Eastlake ornament.

As a result, the affluent sections of suburban Sunbelt cities like Phoenix, Houston and San Jose resemble giant miniature-golf courses. Each building or enclave of buildings has a competing theme. Each is isolated from the others by asphalt and landscaping.

the commercial vernacular

Every culture has accepted ways of doing things—customs that its members take for granted. This concept of the vernacular becomes ambiguous, however, when it is applied to contemporary America. The citizen of today's consumer society is relatively free of the cultural programming that would have been his or her birthright in a nonindustrialized society. Although there are accepted ways of doing things today, such practices are more often the result of technological innovation, marketed by means of advertising, than of slowly evolving patterns of social interaction.

Americans compose their personal cultural identities item by item. Their belief systems come from the organizations they belong to—12-step programs for example—or from one or another breed of pop psychology. Attitudes, touted by experts popularized by the media, are selected by comparison shopping rather than handed down from parent to child. Information on how to cook, relate to peers or define values come from instruction manuals, how-to guides, magazine articles and television programs. Recipes come from Julia Child, not Granny; conceptions of sex come from Dr. Ruth, not Mom.

The predominance of mass-produced goods and services, and their mass consumption, means these cultural values are now commercialized. They do not trickle down from an aristocratic or educated elite. They do not trickle up from a tradition-bound peasant class. America's values are molded in the marketplace through the complex interaction of personal choice and behavioral manipulation.

But just as soap opera has supplanted folklore and story-telling, commercialized architecture has taken the place of the traditional vernacular in the building of present-day America. What makes the study of this architecture so confusing is that as a vernacular it seems so very unvernacular. However, commercial vernacular is part of our economic and social evolution. It is tied to changes in public taste and living patterns.

Traditional folk structures are viewed with nostalgia because they are associated with ways of living that have been outmoded by technological change. Pennsylvania Dutch teams and 19th century California adobe ranch houses have obvious appeal. Car washes from the 1960s and coffee shops from the 1950s are less charming to most observers precisely because they still function as part of everyday life and are not yet obsolescent. But these buildings still constitute a vernacular—a commercial vernacular. The legitimacy of applying the term vernacular to commercial building production has been advocated by the historian J.B. Jackson and the architect Charles Moore, among others.

In *Design Quarterly 128*, J.B. Jackson wrote about commercial vernacular

Third Street in Hancock Park, 1998. The consumerist homestead: house and yard are secondary, obliterated by an army of plastic Santas.

The Burger that Ate L. A., by Solberg and Lowe, at 7624 Melrose Boulevard, Hollywood, 1988, has since been remodeled into blandness as a Starbucks. The economic function of the programmatic architecture speaks for itself.

Buddhist temple on Arlington Avenue, in the Koreatown section of Los Angeles, c. 1990. An example of traditional preconsumerist architecture, a vocabulary of form still embedded in its original cultural context.

William Andrews Clark Mausoleum, Hollywood Memorial Cemetery, c. 1930. Robert Farquhan, architect. Even the dead don't get their civil and cultural due anymore. Funerary monuments and religious and civic institutions once held commonly accepted meaning of the importance of marking graves that has been displaced by the domination of consumerism.

architecture as a continuation of humankind's age-old struggle to be housed and to conduct business with as much comfort and decency as possible. Although there are accepted ways of building commercial vernacular architecture today, these practices are usually the result of technological innovation, advertising and marketing. In earlier times practices became accepted through slowly evolving patterns of social interaction. "Every farmer knew the right proportions and designed his buildings in the same way as his ancestors always had," wrote Lena Ason-Palmqvist of the early Swedish settlers of Minnesota and the farm buildings they constructed.

Traditional vernacular architecture directly accommodated local demands. A building in a northern climate might have a very steep roof to shed snow. A building in a southern climate would have an internal courtyard or a large veranda for shade and ventilation. Such buildings have been admired for the ways they fit their own climate and purpose. They pretend to be nothing more or less than what they are. Traditional vernacular architecture is almost always thought of as consisting of a single style from a particular region, such as the sod house of the prairie states.

But styles of commercial vernacular architecture are as eclectic as the society they reflect, embracing every style from expressionistic modernism to atavistic neoprimitivism. Since consumers shop for novelty as well as for familiarity and consistency, commercial vernacular buildings may pretends to be almost anything: Spanish tile, Tudor half-timbering or colonial American fanlights are slipped onto structures like Halloween costumes. In the early 1960s, apartment houses in southern California were sometimes given steep-pitched front entrances adorned with Tiki idols. Some apartment houses of the same era in Texas had Frenchified, clipped-box-hedge parterres and mansard roofs, while apartment houses in southern California were being given the names of casinos or far-off resorts, such as the Dunes or the Riviera. Just as in the worlds of literature and theater, no one is disturbed by the obvious duplicity of these forms. On the contrary, make-believe—an altered identity—is part of what these buildings are selling.

But consumers are not only shopping for products and services, they are also shopping for atmosphere and experience. This is why novelty is so important in commercial vernacular architecture. Presenting a grocery store as a false-front Western stage set, such as the former Aunt Tilly's in West

Hollywood's Pacific Design Center building, or a group of condominiums as a Moroccan village, such as the Casa Blanca complex in Phoenix, gives it a competitive edge over buildings that do not offer this extra visual metaphor.

As the forces of mass production and distribution take over larger and larger sectors of daily life, anything that seems individual or different takes on enhanced importance. The corner cafe is now a Sizzler and the community bank is now a branch of Citibank.

Phillip Johnson once noted that Late Modernism celebrated the capacity to produce blankness, to create buildings that are not particular, and promulgated the idea that "everybody should have a flat-roofed glass house." Now he went on to say, "We once more want our churches to look like churches and our houses to look like houses and not boxes." His statement presumes that the notions of house and church are defined by the public as much or more so than by the architect.

In *You Have to Pay for the Public Life*, Charles Moore makes the point that the consumer's most important experiences must be purchased. The consumer expects the amusement park, the theme restaurant, and the resort to address emotional needs precisely because the rest of his environment does not. This workaday world has been reduced to utilitarian ends: the provision

Western Plaza Motel, 1066 N. Wilton Place, Hollywood, c. 1984. Consumerism is not a function merely of typology of use, but rather the degree to which a building is being consumed for its experiential qualities. This "no-tell" motel with its windowless street facade makes no experiential claims on its users.

of goods and services and the satisfaction of the needs of daily life. Commercial vernacular buildings after a release from the overwhelming rationality and uncommunicativeness of the rest of the environment.

Consumerist architecture exhibits a love of eclecticism similar to that found in Postmodernism. However, it is an eclecticism founded on the belief that memories of other eras and places can legitimately be represented, rather than ironically deconstructed. Unlike high-art architects, consumerist architects are not free to satisfy only their own artistic concerns. They must try to find common ground with the images already cherished by the public at large.

340 Main Street, Venice, Calif., 1984–91. The architect as product, Frank Gehry is emblazoned on the wall of his Chiat/Day offices.

high-art architecture and consumerist architecture

Because its imagery can be selected from a huge menu of vocabularies, consumerist architecture does not have the same unity of conception between building program and imagery found in earlier vernacular architecture. Consumerist environments such as Knott's Berry Farm may be planned to play upon the emotions of their users, but even manipulative thinking about a building's users is preferable to not thinking about them at all. In contrast to much high-art architecture, consumerist architecture is informed by psychology and the need to communicate; like advertising, consumerist architecture attempts to address directly the needs of its users.

High-art architecture and consumerist architecture are at cross-purposes. Architects are trained to go to elaborate, some might say absurd, lengths to avoid fantasy and literal representation, qualities that are the lifeblood of consumerist architecture. Consumerist architects must communicate with the public clearly and directly. If the public cannot comprehend their work, then the architects of a consumerist building have not done the job that they were hired to do.

High-art architecture, as it has often been practiced in Late Modernism, and even in Postmodernism, may not attempt to communicate with its audience at all. Peter Eisenman may base house designs simply on a series of rotating cubes, in the manner of minimal artists. Frank Gehry may seek to invert normal expectations about building finishes by exposing construction.

Their intent is to create an abstract internally created order, not necessarily to communicate with an audience.

Consumerist architecture has always been comfortable with the use of ornament and historical references, and it needed no sanction from the world of high-art architecture to employ them. Indeed, as the Postmodernist threshold of tolerance rises for nonironical references, and as consumerist-revivalist architecture grows in sophistication and correctness to its sources, it is sometimes difficult to know how to keep the categories separate. The most sophisticated consumerist buildings, such as Jones and Mah's La Borgata shopping center in Scottsdale, Arizona, and the least sophisticated high-art buildings, such as Taft's Mixon House, are roughly comparable.

It is easier for consumerist designers to use historical references, because popular architecture does not demand the unity of conception that high-art architecture does. The individual components of pop and vernacular buildings are often more important than the way they are put together. The inclusion of the requisite amount of neo-Victorian bric-a-brac on Thomas Layman's 1984 office building for Bill Stein in Los Angeles, for example, was much more important than the compositional relationship of the bric-a-brac. Content rules form in commercial vernacular architecture.

The latest formal movement to exhibit such tendencies is Deconstruction, which claims that Postmodern architecture does not confront the present and the current impossibility of cultural consensus. (Here, despite their rejection of any concept of history, many poststructuralist advocates fall into the rhetoric of zeitgeist.) Instead of seeking cultural communication, architecture, in their view, should make explicit its obliteration. Fragmentation, dispersion, decentering, schizophrenia and disturbance are the new objectives; it is from these qualities that architecture is to gain its "critical edge."

This kind of abstraction may be an aesthetic accomplishment, but it contradicts the nature of architecture as a socially based, applied art form. High-art architects have been trained to value the creation of new forms and the expression of individual artistic sensibility above all else. Historically architects have been more impressed by the setting of new precedents than by the following of old ones. However, if one of the true functions of architecture in a consumer society is to create moods and emotional settings (just as literature and theater have traditionally done), then there is no place for accu-

Santa Monica Boulevard and Gower, Hollywood, in 1985. The old fashioned consumerist landscape still looks like this in much of the U. S. The swarm of signs renders any architectural communication superfluous. This signage is part of the long American tradition of plastering cities with posters, signs, banners and wall advertisements that dates well back into the 19th century. In more affluent communities where theme oriented enclaves flourish, such signage is frequently banned because it is considered crass to be so direct about commerce.

French Market Homestead, 3900 Veterans Boulevard, Metairie, Louisiana, 1981. H. B. E. Architects. Even the most solid World War I era beaux artes building never managed to be this boxy. The lack of cornice, the huge span of the third floor balcony and the expanse of plate glass at the entry are inconsistent with the neo-classical vocabulary of the building. Nonetheless, buildings such as this are evidence that the 1980s brought a renewed interest in traditional forms in vernacular and popular commercial, consumerist work.

sations of plagiarism or anachronism. A form that evokes the right associations to do a particular psychological job becomes the correct choice in a formal sense as well.

As Denise Scott-Brown noted in 1980 in the *Harvard Architectural Review*, "Because buildings and cities are big, they inevitably serve wide taste publics; because they last a long while, over the length of their lives, they serve many different people." Consumerist buildings once represented widely shared values that reflected the overall character and organization of society. Now they do so only insofar as they represent a society in which cultural values are exploited as commodities. This is the irreducible irony of consumerist architecture. Still, this architecture genuinely reflects popular attitudes and allows for the expression of a wide range of emotions. It does so in a specific and easily readable form and to an extent that no other sector of building production can match.

If entertainment is a legitimate function of architecture, then the use of forms, details or patterns of composition evoking a time, place or function that has disappeared from modern-day America is quite appropriate in works of architecture intended to be evocative. The success of a project in hitting its particular target, the coherency and appropriateness of its three-dimensional material realization, ought to be the principal criterion by which it is valued, not its conformity to currently accepted rules of contemporary high-art architecture.

Themed consumerist architecture maintains its vitality because it fufills more emotive and narrative roles than any other category of architecture, at least in Southern California. As set forth by Alan Gowans in his essay *Popular Arts and Historic Artifact*, these functions are substitute imagery, beautification, persuasion, conviction and the illustration of events.

Consumerist architecture provides substitute imagery by creating idealized versions of pedestrian environments that have now become rare, such as Port o' Call Village in San Pedro. It offers beautification by including details popularly valued as pretty because of their associations, like the ones employed in New Orleans Square at Disneyland. Consumerist architecture engages in persuasion by reassuring the public that nostalgic views of society still hold true, as in the emphatically domestic ranch houses of the '50s with their dovecotes, wishing wells and garages shaped like hay barns. The frequent use of Spanish Colonial Revival imagery in consumerist architecture in California illustrates the events of the occupation by Spain in a chain of presidios, pueblos and missions.

At the same time, this capacity for metaphor and narrative is the weakness of consumer architecture. Couching one experience in the guise of another can be refreshing in its spirited refusal to accept the tyranny of the world as it is. It is also a direct route to escapism, and a recipe for reductivist kitsch. This appropriation is capable of draining architecture of any enduring cultural meaning because that meaning is borrowed merely for its titillation value and is always up for sale. Such architecture undergoes a continued inflation of meaning. It takes a greater and greater dislocation of syntax and context to satisfy a public grown jaded from its experiences of earlier theme environments. In heavily consumerist environments such as Las Vegas, form itself is no longer enough; staged entertainment and spectacle are required to extend themed architecture's shelf life.

Allison and Peter Smithson wrote in 1956, "Mass production and advertising are establishing our whole pattern of life, principles, morals and aspiration and standards of living. We must somehow get the measure of this invention if we are to match its powerful and exciting impress with our own." So must we take the measure of this increasingly common category of building production, consumerist architecture.

For some two decades now, theorists such as Colin Rowe, Alison and Peter Smithson and Robert Venturi have been attempting to make Modern architecture relevant to everyday life, but consumerist architecture has been matter-of-factly relevant all along. The debate on consumerist architecture, part of the larger debate on the merits of popular culture, has been divided between those who reject it as fraudulent and those who view it as a legitimate form of cultural expression. Exclusionists, such as historian Kenneth Frampton, dismiss the subject of mass culture out of hand, as unworthy of consideration. Defenders of popular culture, such as the critic Charles Jencks, have been known to promote the subject primarily for its titillation value.

Historicist forms and ornament were long forbidden to serious practitioners of architecture in the years following World War II, during the triumph of Modernism. Literal references to the past, pioneered by Charles Moore and Robert Venturi, did not begin to reappear in serious architecture until the 1970s. Actual pediments, cornices and other period-revival decorations were still suspect, however, and had to be laundered through the use

Irony often reverted to mock kitsch in 1980s postmodernism. A cadillac hubcap in the Park Regency Terrace Townhouses, by Venturi, Rauch and Scott Brown. Architects McCleary Associates Architects.

of irony in order to make them respectable. Readily identifiable ornament from the past communicated too well for Modernist-trained architects, since it lacked the required degree of abstraction.

The intensely meaningful imagery and the shared public values that consumerist architecture harnesses endow it with conflicting powers. It is capable of producing architecture with genuine civic and public characteristics, but its manipulative exploitation of forms for commercial purposes tends to contradict and undermine this potential. The task for architects and designers of consumerist architecture is not to avoid the task of addressing consumerism, but rather to invest consumerist architecture with both traditional populist and architectural values.

bibliography

The selection of books included here is eclectic rather than exhaustive.

PERIOD REVIVAL AND MODERNISM IN SOUTHERN CALIFORNIA ARCHITECTURE

Banham, Reyner. Los Angeles *The Architecture of Four Ecologies*. Harmondsworth, England: Pelican, 1974. Banham sorts Los Angeles into a series of communities that are the result of lifestyles, social mores, geography and infrastructure.

Clark, Alson. *Wallace Neff: Architect of California's Golden Age*. Santa Barbara: Capra Press, 1986. The monograph on an accomplished Southern California period revival architect.

Gebhard, David. *L.A. in the Thirties*. Salt Lake City: Peregrine Smith, 1975. A marvelous evocation of Los Angeles architecture, design and planning in the 1930s.

_____*Samuel and Joseph Cather Newsom Victorian Architectural Imagery in California, 1878–1908*. Santa Barbara: UCSB Press, 1979. The Newsom brothers practiced a delightfully exhibitionistic Baroque form of Victorian architecture.

Gebhard, David and Winter Robert. *Los Angeles: An Architectural Guide*. Salt Lake City: Gibbs Smith, 1994. A must for any student or aficionado of Southern California architecture, notable for its catholic taste.

Goldstein, Barbara, ed., with an essay by Esther McCoy. *Arts & Architecture The Entenza Years*. Cambridge, MA. MIT Press, 1990. Selections from the magazine that was the standard bearer of Modernism in Southern California

Heimann, Jim and Georges Rip, intro. by David Gebhard. *California Crazy Roadside Vernacular Architecture*. San Francisco: Chronicle Press, 1980. The chief commentary on buildings built in shapes that mimic their use, such as a doughnut shop in the shape of a doughnut.

Hunter, Paul and Walter Reichardt. *Residential Architecture in Southern California*. Los Angeles: Southern California American Institute of Architects, 1939. A snapshot of the period.

MCoy, Esther. *Case Study Houses, 1945–1962*. Los Angeles: Hennessey & Ingalls, 1977. Esther McCoy was the oracle and pioneering chronicler of modernism in Southern California.

Pilcher, Douglas. *The Regency Style: 1800 to 1830*. London: B.T. Bashford Ltd., 1947. Pilcher's monograph is the best book that I have found on the subject.

Riley, Frank and Riley Elfriede. "Memoirs of a Celebrity Architect". *Los Angeles* magazine, February 1978, pp. 144–7. The best source on architect Jim Dolena.

Smith, Elizabeth, editor. *Blueprints for Modern Living: History and Legacy of the Case Study House*. Los Angeles: Museum of Contemporary Art and Cambridge, Mass.: MIT Press, 1989. A later reappraisal of the Case Study houses program

Street-Porter, Tim. *The Los Angeles House Decoration and Design in America's 20th Century City*. New York: Clarkson Potter, 1995. A good source on decorators of the 1930s.

Wieskamp, Herbert. *Beautiful Homes and Gardens in California*. New York: Harry N. Abrahms Co., 1964. California at the height of 1950s and 60s architectural modernism.

INTERIOR DESIGN

Hicks, David. *David Hicks on Interior Decoration*. New York : Macmillan Company, 1966. David Hicks is full of the high-handed opinions that any good decorator should be full of.

Smith, Jane S. *Elsie de Wolfe A Life in the High Style*. New York: Atheneum, 1982. An essential source of information on the doyenne of American interior decoration.

HOLLYWOOD

Albrecht, Donald *Designing Dreams Modern Architecture in the Movies*. New York: Harper & Row in collaboration with The Museum of Modern Art, 1986. A well-informed discussion of the influence of modernism on movie set design and on the movies.

Anger, Kenneth. *Hollywood Babylon*. Dell: New York, 1975. This is a legendary mishmash of celebrity backstabbing and Hollywood as scandal, vividly written.

Balazs, Andre. *Chateau Marmont Hollywood*. Universe: New York: n.d., c.1997. Balazs has compiled a wild and woolly psycho-sexual-musicological compendium of Hollywood History focusing on the Sunset Strip.

Barsacq, Leon. *Caligari's Cabinet and Other Grand Illusions: A History of Film Design*. Translated by Michael Bullock. Revised and edited by Elliot Stein. Boston: New York Graphic Society, 1976. A useful resource, detailing the contributions of a host of art directors to movie magic-making.

Knight Arthur and Elisofon, Elliot. *The Hollywood Style*. New York: MacMillan Company, 1981. A high glam presentation of Hollywood stars' homes.

Lockwood, Charles. *Dream Palaces, Hollywood at Home*. New York: Viking Press, 1991. Lockwood focuses gossipy attention on Pre World War II movie stars and their living environment.

Mann, William J. *Wisecracker : The Life and Times of William Haines, Hollywood's First Openly Gay Star*. New York: Viking, 1998. The definitive work on the most successful of Hollywood actors turned decorators.

Rosten, Leo. *Hollywood; the Movie Colony, the Movie Makers*. New York: Harcourt Brace, 1941. A classic book summing up all aspects of Hollywood at the time.

CONSUMERISM

Bourdieu, Pierre. *Distinction; A Social Critique of the Judgment of Taste*. Translated by Richard Nice. Cambridge, Mass.: Harvard University Press, 1984. Bourdieu analyzes the relationship between the construction of culture and class and social status.

Butsch, Richard. *For Fun and Profit: The Transformation of Leisure into Consumption*. Philadelphia: Temple University Press, 1990. A collection of essays on specific aspects of consumerism such as the use of children's time.

Chase, John, and Delgado, Michael, editors. *LAICA Journal*. Spring, 1983. *The Garret, the Boardroom and the Amusement Park*, part of a special issue, focused on consumerism and architecture. My first attempt at trying to classify building production according to its relationship with consumerism, This essay was republished in the November 1993, Vol. 47, no. 2, *Journal of Architectural Education* under the same title, under the editorship pf Diane Ghirardo.

_____*Design Quarterly* 131, 1986 *Unvernacular Vernacular*. A redefinition of the notion of vernacular architecture in a more consumerist light.

_____"The role of Consumerism in American Architecture". *Journal of Architectural Education*, August 1991, vol.44, no. 4. .A further evolution of the theories of consumerism and building production that I had proposed in earlier articles.

Crawford, Margaret; "Can Architects be Socially Responsible?' in *Out of Site A Social Criticism of Architecture*. Diane Ghirardo ed. Seattle: Bay Press, 1991. A sharp-eyed analysis of the role of the architect, and the limitations of his role.

_____"The Fifth Ecology". *Fantasy the Automobile and Los Angeles in The Car and the City*. Margaret Crawford and Marty Wachs, eds. Ann Arbor: University of Michigan Press, 1991. Crawford explores the relationships between fantasy, consumption and the automobile.

_____'The World in a Shopping Mall', in *Variations on a Theme Park*. Edited by Michael Sorkin. New York: Hill and Wang, 1992. The best analysis of the history, purpose and function of the shopping center.

During, Simon, ed. *The Cultural Studies Reader*. New York: Routledge, 1993. A large anthology addressing a broad range of popular culture and consumerist issues including essays by Dick Hebdige on culture and hegemony and Raymond Williams on advertising.

Kiernan, Stephen, "The Architecture of Plenty", *Harvard Architecture Review* 6 (1987), 103–113. Kiernan makes the case that the practice of name brand architecture is inherently consumerist.

Lamont, Michelle and Fournier, Marcel, eds. *Cultivating Differences: Symbolic Boundaries and the Making of Inequality*. Chicago: University of Chicago Press, 1992. These essays explore the mechanics and meaning of segments of cultural production and its audience in topics such as food and the constituency for abstract art.

McCracken, Grant. *Culture and Consumption New Approaches to the Symbolic Character of Consumer Goods and Activities*. Bloomington: Indiana University Press, 1990. A thorough discussion of the mechanism by which value is created in consumer culture.

Olalquiaga, Celeste; Megalopolis *Contemporary Cultural Sensibilities* Minneapolis: University of Minnesota Press, 1992. The chapter "Holy Kitschen Collecting Religious Junk from the Streets " cleverly categorizes Kitsch into three orders by character and level of consumption and degree of transformation.

Venkatesh, Alladi. "Changing Consumption Patterns" in *Post-suburban California: The Transformation of Orange County Since World war II* edited by Rob Kling, Spencer Olin and Mark Poster. Berkeley: University of California Press, 1991. This book deals with the relationship between the structure of business and employment and consumption and development patterns.

Zubin, Sharon, "The Post-Modern Debate over Urban Form". *Theory Culture & Society* 7 and 8 (1988) 432–443, 440. Zubin discusses the well known architect as marketable designer label asset to development.

URBAN SPACE

Chase, John; Crawford, Margaret; and Kaliski, John, eds. *The Architecture and Urbanism of Everyday Life.* New York: Monacelli Press, 1999.

Davis, Mike. *City of Quartz Excavating the Future in Los Angeles.* New York: Vintage Books, 1992. This is the book that revitalized the study of Los Angeles history, by a gifted and visionary writer, historian and social critic.

_____*Ecology of Fear, Los Angeles and the Imagination of Disaster.* New York: Metropolitan Books, 1998. Mike Davis charts just what has, and what could, go wrong between man and nature in Southern California.

Ellroy, James. *My Dark Places.* New York: Knopf, 1996. A richly sensationalizing, highly personal, account of a noir Southern California.

Moore, Charles and Allen, Gerald eds. "You have to pay for the Public Life"; in *Dimensions.* New York: Architectural Record Books, 1976. A famous essay that recasts the traditional notion of public space in a new light.

Perin, Constance. *Everything in Its Place, Social Order and Land Use in America.* Princeton: Princeton University Press, 1977. Perin explores the American hostility to multiple-unit housing.

Ray, Mary-Ann; Sherman, Roger; Zardini, Mirko, eds. *The Dense-city After the Sprawl; Lotus Quaderni Documents 22,* 1999. Essay by John Chase "Don't be Dense: Its Common Sense" is an attempt to sum up the general American anti-urban attitude.

Sante, Luc. *Low Life.* New York: Vintage Books, 1992. A riveting tour of New York's nineteenth century underworld, a perfect melding of psychological characterization and physical setting. and milieu.

Seewerker, Joseph. *Nuestro Pueblo: Los Angeles City of Romance.* Drawings by Charles H. Owens, introduction by Lee Shippey. Boston: Houghton Mifflin, 1940. This book is an unabashedly sentimental evocation of the all the indefinable aspects of history that made pre-World War II Los Angeles memorable, illustrated by picaresque sketch vignettes. Never say there aren't any truly romantic books about Southern California.

Watson, Sophie, and Gibson, Katherine. *Post-Modern Cities & Spaces.* Oxford: Blackwell, 1995. Useful for cross-cultural comparisons of social change in urban life, because of the diverse selection of cities examined.

POPULAR CULTURE

Elliot, T.S. *Notes Toward the Definition of Culture.* New York: Harcourt Brace and Co., 1949. The original curmudgeon's definition of the difference between high and low culture.

Gans, Herbert J. *Popular Culture and High Culture, An Analysis and Evaluation of Taste.* New York: Basic Books, 1974. Here you will find a basic theory of the division of society into a series of levels and types of taste preference.

Hine, Thomas. *Populuxe: The look and life of American in '50s and 60's from tail fins and TV dinners to Barbie dolls and fallout shelters.* New York: Alfred Knopf, 1986. The story of sexy product differentiation in the consumer paradise of Post World War II America.

Schlereth, Thomas J., *Material Culture Studies in America.* Nashville, Tenn.:The American Association for State and Local History, 1982. An anthology that places the valuation of buildings in a broad cultural and historical context, see especially the essay by Pierce F. Lewis, "Axioms for Reading the American Landscape: Some Guides to the American Scene"

LAS VEGAS

TCI Magazine, The Business of Entertainment Technology, "Las Vegas Architecture 94." special issue on Las Vegas, May, 1994. This issue carries detailed documentation of the many players involved in the creation of a large themed Las Vegas hotel/casino project.

Anderton, Francs; and Chase, John; *Las Vegas An Architectural Guide*. London: Ellipsis Konemann 1997. One in a series of those tiny square architectural guides, and an attempt to see if there is life outside the strip.

_____*Las Vegas The Success of Excess*. London: Ellipsis Konemann, 1997. Slightly different material than the above guide with more general analysis and less specific references.

Barnard, Charles S. *The Magic Sign*. Cincinnati: S.T. Publications, 1993. A thorough accounting of all aspects of sign design in Las Vegas.

Castleman, Deke. *Las Vegas*. Oakland, Ca., Compass American Guides, 1993. The best guide to Las Vegas, crammed with useful information.

Hess, Alan. *Viva Las Vegas*. San Francisco: Chronicle Books, 1993. The story of how neon signage and sophisticated Los Angeles modernist architecture transformed Las Vegas.

COMMERCIAL VERNACULAR ARCHITECTURE

Jackson, J.B. *Discovering the Vernacular Landscape*. New Haven, Conn.: Yale University Press, 1984. J.B. Jackson is the universally acknowledged master of American landscape description.

Chase, John. *Exterior Decoration*. Los Angeles; Hennessey & Ingalls, 1982. A case study analysis of a small group of buildings in order to better understand what homeowners, (as opposed to what architects) want. The book implicitly flirts with the question of is there such a thing as homosexual taste in architecture, and interior decoration. I view this book as nostalgia as I doubt I will ever again have a chance to spend that much time researching so obscure a subject.

Cromley, Elizabeth Collins and Hudgins Carter L. eds. *Gender, Class and Shelter Perspectives in Vernacular Architecture*. Knoxville: University of Tennessee Press, 1995. Of note: Christopher L. Yip Association "Residence and Shop: An Appropriation of Commercial Blocks in North American Chinatowns'" and Annmarie Adams "The Eichler Home: Intention and Experience in Postwar Suburbia".

Fishwick, Marshall; and Neil, J. Meredith, eds. *Popular Architecture*. Bowling Green, Ohio: Bowling Green Popular Press, n.d., c. 1973. One of the earliest publications to address the subject, and still a valuable source.

Hess, Alan. *Googie: Fifties Coffee Shop Architecture*. San Francisco: Chronicle Books, 1985. A thorough history and examination of a decorative and now vanishing building type, that sheds light on the role of style in creating a building type.

Jencks, Charles. *Daydream Houses of Los Angeles*. New York: Rizzoli Publications, 1978. Charles Jencks finds amusement in the popular architecture of Southern California. I disagree with Jencks on the seriousness of the houses—he sees them as architectural *jeu d' esprit*, I see them as earnest vernacular attempts to lay claim to a certain social status or taste culture.

Langdon Philip. *Orange Roofs, Golden Arches*. New York: Knopf, 1986. Langdon demonstrates the care that goes into crafting the physical environment of fast food, showing just how integral to the consumption of the food is the consumption of the building.

Lovett, Anthony R. and Maranian, Matt. *L.A. Bizarro: The Insider's Guide to the Obscure, the Absurd, and the Perverse in Los Angeles.* New York: St. Martins Press: 1997. A collection of all the corniest, kitschiest aspects of Los Angeles written with terrific moxie and shameless humor.

Nero, Bob. "The Blooming of the Plastic Apartment House". *Los Angeles Times West Magazine,* 1972, pp. 24–31. The first article on the stucco box apartment house, replete with plenty of quotes from Stucco Box king "Packing Jack" Chernoff.

Moore, Charles W.; Smith, Kathryn; Becker, Peter. *American Vernacular Architecture Home Sweet Home.* New York: Rizzoli and Los Angeles, Craft and Folk Art Museum, 1983. This anthology contains the article I wrote with John Beach, "The Stucco Box." It was later reprinted by Barbara Goldstein in her late, and much lamented, *Arts and Architecture Magazine* in 1984 under the title *Stucco Boxes Apartment Buildings* in vol. 3, no. 3, pp. 42–47 accompanied by Judy Fiskin's photographs.

Papademetriou, Peter. "Aspects of a New Urban Vernacular," *Harvard Architectural Review* 1 Spring , 1980, 123–26

Ruscha, Edward. *Some Los Angeles Apartments.* Los Angeles: G. Wittenborn, 1965. The first portrayal of the post World War II vernacular apartment house.

Winter, Robert. *The California Bungalow.* Los Angeles: Hennessey & Ingalls, 1980. A good source for the study of building production and popular taste in California.

Articles on small apartment buildings relevant to the study of the Stucco Box apartment appeared in *Arts & Architecture* magazine, May 1951 Campbell & Wong, pp. 32–33, "Hillside House by Carl Louis Maston", November 1952, pp. 32–33 "Small Apartment by Raymond Kappe Architect" January 1955, p. 27 House by Craig Ellwood, October 1952, p. 30 'Rental Housing designed by Greta Magnusson Grossman", May 1952, p. 32 "Small Apartments by Carl Louis Maston" Architect September 1952, p. 24 "Six-Unit Apartment Carl Louis Maston, architect", February. 1952, p. 27 and apartment building by Gregory Ain, April 1965, pp. 20–21 *see also House and Home* magazine February 1952, pp. 86–88 on "Googie Architecture", article on John Lautner's work 89–91 and article on Raphael Soriano's Colby Apartments pp. 67–73. For a discussion of the tradition of stucco-box building see David Gebhard's article "L.A., the Stucco Box" *Art in America* 58, 1970, pp. 130–133.

HISTORIC PRESERVATION

For a discussion of the merits of preserving the commercial architecture of the recent past see Richard Longstreth's article in the October,1992 *Forum Bulletin of the Committee on Preservation in the Newsletter of the Society of Architectural Historians.*

Slaton, Deborah, and Shiffer, Rebecca A., eds. *Preserving the Recent Past .* Washington D.C.: Historic Preservation Education Foundation, 1995.

BUILDING TYPOLOGY

Clay, Grady. *An Unconventional Guide to Real Places, America's Generic Landscape.* Chicago: University of Chicago Press, 1994. An imaginative division of American space into an all inclusive typology.

Franck, Karen A., and Schneekloth, Lynda H. *Ordering Space Types in Architecture and Design.* New York: Van

Nostrand Reinhold, 1994. This book focuses on the concept of typology as applied to building.

Groth, Paul. *Living Downtown The History of Residential Hotels in the United States.* Berkeley: University of California Press, 1994. Paul Groth sums up the neglected tale of hotel life in the US and the class distinctions between different types of lodging.

Longstreth, Richard. *City Center to Regional Mall: Architecture, the Automobile and Retailing in Los Angeles, 1920–50.* Cambridge Mass.: MIT Press, 1997. A cogent and meticulously researched history of the trajectory of large-scale retail as it accommodates the automobile and moves from downtown to suburbia.

Margolies, John. *Miniature Golf.* New York: Abbeville Press, 1987. A seductive presentation of the history of miniature golf courses, charmingly discussed and lushly illustrated with photographs.

Markus, Thomas A. *Buildings & Power Freedom & Control in the Origin of Modern Building Types.* New York: Routledge,1993. A re-thinking of the notion of building types by their social relationships.

Pevsner, Nikolaus. *A History of Building Types.* The A.W. Mellon Lectures in the Fine Arts 1970. Princeton, New Jersey: Princeton University Press, 1976. The primary text on historic building types, arranged in relatively broad groupings.

Polyzoides, Stefanos; Sherwood, Roger; Tice, James; photos by Julius Shulman. *Courtyard Housing in Los Angeles: A Typological Analysis.* Berkeley, University of California Press, 1982. A study of the bungalow court and Hispanic courtyard housing tradition that focuses on the morphology of the courts.

THE HAYMARKET SERIES

EDITORS: MIKE DAVIS AND MICHAEL SPRINKER (1950–1999)

The Haymarket Series offers original studies in politics, history and culture with a focus on North America. Representing views across the American left on a wide range of subjects, the series will be of interest to socialists both in the USA and throughout the world. A century after the first May Day, the American left remains in the shadow of those martyrs whom the Haymarket Series honors and commemorates. These studies testify to the living legacy of political activism and commitment for which they gave their lives.

Recently published in **THE HAYMARKET SERIES:**

MAGICAL URBANISM: Latinos Reinvent the US Big City
Mike Davis

CANARIES ON THE RIM: Living Downwind in the West
Chip Ward

FROM PEARL HARBOR TO SAIGON: Japanese American Soldiers and the Vietnam War
Toshio Welchel

CULTURES IN BABYLON: Black Britain and African America
Hazel Carby

THE WAGES OF WHITENESS: Race and the Making of the American Working Class (new edition)
David Roediger

A PLAGUE ON YOUR HOUSES: How New York was Burned Down and National Public Health Crumbled
Deborah Wallace and Rodrick Wallace

DEVELOPMENT ARRESTED: The Blues and Plantation Power in the Mississippi Delta
Clyde Woods

MECHANIC ACCENTS: Dime Novels and Working-Class Culture in America (new edition)
Michael Denning

THE CULURAL FRONT: The Laboring of American Culture in the Twentieth Century
Michael Denning

PICKUP ARTISTS: Street Basketball in America
Lars Anderson and Chad Millman

THE INVENTION OF THE WHITE RACE, VOLUME 2: The Origin of Racial Oppression in Anglo-America
Theodore Allen

RED DIRT: Growing Up Okie
Roxanne Dunbar-Ortiz

STRUCTURES OF THE JAZZ AGE:
Mass Culture, Progressive Education and Racial Discourse in American Modernist Fiction
Chip Rhodes

SELLING CULTURE: Magazines, Markets, and Class at the Turn of the Century
Richard Ohmann

3.Sep.2000 NTI 31.50 (35.00) 78751